WORLD TRADE CENTER
THE UNITED NATIONS TWENTY FIFTH 1945 1970
SMOOTH N'JUICY
SPORT SCORE
Queen Mary
BUSINESS
THE ICEMAN COMETH
REVLON
Stouffer's Inn On The Square
PBS
Luther
WOMEN
AVANT GARDE GOTHIC
fact book
oh! ah!
NY, NY
DIMENSION
NBC ABC CBS
Thirteen wnet
ZEBRA
U&lc.
MONEYSWORTH
COOPER UNION
The Saturday Evening Post
AMERICAN STAGE
Family Circle
The Sound of Music
L'eggs
Scruples
Volk
fact
THE EMPIRE STAKES
Grumbacher
13¢ USA
Friday
Ice Capades
3 SUISSES
THE COOPER UNION SCHOOL OF ART & ARCHITECTURE
ad 1234 5678 90
MOTHER & CHILD

ENDPAPERS:
Lubalin's rough sketch and finished poster showing a montage of logo designs produced by himself and the designers in his studio, Tom Carnase, Tony Di Spigna, Roger Ferriter, Alan Peckolick and Ernie Smith.

HERB
LUBALIN
ART
DIRECTOR,
GRAPHIC
DESIGNER
AND TYPO-
GRAPHER.

AMERICAN SHOWCASE, INC., NEW YORK

Distributed in U.S. by:
Rizzoli International Publications, Inc.
597 Fifth Avenue
New York, NY 10017
Rizzoli ISBN 0-8478-0880-7

For Sales outside U.S.:
Rotovision S.A.
10, Rue de l'Arquebuse
Case Postale 434
CH-1211 Geneve 11/Switzerland

Distributed in Canada by:
Firefly Books
3520 Pharmacy Ave. Unit 1-C
Scarborough, Ontario Canada
ISBN 0-931144-28-0 (Hardcover)
ISBN 0-931144-52-3 (Paperback)

Design by: Alan Peckolick

Printed in Japan: Third Printing
First paperback edition

Library of Congress
Catalogue Card No. 84-072129

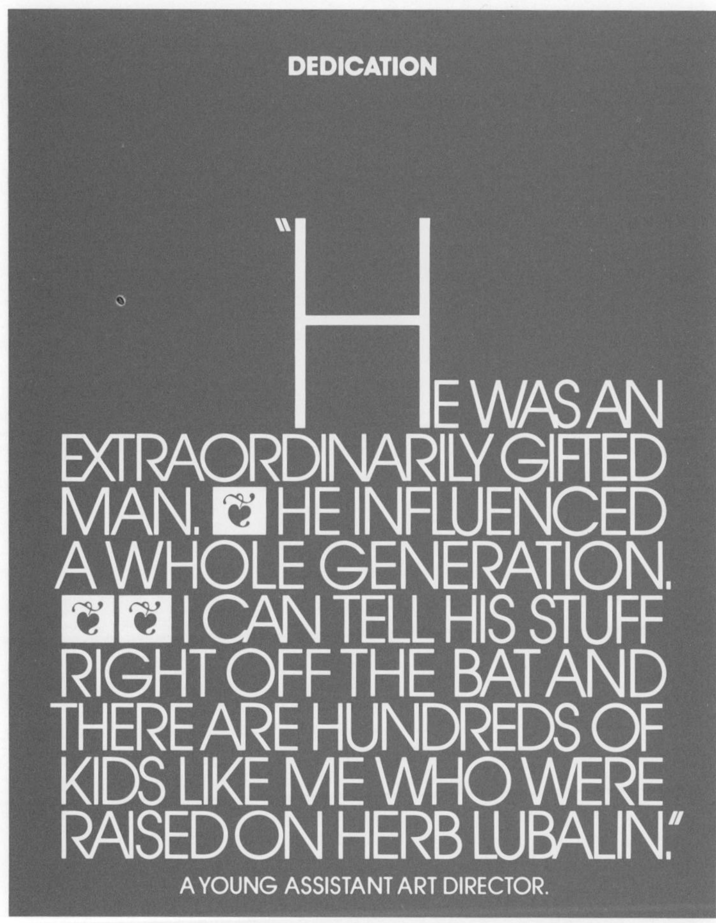

HERB LUBALIN 1918-1981

ACKNOWLEDGEMENTS

IN GRATITUDE TO THE FOLLOWING ASSOCIATES OF HERB LUBALIN FOR THEIR MANY CONTRIBUTIONS TO THE PROJECTS PICTURED IN THIS RETROSPECTIVE:

TOM CARNASE
TONY DI SPIGNA
ROGER FERRITER
ERNIE SMITH

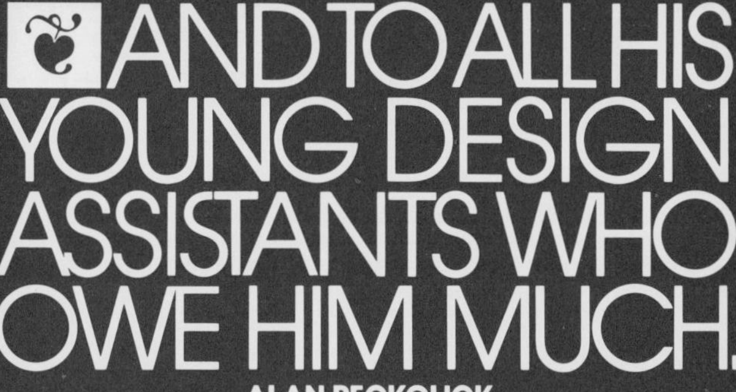

AND TO ALL HIS YOUNG DESIGN ASSISTANTS WHO OWE HIM MUCH.

ALAN PECKOLICK

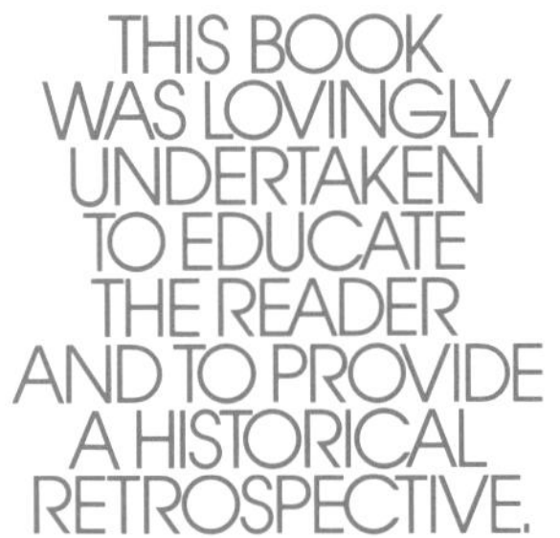

HERB LUBALIN

His father-in-law, Solomon Kushner, wondered "if he'll ever amount to anything." Sylvia, Mr. Kushner's elder daughter, had married a skinny, colorblind, left-handed artist who didn't speak much. But, Mr. Kushner was a men's tailor, not a prophet. He wasn't in business to predict the future. He couldn't foresee that Herbert Lubalin would become one of America's foremost graphic designers—an internationally honored giant in a giant industry whose well-being reflects the national economy.

The graphics in this book are mute testimony to the monument Herb Lubalin erected.

The text comes from talks with people close to him, but to whom he was unable to speak intimately. It's about his work methods, of which he talked voluminously. It's about his influence on the way an industry looked and talked to the public. It's about the words he designed that, on the printed page, revealed his tacit capacity to be tender, funny, provocative, and loving. The words he set were the words he said.

This text is about the things that made Lubalin tick. Herb rarely talked, but he did tick....

Lubalin's magic marker roughs on tracing paper were as decisive as his colleagues' comps. He was a non-verbal designer fascinated by the look and sound of words, and he expanded on their message with typographic impact.

He was a tenacious typographer who left-handedly wielded a razorblade on type proofs to juggle hairline spaces between letters, to shorten or lengthen the serifs, and to adjust ascenders

Lubalin's rough sketch and final design for a page in U&lc. **See page 101.**

Two rejected postage stamp designs.

and descenders to his finicky satisfaction.

The graphic artist's job is to solve the client's problem—to give convincing visual testimony to the printed message, to sell products. The essence of Lubalin's multi-faceted role was to package ideas visually and exquisitely. He avoided the limitations of specialization. His intricate design encompassed a range from postage stamps, packaging and advertising, to the preparation of travelling exhibits for the United States government. It rose to physical heights with skyscraper signage for the Ford Foundation building in New York City.

His graphic concept employed copy, art and typography, and he used available production methods to underline the drama inherent in the message. Idea preceded design.

An innovative graphic communicator whose intelligence responded to the world he lived in, an elegant man with a sense of the provocative, a sensitive artist of unexpected wit, Herbert Lubalin would have agreed that "to catch a mouse, make a noise like a cheese." He would have transcribed into type words even a well-fed mouse would nibble on.

Impeccably professional, his low-pressure personality thrived on long hours of work in the high-pressure environment of graphics and advertising, wherein he made the irrevocable contribution of his genius.

Early in the 19th century, advertising consisted primarily of crudely rendered one-sheet announcements or cards telling where to buy what, and for how much. Advertising competition wasn't intense. In the late 1800's, the heaviest advertisers were manufacturers of patent medicine. Collectively, they spent only seven million dollars, and there were fewer than 100 advertising agencies.

In 1984, there were nearly 10,000 advertising agencies, and the 100 wealthiest American companies alone spent more than 12 billion dollars to promote the sale of products through advertising in newspapers, magazines, on bus, subway and train cards, on radio, TV and electric signs, through audio visuals and film.

Herbert Frederick Lubalin took the first step to international graphic renown in New York City. He was born in 1918, the younger of fraternal twin boys, into a large, loving, unlikely amalgam of artists, musicians and businessmen. Rooted in the melting pot, his family was German on his mother's side, Russian on his father's. His mother, one of 18 children, was a singer; his father, who

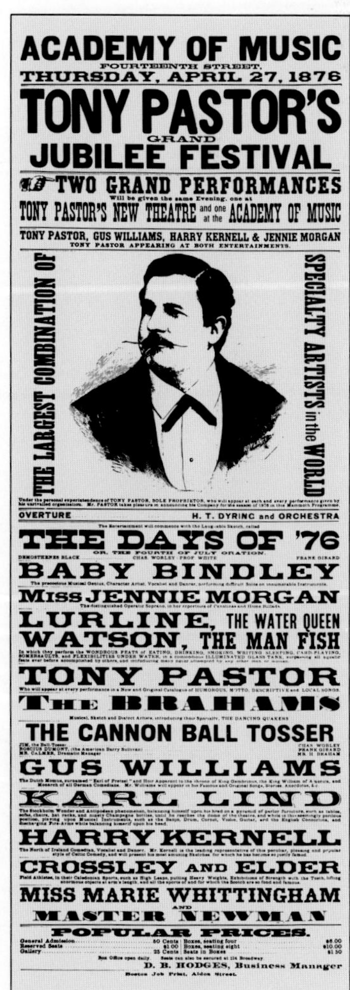

Billboard poster, 1876.

played the trumpet with a professional orchestra, became a member of the first classical orchestra at the American Broadcasting Company.

As children, the twins and their older sister were surrounded by a warm, jovial and active group of aunts, uncles and cousins living within easy radius of each other. Ever quiet, skinny Herb was particularly beloved by the family. His early interest in art was encouraged, although he was colorblind, as was his twin. Figures he drew with crayon had startling purple hair.

Neighborhood youngsters formed an after school sports club, saved monies for team jackets emblazoned with the team name—Bruins of Edgemere. Herb was the smallest boy in the group, but he was also the most daring, perhaps because he had to push so hard to excel.

The Lubalins lived close to the Atlantic Ocean and Sheepshead Bay; it was natural to fish summer and winter. The brothers overturned rocks while hunting for bluefish bait. They knew where to find sandworms, bloodworms and killies.

Every Saturday night, the family of musicians gathered to entertain themselves with classical music, operettas and folk songs from the homelands. Family members reinforced each other, and the children were given inordinate freedom to take risks, to grow and to attempt to exceed what had been done before.

Herbert was a good art student in high school, despite his inability to draw recognizable images. His teacher encouraged his feelings for design and lettering, knowing one can develop as an artist without relying on drawing accurately.

Further schooling in art was accidental. To have an art career wasn't in Herb's original plan, although, typically, he expressed no thought for a future. The family's finances were on shaky ground during the Depression of the '30's. His father hoped Herb and his brother would achieve a financially secure future in medicine; his mother would have been pleased if the boys studied law. But Herb's high school academic standing was so low he wasn't accepted by the tuition-free College of the City of New York, where his twin was enrolled.

What happens when a poor kid with bad grades can't afford to go to a regular college? He applies to a free art school.

In 1935, Herb passed the entrance exam ("mostly in the form of an intelligence test") to the prestigious Cooper Union. "I was 64th out of 64 applicants."

The Cooper Union for the Advancement of Science & Art.

NAME TR. LUBALIN, HERBERT F.
AGE 17 ENTERED Oct. 1935 GRADUATED
Ex marks: Re 8 Sp 16 Art 16 Draw 57

1935-36 FIRST YEAR PREPARATORY

COURSE	OCT.	NOV.	DEC.	JAN.	FEB.	MAR.
FREE HAND DRAWING Daniel 6 hrs.	1 absence			B−		
MODELING Rudy 6 hrs.						
ELEMENTARY DESIGN C. Harrison 6 hrs.	2 absences			B+		
COMPOSITION						
LETTERING Shaw 3 hrs.	(0 absences)			B−		
HISTORY OF ART						
Cl. of Arch Shaw 6 hrs.	(2 absences)			C		

1937-38 THIRD YEAR

COURSE	OCT.	NOV.	DEC.	JAN.	FEB.	MAR.
LIFE DRAWING 15 hours per wk.				B−		
ILLUSTRATION						
DECORATIVE DESIGN						
PICTORIAL DESIGN						
COSTUME DESIGN						
MODELING						
PORTRAIT PAINTING						
Adv. Design - Westervelt 15 hrs				A		

ADDITIONAL RECORD
Birthday. Mar. 17, 1918
Bronze medal in general preparatory work 1937 Exhibition.

Jan. 16, 1939 – Mr. Lubalin granted permission to drop painting and work full-time in adv.

Schedule hrs: 1st semester
Painting 16 wks: – 15 hrs wk.
adv. Design 16 " 15 " "

hours 2nd semester:
adv. Design 16 wks - 30 hrs. wk.

Registered in typography class n.a.s.
Jan. 1939 – 16 wks. only 6 hrs. a week.

5th yr. - N.A.S 1939-40 (no credit)
Painting - Mr. Mangravite - (3 hrs.) Jan B.

Lubalin's four-year report card from The Cooper Union.

His reward was four years of superior art school instruction. Herb's original intent of not pursuing an art career changed with his grades.

"For the first two years, I was the worst student in the school. In the last two years, I was about the best."

The turning point was a class in calligraphy. The angle of the flat pen point used in calligraphy prescribes that the art be done with the right hand. Herb drew with his left hand. The instructor told Herb he'd have to learn to use his right hand on the assignment.

"I didn't tell her I wrote with my right hand. Since calligraphy really is handwriting, it was easy for me. I got the highest mark in the class, not because I was the best, but because the teacher felt I'd overcome a great handicap.

"I guess this gave me confidence, because from that time on, I did very well."

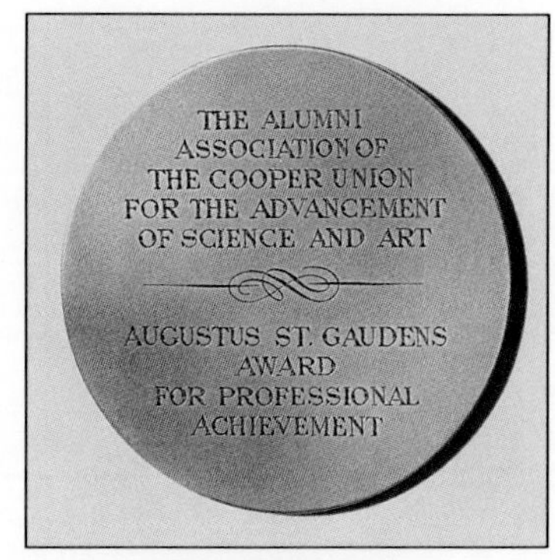

St. Gauden's Medal, 1973.

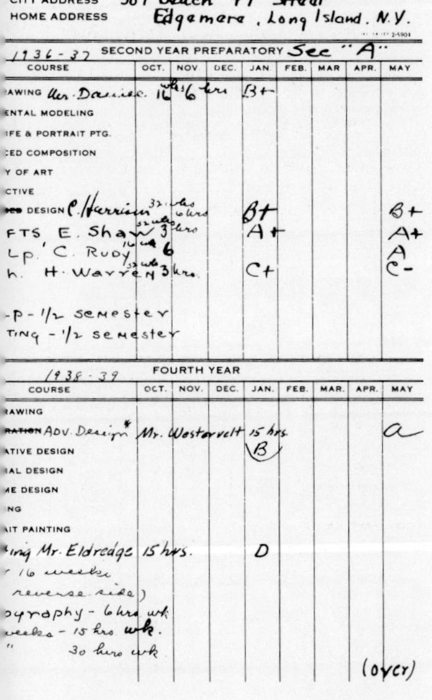

Far. Rock. 7-5421
CITY ADDRESS 307 Beach 47 Street
HOME ADDRESS Edgemere, Long Island. N.Y.

1936-37 SECOND YEAR PREPARATORY See "A"

COURSE	OCT.	NOV.	DEC.	JAN.	FEB.	MAR	APR.	MAY
…AWING Mr. Davies. 16 wks 6 hrs				B+				
…ENTAL MODELING								
…IFE & PORTRAIT PTG.								
…CED COMPOSITION								
…Y OF ART								
…CTIVE								
… DESIGN C. Harrison 32 wks 6 hrs				B+				B+
…FTS E. Shaw 32 wks 3 hrs				A+				A+
…Lp. C. Rudy 16 wks 6								A
…h. H. Warren 32 wks 3 hrs.				C+				C-
…p - 1/2 semester								
…TING - 1/2 semester								

1938-39 FOURTH YEAR

COURSE	OCT.	NOV.	DEC.	JAN.	FEB.	MAR.	APR.	MAY
…RAWING								
…RATION ADV. Design* Mr. Westervelt 15 hrs.				(B)				a
…ATIVE DESIGN								
…IAL DESIGN								
…ME DESIGN								
…NG								
…IT PAINTING								
…ing Mr. Eldredge 15 hrs.				D				

… 16 weeks
… reverse side)
…ography - 6 hrs wk
…weeks - 15 hrs wk.
" 30 hrs wk

(over)

Many awards later, indisputably an achiever in his profession, Lubalin received the Award for Professional Achievement from the president and trustees of his Alma Mater. By now, the privately non-verbal Herb was a blithe and glib, experienced public speaker. At the presentation ceremony, he openly confessed to a distinguished audience that he had not been innocent of the agility of his right hand, and that his duplicity in the calligraphy class "helped me cheat my way into the art profession."

He had entered Cooper Union unaware of two impending romances that would change his life. One lasted three decades, the other, until his death.

The first big excitement was to meet a classmate, the petite and beautiful Sylvia Kushner. Four years later, the two artists were married, after they had been graduated, Herbert with the Student's Medal for General Excellence. He was quite a catch, Mr. Kushner.

Herb and Sylvia had three sons and 32 years together.

Lubalin considered his wife "the most talented graduate of Cooper Union." Yet, she put her career on hold to attend to a household of three children and a rising, driven husband who didn't speak much and brought work home weekends. Before her death, she was emerging as a gifted watercolorist.

Someone once observed that the beginning of typographical wisdom is the love of letters. At Cooper Union, Herb became enamored also with typography, and this love had far-reaching effects on the worlds of advertising and graphic design. He learned the technical language of points, picas and leading. He was seduced by the myriad of typefaces. He was intrigued to discover that the same word set differently created a different image.

Lubalin was known to comment that even though there were more than 2,000 typefaces to choose from, an art director should know the strong points of all of them. In his career, he demonstrated the resiliency of type. He stretched it, pulled it, tore it, and when it resisted, he redesigned it.

In 1939, for his first job as a professional artist, Lubalin worked on displays. He was fired from this job for asking for a $2 raise on top of his weekly $8. Then, he served time sporadically working on staff for small studios and agencies, and freelance designing, sometimes of classified ads.

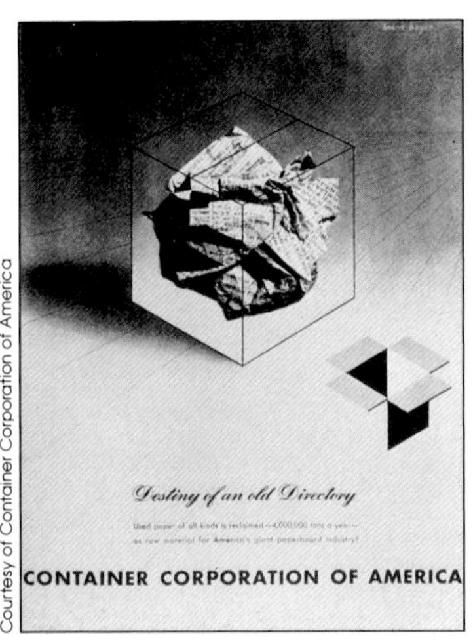

Courtesy of Container Corporation of America

Paul Rand cover for <u>Apparel Arts</u> magazine, 1939.

Herbert Bayer ad for Container Corporation of America, 1939.

Advertising agency structure in the '30's serviced copy. Layout played a secondary role. Large agencies employed one art director to whom layout artists reported. It wasn't the job of layout people to deal with ideas, but to mechanically position art, headline and copy in the allotted space. The conceptual graphic designer had yet to be born.

However, outside factors were working to transform the static approach to graphics. The Second World War had begun. The first obligation of factories was to the nation's armed forces and those of its allies. This reorientation affected the production of consumer goods and communications in many ways. For example, the American Tobacco Company's peacetime slogan, "Reach For A Lucky Instead Of A Sweet," was superceded by the copyline, "Lucky Strike Green Has Gone To War." The green ink on the cigarette package was dropped, for it had a metallic component that was donated to the war effort.

At the same time, America was on the brink of an unparalleled technological breakthrough—television. There was accelerated competition for the eye and ear of the consumer.

With the threat of war in Europe, eminent designers emigrated to America, thereby influencing U.S. graphics. Bauhaus-trained Herbert Bayer worked for Container Corporation of America. <u>Vogue's</u> M.F. Agha and <u>Harper's Bazaar</u>'s Alexey Brodovitch were exploding the editorial page with their radical use of bleed photographs. They made a positive of negative space and created a showcase for new talent. Agha's assistants were Cipe Pineles, who became the first woman member of the Art Directors' Club, and William

Animated sequence for on-air television spot for PBS designed by Lubalin.

Golden, designer of the omnipotent CBS eye. Brodovitch commissioned a young photographer named Richard Avedon. Paul Rand, who had studied with the German expressionist George Grosz, was only 23 years old when he became art director of both Esquire and Apparel Arts simultaneously.

Better art schools in America were teaching the functionalism of the Bauhaus, the simplicity of De Stijl, and the discipline of the Wiener Werkstätte. Young art school graduates with refreshing European concepts began applying for jobs. Along with rebellious layout people, they altered the established focus in advertising. Both groups were eager to communicate. Effectively combining word and image, they reached out to make a visual and emotional impact on the public.

These new designers set about educating their clients. Layout people became articulate art directors working as a team with writers; they were artists who respected the mechanics of business, and who gained stature as visible members of the agency. They met with the client; they explained the designer's point of view and demonstrated the persuasiveness of graphic punctuation in sales.

All this when returning GI's and women who had entered the work force during the war had income to spend on housing and family needs. New consumer products were created for the efficiency-minded, two-salaried household.

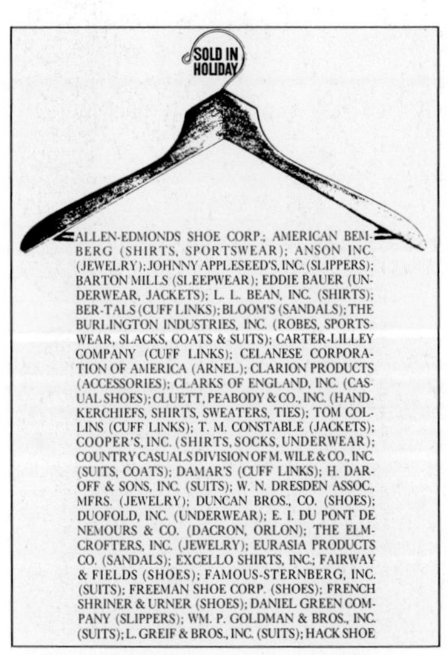

Sudler & Hennessey promotion piece for Holiday magazine, 1958.

Lubalin's need to fill O's flourished in this piece designed in 1957.

The momentum of equipping a huge fighting machine had also accelerated medical techniques. Miracle drugs like sulpha that treated battlefield wounded were soon available for the peacetime market. They were introduced to the medical profession through educational, noncompetitive advertising. It was important for graphics to generate the excitement inherent in the products.

The conservatism of the old order yielded to new procedures and innovative thought in the graphic arts. The new generation of artists and designers was ready.

So was Herbert Lubalin.

In 1945, Lubalin became art director at Sudler & Hennessey, a studio specializing in pharmaceutical ads and promotions. He worked with a bullpen of 20 illustrators, photographers, comp people, letterers and retouchers who followed through from Lubalin tissues—tissues on which the Lubalin legend began.

Ernie Smith, now Executive Vice President, Creative Director/Art, at Sudler & Hennessey, was given his first job by Lubalin more than 30 years ago. They became friends, partners and fishing companions. Smith recalls Herb's awesome professionalism, his two-dimensional pyrotechnics, the unerring instructions on Lubalin's 18″ by 24″ tracing paper pad roughs.

"It would be hard to misinterpret a Lubalin tissue, even though what was on it sometimes seemed like a scrawl torn from the corner of his pad. But every important design decision was apparent in them. He marked here and there—'make this red,' 'make this Franklin Gothic Bold, 12 point, flush left, no leading, U&lc.' He wrote all the instructions, and the tissue reflected the whole solution. It was a blueprint.

"The art director who got a Lubalin tissue to follow through on couldn't take credit as the designer. You tightened it up and refined it; but the idea, the major spatial relationships, the elegance, was built into it. Once Herb made the tissue, the ad or booklet was designed.

"In the realm of ideas, it was the same way. He worked out all the crazy folds and the die-cuts; he never left anything open."

As this rough logo sketch shows, Lubalin approached design and type choice as one continuous thought.

Lubalin's dexterity was impressive. A staff member who had completed a job would say, "I'm up," jargon for being free for a new assignment. Lubalin would reach into his thick pile of blue job folders and see for the first time the suggested copy. He often ignored the original words to suit his creative needs. With the young artist standing by, Lubalin would begin to sketch, and the idea, perhaps a new headline, unfolded easily. He became adept at devising copy lines before he drew. This gave him a hook on which to hang a design.

He'd slip another tissue over the first, and then another, to make adjustments. Sometimes he'd tear a small squiggle from the corner of the pad, and tape it in place on a new sketch. The impressive pile of discarded tissues became collector's items as assistants salvaged the discards. Fifteen to 20 pads a week made their contribution to art.

Smith says, "Herb visualized the headline. There was no need to set it several ways. He put his ideas down simultaneously, like stream-of-consciousness designing.

"On mechanicals of his tissues, he made no alterations, no adjustments. Didn't make something bigger or smaller. Didn't alter a curve, add a line."

At about 6 P.M., free-lancers arrived, and he'd distribute work to a cadre of artists. He'd give two or three jobs each to illustrators, photographers,

First sketch for an ad for the Irish Tourist Board. Lubalin wrote the headline as well.

comp people. All the tissues were designed with the artist at his side. He'd say, "We'll do this..." and make his left-handed sketch, give the tissue to the artist, and reach for the next folder with the next assignment. It was a dazzling display of on-the-spot design.

His daily output was staggering. He went through the day seemingly calm, saving energy for work. Except for meetings, he rarely left his desk to walk around, chat or relax.

He was never satisfied, always struggling, searching, scribbling, accepting ideas from others. "A great art director knows when someone else has a better idea." He pushed a thought until he could say, "Alright. That's it. It's beautiful."

Lubalin at Sudler & Hennessey, 1956.

And the clients were pleased. And the studio prospered.

Every few days, he looked through an accumulation of portfolios left by artists. He recognized top talent, and when he saw work he liked, would design for it specifically. Ernie Smith, an authority on jazz, likens this to Duke Ellington, who composed to feature talented new musicians.

Lubalin began to have too much work to handle by himself. As Sudler & Hennessey grew, due to its award-winning art department, Herb created an exciting working atmosphere. He hired only artists and writers of the finest caliber, adding more than 40 people to the staff.

Many esteemed members of the profession are illustrious alumni of Sudler & Hennessey—Aaron Burns, Seymour Chwast, Bob Fiore, Gerry Gersten, Irwin Glusker, Helmut Krone, George Lois, Fred Papert, Larry Muller, Sam Scali, Arthur Singer, Bernie Zlotnick.

Reward for Intrinsic Merit
You have convinced the toughest of all juries when your advertising convinces customers to part with their money for your product. If you believe, as we do, that only creative advertising achieves outstanding results in to-day's competitive market, we suggest you investigate S&H as a source of creative ideas, art and design. It has been our pleasure to share over two hundred awards with leading advertisers over the past three years-and there is no charge for medals at Sudler & Hennessey. PL.1-1250

Institutional ad for Sudler & Hennessey, 1957.

George Lois, Chairman of the Board, Lois, Pitts, Gershon, speaking of "the greatest southpaw in the business," says, "Herb was probably the finest judge of talent I have ever seen."

Herb's laidback manner encouraged superb teamwork. People who worked for him wanted to please; they knew he sought the best, and they produced. He loved working with people who understood ideas; he'd look at something his staff had done, something he admired, and murmur his ultimate praise: "Goddamn."

His gentle quietude inspired loyalty that in one instance was unique and unsought. A pregnant assistant "was taking La Maze classes. I was so devoted to Herb that in those final weeks of pregnancy, I gave up my last class to help him hang an exhibit at the Type Directors' Club."

Conversely, exasperated artists have been critical of Lubalin's almost pathological inability to communicate verbally one-to-one with his craftspeople and partners.

It's an understatement to say Herb wasn't vocal about his feelings on work he had commissioned. As fine a communicator as he was professionally, in human relations, Lubalin said little. A range of grunts, a few words. Friends, assistants, secretaries would come to his office to chat, or for help with a specific job or problem. They talked. Herb worked. The number of words most people speak during the course of a day would equal Herb Lubalin's verbal output for a week.

His silence could be devastating. He'd look at work, nod and tell the artist or writer to leave it and send a bill. The artist or writer had no sense of success or failure.

The approval of his peers was manifested by the Gold T-Square, the highest industry award, given by the National Society of Art Directors, 1962.

One secretary summed it up for all his secretaries. "He couldn't say he liked a job, and he couldn't say he didn't like it. If he didn't like it, he'd put the job aside, and hire someone else to do it. When our offices moved, I found a stack of rejected jobs in the storeroom.

"The artists were bewildered constantly. I'd say, 'Herb, why didn't you say something?' He'd say, 'Why can't people be satisfied with doing their work? Why do they always want to be patted on the head?' He felt if you knew what you were doing, and if you did it well, that should be enough. I told him most people need a little more.

"But for himself, he had to have his pat on the head—the approval of his peers, and winning awards."

Lubalin at work at Lubalin, Smith, Carnase, 1975.

A young designer who worked closely with Herb at Lubalin Associates brings the early pattern up-to-date. "He was the quietest person. You almost had to use sign language to communicate. Little nods. Little finger movements. 'Do this. Do that.'

"He wasn't good with a compliment. If he looked at a job, grunted, and walked away, that was approval.

"He had no outside interests except as they pertained to design. He loved design, ate, slept, and drank it. He had the most fun sitting at his desk, drawing with his marker. Piles of tissues. It was terrific."

Herb's reluctance or inability to talk in depth made most personal relationships uncomfortable. A writer who was an intimate had difficulty with Herb's non-verbalizing. "We drove to work together for years, and never talked about anything personal. We'd talk about advertising, business and cars. Whenever I brought up anything personal, he'd sail right past it."

Closer to the bone, far more poignant, one of his sons says wistfully, "I loved my father, but we only exchanged maybe a few hundred words in his lifetime."

Herb's closest relationship was with his twin, Irwin. Laconic Herb became loquacious in Irwin's presence. At family dinners, their constant banter was a verbal tennis game. Irwin says when Herb felt passionately, he spoke up. It wasn't easy for him to argue because he had such difficulty articulating. In disagreement, he could become angry and abusive, and would withdraw.

First long pants. Irwin, left, and Herb, right, on the roof of their father's music store in Oyster Bay, New York, 1922.

Lubalin as guest lecturer.

In private conversation, his humor was subtle, not always understood, or he could spout from an ever-refurbished repertoire of jokes, most of which were obscene. And hilarious.

Given preparation time, as in his public-speaking, he was relaxed. Audiences testify he was "as funny as the Marx brothers." The evening he received the crowning jewel of his awards, the medal from the American Institute of Graphic Arts, he was openly revelatory, announcing joyfully that he was "engaged to be married" to the immensely charming Ms. Rhoda Sparber. "I'm lucky that the two most beautiful women I know agreed to marry me."

Ultimately, Sudler & Hennessey the studio, became Sudler, Hennessey & Lubalin, an advertising agency with Lubalin as creative director.

Still, there has been criticism of Herb's talents. "Lubalin's an exquisite designer, but he can't do an ad." One of his designers disputes this. "I can think of dozens of campaigns he turned out literally in hours, all of them brilliant. He was as good at ads as he was at design."

Lubalin on advertising: "The most intriguing thing about advertising is writing the headline. I think more about creating an idea, writing the headline, than designing the ad."

New logo for Sudler, Hennessey & Lubalin.

The influence of people barring the way between creator and consumer was disturbing to him. "You have account executives, agency presidents, copywriters, marketing experts, media and production people. If there's a choice between going with a good ad or changing it, an account executive will change it. Since I know better than anyone else what I'm doing, the only way I can function is to deal directly with the client."

He always rejected advertising a product or a political candidate he considered unethical. "I don't like to sell a product I don't respect. If you do a beautiful campaign and the consumer is disappointed in the quality of the product, you've wasted your effort."

His designer's responsibility was to educate the consumer to the aesthetics of good graphics. To him, advertising offered the most exciting form of communication. One of Lubalin's most memorable ads featured a drug to counteract muscle spasm. He came to the office with a Slinky®, a coil-like toy that could "walk" down stairs, slither across the floor, tumble end over end.

"See how it expands and contracts. Sort of says 'spasm.' We'll make it into a Spasm Campaign."

To Carl Fischer, "Make some pictures for me."

Fischer recounts, "He asked me for experimental pictures. He didn't know how he was going to use them, but he knew he was going to make a stomach spasm from them.

"I saw him giving birth to this, and it was effortless. Not the struggle we associate with the conception of an idea, but a joy, a delight to see. And it worked."

Lubalin, Smith, Carnase, Inc., 1967-1975.

Many art directors seem overwhelmed by their workload. But Lubalin never indicated the job demanded more than he could give. He never complained about the number of meetings or countless jobs he had to design and assign. An efficient administrator, he relied a great deal on his secretary and delegated freely to his staff.

His passion for design was diverse. "Advertising alone isn't enough. I love to create advertising, but in the right amounts, with the right people. It's the area I'm most interested in, as long as I don't have to do it all the time."

Logos reflecting the success and growth of Lubalin's design office. Herb Lubalin, Inc., 1964-1967.

In 1964, Lubalin left Sudler, Hennessey & Lubalin to give himself the fluidity he craved. From that day, as president of Herbert Lubalin, Inc., and through a successive series of partnerships, only about one-third of the studio output was on national consumer ads. Most of the accounts were commissions for logos and letterheads, books and book jackets, posters, packaging for bubble gum and tuna fish, and typeface design for architectural, editorial and industrial clients.

From 1964 until his death, only failing health could restrain his talent. He soared high and free, ever disciplined. He was as unconfined in his gusto for work as his inhibited nature allowed.

LSC&P, Inc., 1975-1978.

Lubalin opened editorial floodgates with Eros and Avant Garde, magazines which rocked the reading world with their erotic subject matter and bold graphic treatments. He designed typefaces reflecting both his humor and respect for the limitations of printing. He broke tradition and modernized ligatures unnoticed for centuries, except by scholars of illuminated manuscripts.

He found his ultimate niche as editor and designer of U&lc, (which he named, an abbreviation for upper and lower case type), a trade newspaper for the typographic industry with an international readership of 1,000,000. U&lc, the brainchild of Lubalin's friend, Aaron Burns, is a quarterly, direct mail promotion of 100-plus pages that features four new typefaces each year.

Lubalin was Executive Vice President of International Typeface Corporation, of which Burns is founding father and president. Burns believed that designers had withdrawn from creating typefaces because they weren't receiving royalties on each usage. The advertising industry was the loser. ITC opened a worldwide market for well-designed new typefaces by offering them to manufacturers at no cost except for a royalty fee, which designers share with ITC.

HERB LUBALIN
ASSOCIATES, INC.
TOM CARNASE
TONY DiSPIGNA
HERB LUBALIN
ALAN PECKOLICK
ERNIE SMITH
217 EAST 28TH ST.
NEW YORK, N.Y.
10016. OR9-2636

Herb Lubalin Associates, Inc., 1978-1980.

Lubalin worked on U&lc at his office on 28th Street. He arrived at 8 A.M. and solved The New York Times crossword puzzle before breakfast. When the staff came in, someone would prepare his coffee, for which amenity Herb cleared his throat to signify "Good Morning." He'd carry his breakfast on a tray to his desk, eat and work there until someone would stop him for lunch.

He halted reluctantly. At his desk, he lunched on hot food gone cold, and said he liked cold scrambled eggs, then worked long after the staff had left for the day.

When his signature was needed on business papers, his left hand worked on tissues, his right hand signed checks; the tissues piled up, the checks cleared the bank. No momentum was lost.

A woman staff designer discussed the disciplined demands of working on U&lc, the delicacy of making type conform to design.

"Herb scribbled most of his layouts. He knew exactly what he wanted. Sometimes, he gave me the scribbles, and it was my job to order type, get the art, put the whole thing together, and bring it to him when it was finished.

"He was open to suggestions, yet got things done the way he wanted. For an employee seeking creative freedom, it wasn't an ideal job. You were working with God. He didn't have 20 people going off in 20 directions. Quietly, subtly, without his giving orders, or standing over your shoulder, things were done the way he wanted,

Lubalin, Peckolick Associates, Inc., 1980-1981.

the way he needed, to keep the studio running.

"The first time I did a layout with a ragged bottom edge, he said, 'What the hell is this? Only a lazy designer does that.'

"That's one of the lessons I learned from him—not to be fast and lazy, but to take the time to do it right.

"To make everything line up, you've got to do it over and over again, and then, if the client alters the text, you've got to redo the whole thing. To him, it was worth it. How long it took or how much it cost wasn't as important to him as it was to other designers.

"On proofs for U&lc, when we wanted copy to flush, we would cut the L's, cut the E's, redraw the R's, overlap the O's. You can take two words of different length, and by carefully designing and spacing, make them align left and right. It may take all day. It may take several days. You've got to make it look as though they grew that way."

"Don't draw before you think" was Lubalin's rationale. He told his students, "You can't say why you do the subconscious things a good art director does. The guys who can explain are those who can't do things well."

There were many outside artists and writers working on U&lc assignments, primarily under instruction to "make it look good." Many of the studio designers were occupied with Lubalin's tissues. For each article, there were diverse pieces to keep tabs on, and Herb was always on top of the traffic flow and production schedules. He knew who was working on what, the status of every job, and when they were due. He kept mental notes of endless detail.

In setting type for U&lc, the telephone was the medium for the message. Lubalin phoned Matthew Baumwell of TriArts Press, and said, "I've got this job I need tomorrow. I may have a problem. I'll send it over. Tell me what you think."

Baumwell: "He'd send a rough and a few scribbled words. I'd use a few hundred words to instruct my people as to what he wanted. We'd give him 90% of it on the first proof.

"Then he'd phone. 'How about...,' and we'd discuss the 'how abouts....' I'd warn him of the pitfalls. Let's say the lines were underleaded. I'd say, 'If you put them any closer, you'll have the unfortunate overlap of ascenders and descenders.' He'd say, 'Let's worry about that when it happens,' or, 'Can't you control that?'

"So, we'd set the job, send the proofs, and Herb would call. 'I know what we can do. Insert the word 'the' in the middle of the second line, and

Beginning with *Scriptura '71*, a glorious series of lettering arts calendars has issued from the publishing house of Wilhelm Kumm in Offenbach, West Germany. Mr. Kumm was once a student in the Offenbach Workshop of the legendary Rudolf Koch, and there learned lettering as a "life-elixer." Today he is a publisher of fine editions, noted for the quality of their calligraphy, typography, and illustration.

The *Scriptura* calendars are manifestly more than productions for bibliophiles, for each calendar is dedicated to a different universal lettering theme and displays a dazzling variety of images within its twelve pages. The series is edited by the versatile and ebullient Dr. Hans Halbey, formerly the Manager of the Klingspor Museum in Offenbach and now the Director of the Gutenberg Museum in Mainz.

In 1978 Dr. Halbey arranged the greatest homecoming in the history of the printed book by securing the purchase of a copy of the Gutenberg Bible for the Gutenberg Museum, thus returning the book to its birthplace in Mainz after an absence of some 522 years! Dr. Halbey is so well-known in the book industry that on one occasion when he wanted to attend the Frankfort Book Fair to actually look at the books rather than to speak to his many acquaintances, he went disguised in a false moustache, beard, trenchcoat, and beret. The ploy worked.

Dr. Halbey selects the majority of the images for each year's calendar from the archives of the Klingspor Museum, a mecca of 20th century lettering art. In addition to major holdings of the work of German-speaking writing masters such as Rudolf Koch, F.H. Ernst Schneidler, Rudolf von Larisch, and Emil Rudolf Weiss, the Klingspor has a broad range of works from Europe and the world. On occasion, a new work is commissioned especially for a *Scriptura* calendar, and is then placed in the permanent collection of the Klingspor. Some other pieces in the *Scriptura* series are reproduced from originals in the private collections of the artists.

Each calendar generates a tangible excitement by the combination of an ingenious and thought-provoking theme with original and arresting images. In these pages the letterforms have been released from their humble and pedestrian labors and stand ready to fly like the spirit of Ariel freed from bondage by Prospero. By varying the theme each year, and representing each artist only once in a decade, Dr. Halbey has given the series a freshness and diversity seldom seen in compilations of lettering art. Many of the works have never been seen in the U.S.

For example, in the 1979 calendar, devoted to "Scriptural Drawing and Painting," the month of May shows a hauntingly subtle combination of collage and watercolor by Eva Aschoff, one of the dozen women represented in the series. Ms. Aschoff's abstract and painterly handwriting echoes the formal sensitivity of her teacher, Ernst Schneidler. In August of the same year is a writing-like network of lines with splotches by Heinz Trökes, and in November a curious abstract piece by Paul Klee.

For sheer depth, subtlety, and abstraction, it is hard to equal the character "Tao" calligraphed by Shiryu Morita in the November, 1973 calendar, the theme of which is "Speech and Writing." As the current wave of experimental calligraphy in America gathers momentum, it is clear that a major source of guiding inspiration is coming from images like Morita's, with its multiple levels of tonal value and nuances of spiritual expression. In April of the same year there is the matchless power of Rudolf Koch's woodcut textura Ten Commandments.

Lubalin was a perfectionist about type. After the first setting, he would make final adjustments to get precisely what he wanted. Here is a typical Lubalin marked-up type proof.

Lubalin's tissue for spread in U&lc. It pinned everything down, from type spec to the size and position of illustrations.

that will move all the words ahead....'

"We'd make these adjustments all the time over the phone. When the discussion ended, Herb would never say 'goodbye.' He'd mumble 'uh-huh,' and hang up."

Two professionals doing what they do best.

Baumwell adds, "Herb was innovative, but there were still limitations to typesetting, which is why he was so delighted with the new technology of photographic typography. The mechanical constraints he had lived with were changing. He became free from the concept of square letters: one letter butted *through* the other. He was able to make his wonderful interplay between letters, between lines.

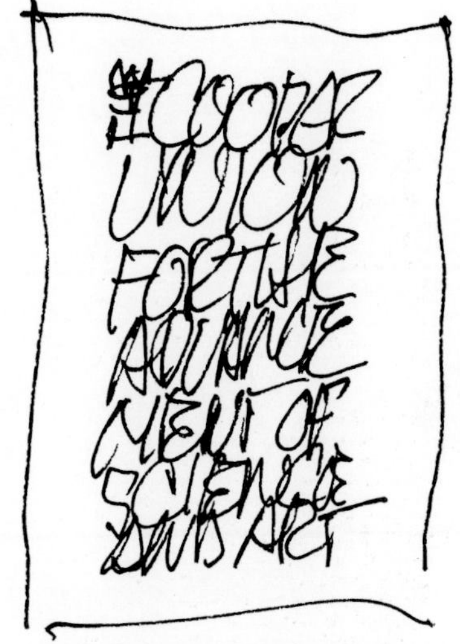

Initial rough, scribbled on the back of a memo pad, for a logo for Cooper Union. See page 56.

"The result excited him, not the technology. What intrigued him was not, 'What is it?' but 'What does it do that it didn't do before?' "

An assistant remembers: "He loved letterforms, characters in an alphabet. His design or logo was expressive typography; as illustration, it speaks for itself. I never knew him to put the final type proof on a mechanical without cutting a dash, respacing a line, using his sensitivity to turn text into his reflection of what type should be."

In a Cooper Union class on typography, Lubalin posited, "We've been conditioned to read the way Gutenberg set his type, and for 500 years, people have been reading widely-spaced words on horizontal lines Gutenberg spaced far apart. Even with advances in typesetting, typesetters still maintain the pattern. We read words, not characters, and pushing letters closer or tightening space between lines doesn't destroy legibility; it merely changes reading habits."

So Lubalin would cut, chop and tailor to the finest detail. He'd outline space dimensions, tell an artist he trusted, "Put it in here. Make it work."

Just as sound can't be explained, the understanding of letterforms and design nuances can't be verbalized. Before he revised a letter shape, Lubalin would rarely pinpoint a specific fault. Instead he would say, "Look at the connecting letters. Something's wrong. It doesn't feel right."

Even after years of viewing Herb's adaptability to rush jobs, Alan Peckolick was impressed by his partner's response to a particular eleventh-hour telephone request to plan an ad campaign.

"Lou Dorfsman phoned for a series of prototypes for a CBS News campaign. Herb, who was leaving for Europe that night, ground out tissues in a frenzy. At 6 P.M., when he had to make his flight, he came to me with his luggage, a fistful of

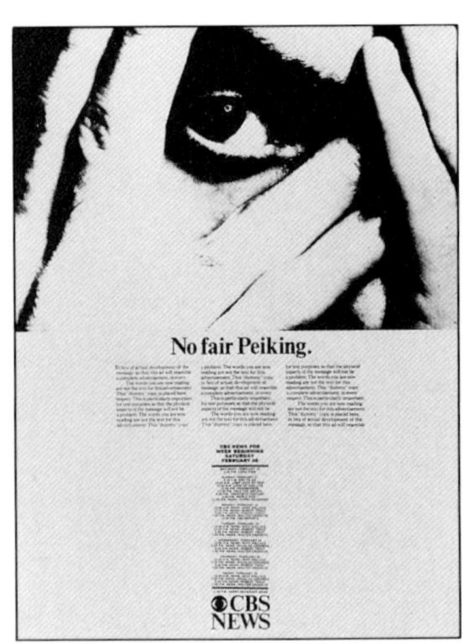

CBS News ad.

tissues, and instructions that 'these have to be comped up, and delivered tomorrow.'

"I looked through Herb's scribbles for 30 or 40 ads with the headlines written out to say something about China, 36 point Times Roman Bold. No break in his thought, no break in the writing. One continuous line, yet anyone familiar with design knew where the headline ended and the type spec began."

For Lubalin the businessman, business would have been much more enjoyable if he didn't have to deal with so many clients.

When a meeting was scheduled, he often begged off, leaving the matter to a partner or a trusted assistant. Sometimes he had to be there. If he became irritated, Lubalin's high-pitched voice would grow dominant, authoritative. He knew his subject, believed in his presentation.

For the most part, clients understood this. However, if they were unreasonably resistant, Herb would declare, "This is the way it's going to be if you're going to work with me." The persuasive factor was his incredible track record of increased sales through graphics.

Still, the most consistent criticism from a client was, "It's beautiful, but I can't read it." And the saying amongst competing designers was, "If it's readable, Lubalin didn't do it."

A partner analyzes: "A good businessperson makes money, worries about overhead and how to invest. Most designers aren't good at business. Herb was happy if rent and salaries were paid, and there were assignments on his drawing board.

"True, his priority was to make money, but the reason he came to the office every day was to do his work. Negotiating contracts, fees and royalties were not his forte. Our income suffered because many of our jobs were underpriced so Herb could get them in-house. Also, he hired new talent whether or not the ratio of work could sustain an additional salary. Once, we had a staff of 26 in addition to 5 partners."

"What's a schmuck?" Lubalin once asked. His answer: "An art director who doesn't get royalties on his designs."

Herb's pejorative question rests in his chagrin at the result of a business deal he handled on his own. A movie company wanted a program for a forthcoming film, a book to be sold in theatres across the country and abroad. Instead of accepting a lesser fee than the studio's norm, with a percentage of royalties from the book, he asked for his usual fee without royalties. The film com-

Photo for article in Graphis on Lubalin's partners, Di Spigna, Peckolick and Smith.

pany met his price and Herb lost all the royalties from the book, The Sound of Music, which has sold almost as many copies as the Holy Bible!

In the long run, Lubalin's work relied on the strength of its graphics, to which color was secondary. "Yet, his color selectivity was exquisite, especially for someone who was colorblind," observed an assistant.

Herb's colorblindedness wasn't as much of a handicap as the myth indicates. He could see red and green clearly, but couldn't estimate the amount of red or green in other colors. Was the yellow hot or cool? He told of buying a pair of "golf-course green" slacks believing them to be olive drab.

Some of his colored pencils had their names printed on them.

Jokingly, he explained that being colorblind was an advantage for an artist. "We don't get confused seeing all the colors there are. The eye compensates by being more perceptive to the other things it sees."

Typographic self-portrait for an exhibit at the American Institute of Graphic Arts.

Eros was the launching pad that propelled Lubalin into the spotlight, spreading his name to a new generation, and culminating with the international prestige he found as designer of U&lc.

Ralph Ginzburg, publisher of Eros, Avant Garde, Fact, and Moneysworth, recalls, "I didn't know what to make of him, which is the reaction of most, meeting him for the first time. He seemed unresponsive, yet when we talked about design problems, his solutions were instantaneous and breath-taking. I thought he was doodling as I articulated the problem, but I saw that he had roughed out a terrific sketch, right there on the spot. There was no design problem he couldn't tackle with ease and gusto.

"If he had several solutions, he gave me my choice. In our 20 years of working together on projects, ranging from proposals for periodicals to specific articles, ads and direct mail pieces, he never disputed my selection. He was confident of everything he presented. He didn't allow me to see anything he didn't like himself.

Lubalin used this phrase often. Ernie Smith had it embroidered, and Lubalin displayed it prominently in his office.

"Argue? Never editorially. He had accepted me as a client with the proviso he have full design control. But, he thought many of my ads and merchandising were vulgar. 'It stinks,' his favorite put-down, was probably right. A few of my promotions really did stink. Of course, they were the ones that worked best.

"Herb and I had a professional relationship like none I know. We were in constant touch by phone. I would call the minute I suspected he might be awake. Usually, I was wrong by a couple of hours. I'd call at 7 A.M. before he left for work, and on weekends I'd race over to his house. Many of the jobs were done on the table at his bedside.

"For a new publication, I wrote lengthy notes with my overall concept. The format was his decision. He would have three or four ideas and would design logos. I would do whatever research the section heading required and find samples of all typography.

"The publication, Avant Garde, began as the single most difficult collaboration we had. I had the distinct idea that it should be a voice of art and politics for the '60's. He said that concept was atrocious, and that the very name of the magazine came out of the '20's.

The Type Directors Club asked Lubalin to write the introduction to their first Annual. On the facing page, was his design incorporating all 26 characters of the Avant Garde typeface.

"His first logo was in Hebrew. He thought that was funny. Then he did it in Coco-Cola script. We went through a dozen logos, masterfully executed. One day, he called me before he left for work, 'I've got it, Ralph!'

"Herb's genius made Avant Garde appear as an expensively produced periodical. It was so magnificently designed, few were aware it was printed on newspaper stock."

The Avant Garde alphabet grew out of its logo. Ginzburg had amassed Picasso erotica, and asked Herb to use it in a sales promotion for Avant Garde. Lubalin wanted titles for the engravings to match the logo, and an alphabet was born, acknowledged by the industry as the most successful new typeface of the 20th century.

Three designers worked against the clock on 26 letters, checking weights. Alternate characters were provided to give users leeway in designing with display type. Another partner, Tony DiSpigna, a type designer and one of the country's finest hand-letterers, says, "The first time Avant Garde was used was one of the few times it was used correctly. It's become the most abused typeface in the world."

Ed Benguiat, a Vice President of Photo Lettering agrees. "The only place Avant Garde looks good is in the words Avant Garde. Everybody ruins it. They lean the letters the wrong way."

The Lubalin residence in New York.

Lubalin's personal style was reflected by all things around him. He drove the newest imported sports cars and enjoyed the admiration of passing motorists when stopped in traffic. He worked and lived in refined ambiance. He was fond of Victoriana, and accumulated Art Nouveau posters before it became fashionable. He loved ornate furniture and natural wood, and he responded to the craftsmanship of carpentry. In his working environment and in his houses, he was surrounded with taste. His offices in the building vacated by Hook and Ladder Company #7, his small mews in the city, and his rambling house in the country all projected his graceful control of space. His sense of form and texture was apparent in the glistening wood, the brass trim, beveled glass, the art and selective found objects displayed on the walls.

Hook and Ladder Co. #7, home of Lubalin, Peckolick Associates.

"I studied architecture, you know," he'd say, to explain his confidence in the seemingly foolhardy and extensive renovations he commissioned from his own plans.

Lubalin's young staff saw beyond the facade of this work-driven man. Most of them adored him. Young women mothered him. All made festive occasions of his birthdays. His response would be a twinkle, his thanks, a shy smile, gratitude, the offer of a lift home, and, rarely, a quick hug. For Christmas, he'd invite his office family to a weekend in the country.

Ralph Ginzburg was astounded to hear that Herb was not well. "A year before he died, I heard he was severely ill. I called. 'Do you want the whole story?' he asked. And he recited the list of cancer removal operations he had undergone. I was dumbfounded. There was a long telephone silence. To diffuse the situation, Herb quipped, 'Hey Ralph, look at the bright side....'"

Lou Dorfsman, Vice President, Creative Director, Advertising and Design, CBS Inc., and his wife, Ann Hysa, a curator at the Cooper Hewitt Museum, were Cooper Union classmates with Herb Lubalin and Sylvia Kushner. The four young people were married on the same day and for a while, shared living quarters. At the outset of their careers, Herb and Lou shared portfolios.

Professionally, Herb and Lou also shared the public podium and presented each other with competitive honors. On a more personal level, there were years and memories that were carefree, pungent and tragic. There were children, vacations, and a circle of other classmates bonded in closeness during 45 years.

The final time Dorfsman offered public tribute to Lubalin was at Herb's memorial service at The Great Hall of Cooper Union.

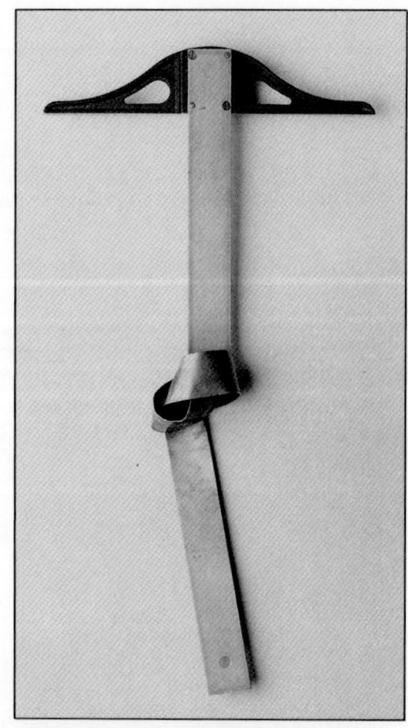

A gift from his design staff in the early 60's. The knotted T-square is inscribed: "To Herb Lubalin for successfully ignoring this instrument for so many years."

"Herb had the joy of knowing as a certainty that his existence was no empty absurdity, that he made an important contribution to, and revolutionized, his profession, and had set its course for decades to come."

You needn't have worried, Mr. Kushner. Your son-in-law turned out just fine.

THE EVOLUTION OF A LUBALIN LOGO

These logos were designed for PAS Graphics, distributors of art supplies. When Lubalin approached an assignment like this, he would first sketch his ideas on tissues—anywhere from three to 30. He edited the tissues down to a select few which he would present to the client, and turned these over to a handletterer for tighter rendering. When the comps were returned, Lubalin would often take an element from one, and with it, develop an additional logo. When he made his presentation to the client, he would indicate which logo he preferred.

These pages show the clarity of Herb's initial concepts. The final result needs little modification from the tissue. Note the tissue sketch at top of page 26. At the bottom of page 27 is a finished logo featuring the symbol from the tissue. This is the logo chosen by the client.

THE CBS WALL

PROSCIUTTO
SQUAB
CAKE
MARMALADE
Strudel
TOM &
MINT JERRY
BASS
OATMEAL
DELICATESSEN
OKRA
FINNAN HADDIE
CORN
PIE
BOUILLABAISSE
SHORT BREAD
PUMPERNICKEL
Menu
CRAB
AVOCADO
BUTTERSCOTCH
FIG
BEEF
KNOCK WURST
CHEF
TUNA
TANGERINE
COGNAC
ALE
WATER MELON
ROE
MILK & COOKIES
EXIT
FRUIT JUICE
SAND WICH
LASAGNE
FONDUE
TAMALE
HOT TAMALE
WELSH RABBIT
HALVAH
LAMB CHOP
LOBSTER
THYME
rice
PRETZEL
SCRAMBLED
BOILED
POACHED
FRIED
SHIRRED
EGG
Hamburger & Roll
STEW
HAM
FINOCCHI
PIGS FEET
NUT
GARLIC ONION
GOOSE LIVER
PLUM
CAT
SUP
RAGOUT
CRANBERRY
BAR & GRILL
ROAST
TOAST
SALT
BRIE
CAMEMBERT
BLUE
ROQUEFORT
EDAM
BEL PAESE
GOUDA
GRUYERE
PORT DU SALUT
CHEDDAR
MUENSTER
SAGE
BRIOCHE
Dill
Eat Drink and Be Merry
PORK
EAT
HOT DOG
RHUBARB
BORSCHT
PEA
APPLES
SELTZER
CURACAO
TEA
ANCHOVY
MOZZARELLA
CUMQUAT
ARTICHOKE
CHICKEN PAPRIKA
BUCKWHEAT PANCAKES
BUN
SPAGHETTI
BANANA
FUDGE
HASSENPFEFFER
caviar
SAUERKRAUT
ICE
QT
LB
PT
OZ
STRAW BERRY
Soda
Gefüllte Fish
MUSSEL
OYSTER
SCALLOP
SHRIMP
DANISH PASTRY
raisin
EEL
BAGELS & LOX
scone
LIME

Lubalin worked with Lou Dorfsman on many CBS projects One of the most spectacular was the 40 x 8½′ three-dimensional "food" wall in the CBS cafeteria.

The idea for the project belonged to Dorfsman. After solving the problems of engineering, construction and measurement, Dorfsman hired Herb Lubalin to execute rough layouts to scale for all of the panels on the CBS wall. Herb worked from Dorfsman's single panel mock-up, allowing for staggered areas where Dorfsman intended to insert real three-dimensional food objects.

When the roughs were approved, Lubalin asked Tom Carnase to do the intricate hand-lettering.

Upon its first "unveiling," the CBS wall created a stir in the industry, and many articles have appeared to describe it. Summing it up best is Dr. Frank Stanton: "The wall never ceases to excite the imagination. To me, it represents one of the most arresting design creations seen anywhere."

The wall is an eye-stopper—a visual example of what can be achieved by designers who have spent their best energies polishing their craft.

TUNA
COGNAC
ALE
VICHYSSOISSE
WATER
MELON
GOOSE
LIVER
A LA CARTE

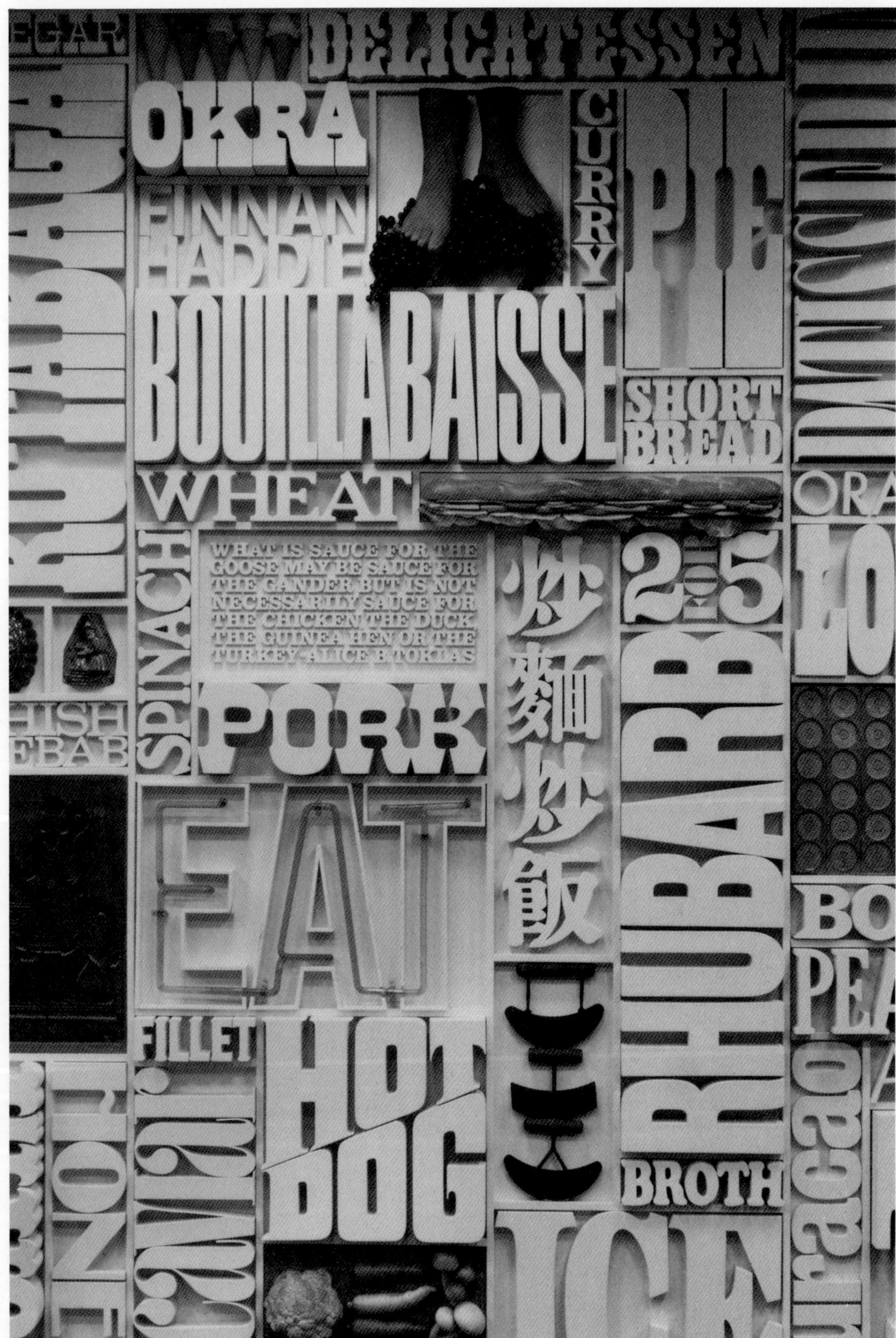

PROMOTIONS FOR THE LUBALIN STUDIOS

1.

2.

3.

4.

1. Announcement for the new office opening, 1964.

2. Ad in the Cooper Union fund-raising book.

3. Announcement for the Lubalin, Smith, Carnase exhibit in Paris.

4. Ad in a trade magazine reporting on the growth of Herb Lubalin, Inc.

5. Christmas card reads upside down and right-side up, 1972.

6. House ad in trade magazine.

7. Christmas card.

5.

6.

7.

8. Christmas card.

9. Poster announcing a 20-year retrospective of Lubalin's work.

8.

A retrospective exhibition of
the old work of Herb Lubalin
which includes his new work
which is now old.
ONE
BICENTENNIAL
TH '54 '74
"20 Years at Hard Labor"

9.

POSTERS

MARRIAGE

1.

ANNOUNCING A
NATIONAL
TYPE FACE DESIGN
COMPETITION
SPONSORED BY
VISUAL GRAPHICS
CORPORATION
MIAMI, FLORIDA
NEW YORK, NEW YORK

"A ABCDE
FG,HI
JKLMNO
P,QRSTU
&V,W abcde
XY& fghijk
Z"!?/?: lmnop
qrstuv
wxy&z
$1234567890¢

2.

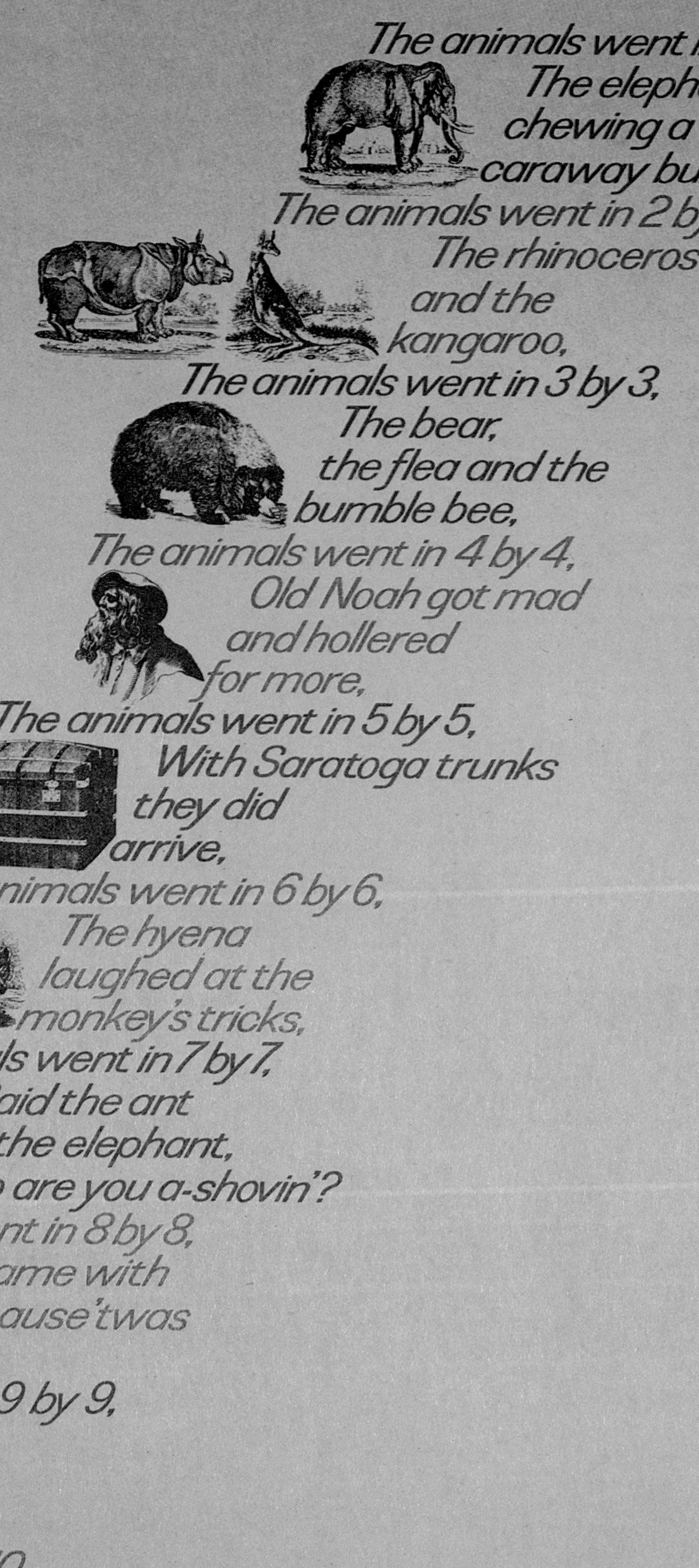

The animals went in 1 by 1,
The elephant
chewing a
caraway bun,
The animals went in 2 by 2,
The rhinoceros
and the
kangaroo,
The animals went in 3 by 3,
The bear,
the flea and the
bumble bee,
The animals went in 4 by 4,
Old Noah got mad
and hollered
for more,
The animals went in 5 by 5,
With Saratoga trunks
they did
arrive,
The animals went in 6 by 6,
The hyena
laughed at the
monkey's tricks,
The animals went in 7 by 7,
Said the ant
to the elephant,
who are you a-shovin'?
The animals went in 8 by 8,
They came with
a rush 'cause 'twas
so late,
The animals went in 9 by 9,
Old Noah
shouted,
"Cut that line!"
The animals went in 10 by 10,
The Ark
she blew her
whistle then.

3.

Visual Graphics Corporation manufactures photostat and typesetting equipment. In 1964, they held a competition for designs of new typefaces which VGC would adapt for production, and for which they would pay royalties.

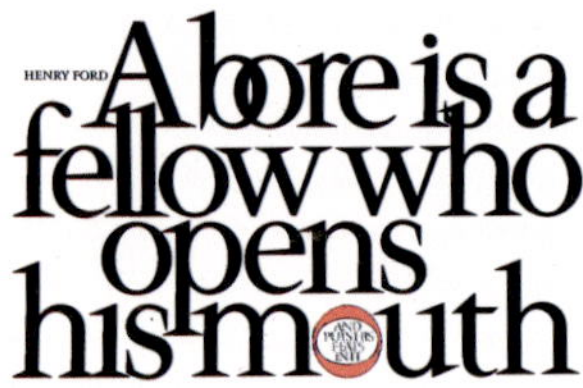

4.

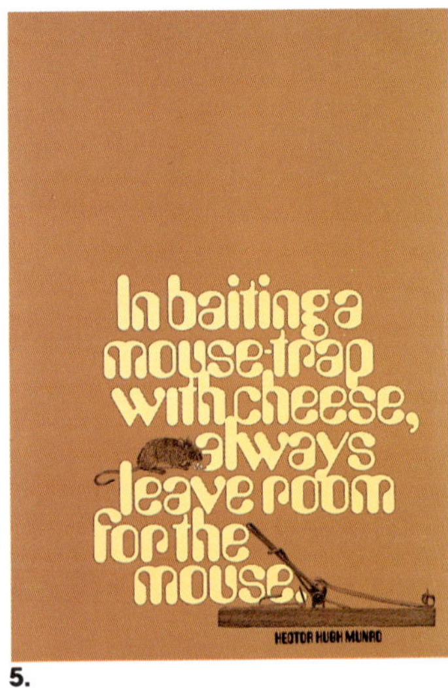

5.

6.

7.

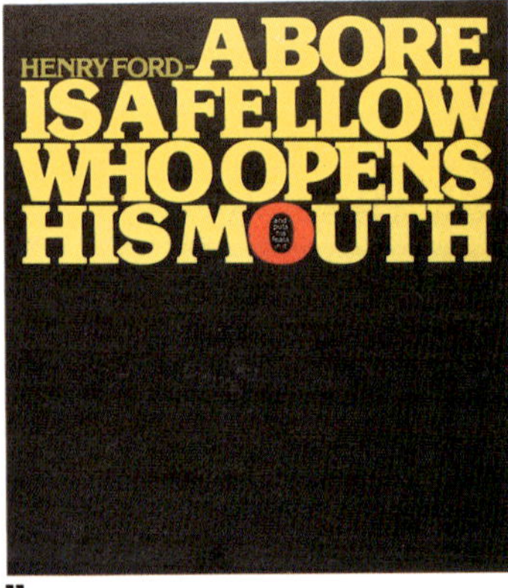

11.

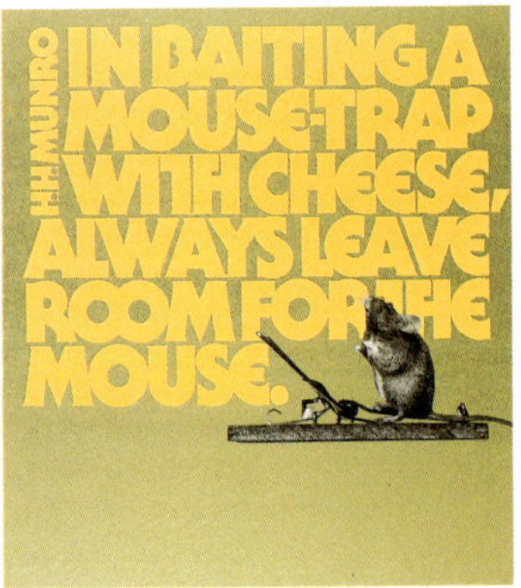

12.

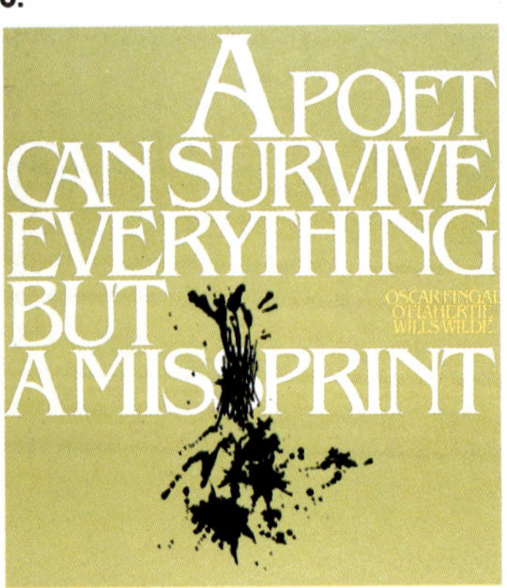

13.

14.

2. Announcement of the VGC competition.

1.,3.-10. Lubalin was one of the judges. These posters were designed by him, using winning typefaces from the competition.

11.-17. Later, in 1978, Lubalin redesigned the posters, using faces that were created after 1964. These posters were not for distribution, and were used only for an article in U&lc.

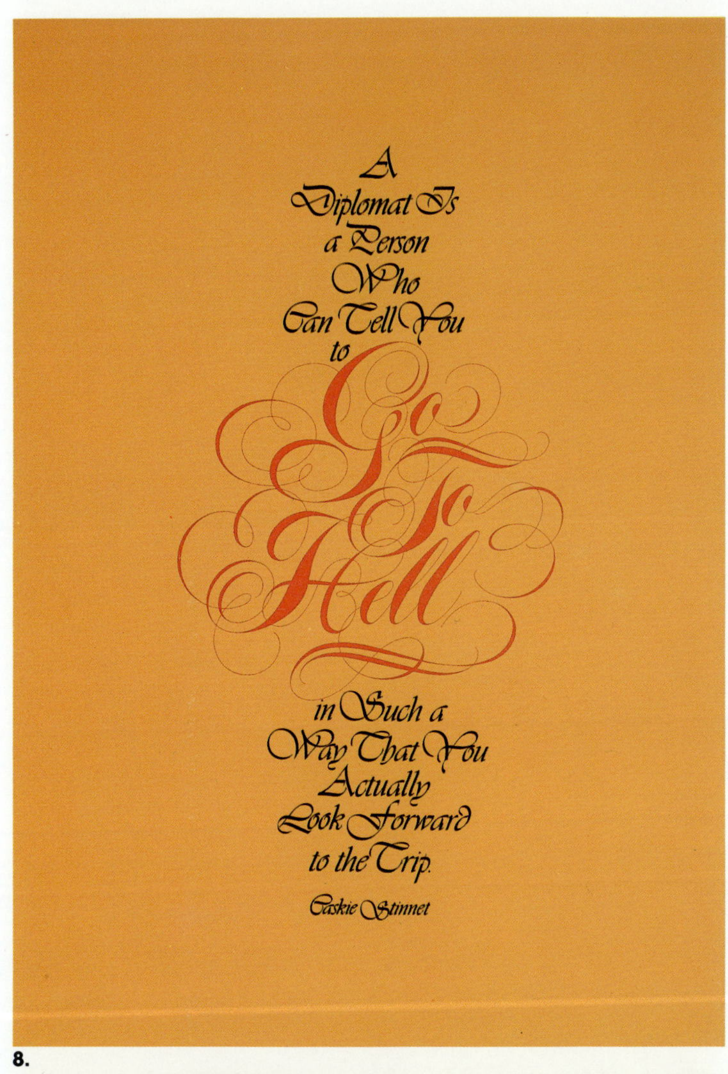

8.

Nothing
exceeds
like
excesss.
Robert Moses

9.

10.

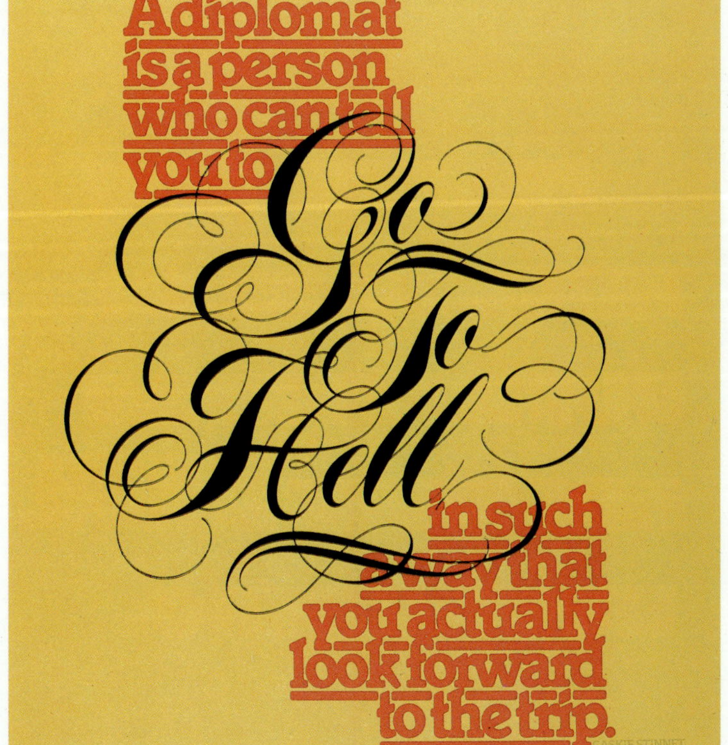

15.

16.

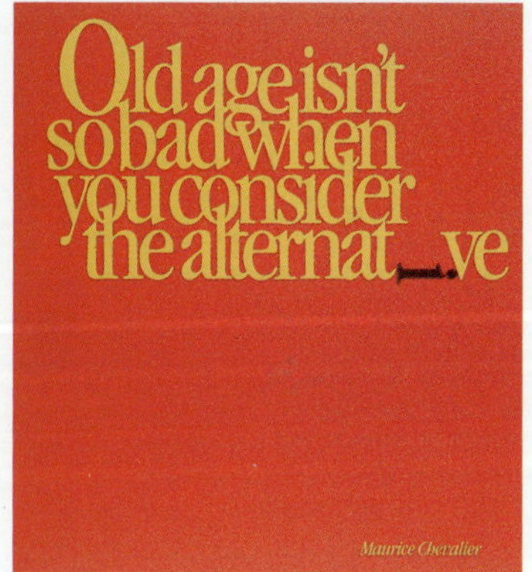

17.

18.-25. Additional posters using VGC award-winning typefaces. The top two-thirds of #20 features original Lubalin art.

Benjamin Franklin

I WISH THE BALD EAGLE HAD NOT BEEN CHOSEN AS THE REPRESENTATIVE OF OUR COUNTRY; HE IS A BIRD OF BAD MORAL CHARACTER; LIKE THOSE AMONG MEN WHO LIVE BY SHARPING AND ROBBING, HE IS GENERALLY POOR, AND OFTEN VERY LOUSY. THE TURKEY IS A MUCH MORE RESPECTABLE BIRD, AND WITHAL A TRUE ORIGINAL NATIVE OF AMERICA

18.

19.

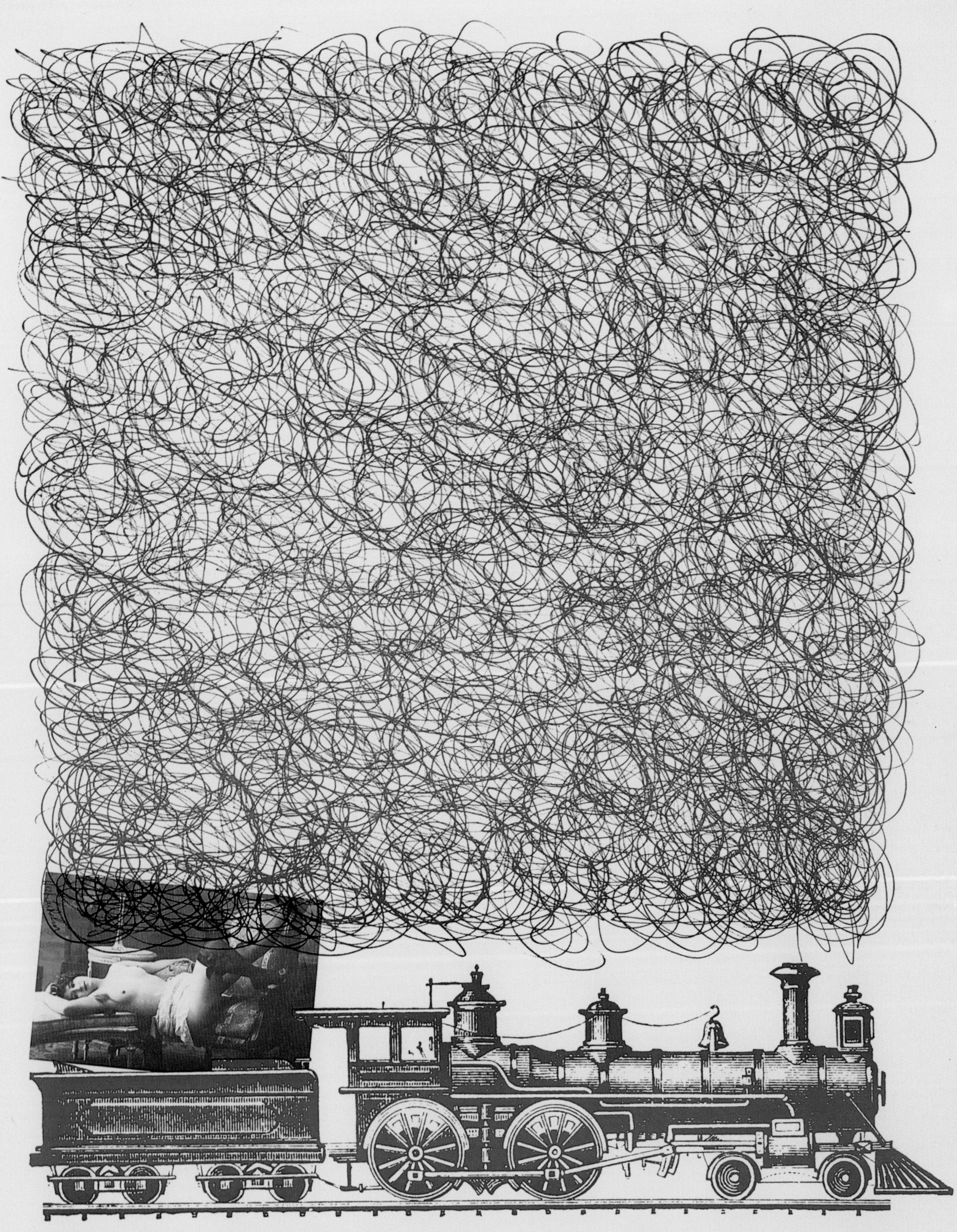

20.

THIRTY DAYS HATH SEPTEMBER (),

Fair summer gently fades away,
And withering flowers fortel her doom;
Thus will earth's brightest joys decay,
And bear us with them to the tomb.

APRIL (), JUNE AND ()

Though Nature smiles when comes her time,
And decks the fields in verdant green,
Yet in our cold New England clime
Few pleasant days this month are seen.

Fair Summer reigns o'er all the land-
How mild and gentle is her sway;
She scatters with a liberal hand
Choice blessings round us every day.

NOVEMBER (); ALL THE REST HAVE

Now sombre clouds o'erspread the skies,
And cast a gloom o'er hill and lea;
Cold is the wind, bleak storms arise,
And tune their mournful minstrelsy.

THIRTY-ONE (),( ),(),

How fierce the wintry tempests howl,
How cheerless is the naked grove;
The skies assume an angry scowl,
And lakes and steamlets cease to move.

The dreary winter months are gone,
And Sol prolongs the hours of day,
But yet no music hails the morn,
No verdure clothes the leafless spring.

The blooming beauties of the spring
With balmy odors fill the air;
And birds with cheerful music sing,
To drive away corroding care.

(),(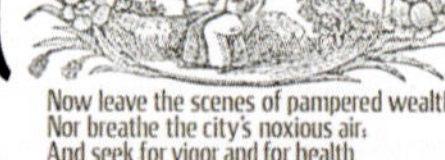),(),(),

How grateful is the cooling shade
To those who toil or roam the plain,
When Sol, in glowing robes arrayed,
Resumes o'er all his sultry reign.

Now leave the scenes of pampered wealth,
Nor breathe the city's noxious air;
And seek for vigor and for health
In verdant fields and woodlands fair.

Though blooming verdure smiles no more,
And dreary is the landscape round,
Yet autumn's rich and bounteous store
Cause joy and gladness to abound.

Another year its course has run,
And all its scenes forever fled;
How soon will mortal life be done -
And we all numbered with the dead!

EXCEPTING FEBRUARY ALONE (),

Yet time so rapidly moves on,
That snowy fields and wintry skies
Will like a phantom soon be gone,
And other scenes before us rise.

WHICH HATH BUT TWENTY-EIGHT, IN FINE,

TILL LEAP YEAR GIVES IT TWENTY-NINE.

21.

In the beginning
God created
the heaven
and the earth.
genesis

22.

FOR MOST MEN
LIFE IS A SEARCH
FOR THE PROPER
MANILA ENVELOPE
IN WHICH TO
GET THEMSELVES
FILED.
CLIFTON FADIMAN

23.

Speech
Silence

24.

ETER
IPER
ICKED A
ECK OF
ICKLED
EPPERS;
A
ECK OF
ICKLED
EPPERS
ETER
IPER
ICKED.
IF
ETER
IPER
ICKED A
ECK OF
ICKLED
EPPERS,
WHERE'S THE
ECK OF
ICKLED
EPPERS
ETER
IPER
ICKED
?

25.

26. Lubalin wrote the copy and designed this anti-war poster for an American Institute of Graphic Arts exhibition.

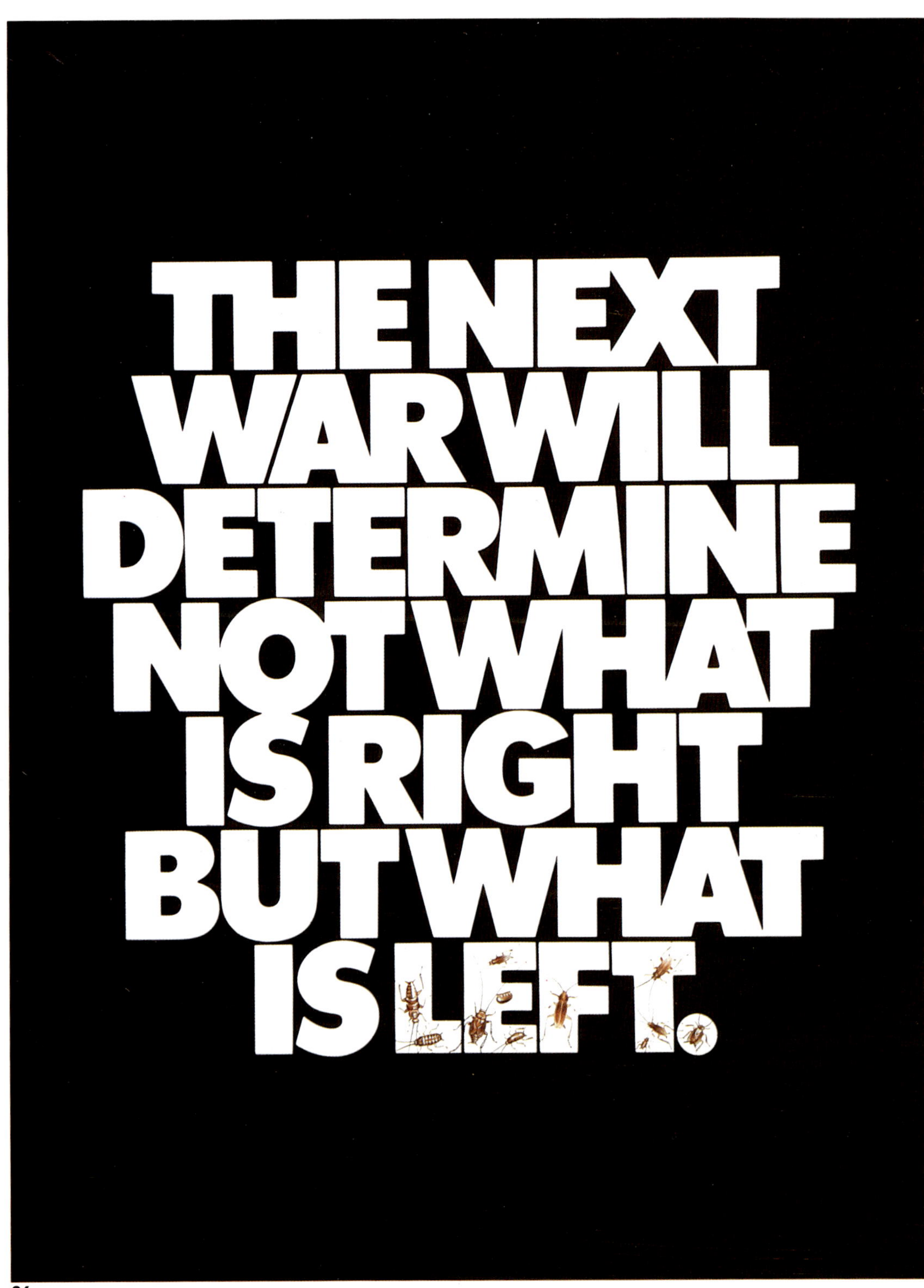

26.

27. Announcement of Avant Garde's anti-war poster contest.

28. Announcement for the opening of the International Typeface Corporation Exhibition Center of the Graphic Arts. Lubalin asked 26 illustrators to each illustrate a letter of the alphabet.

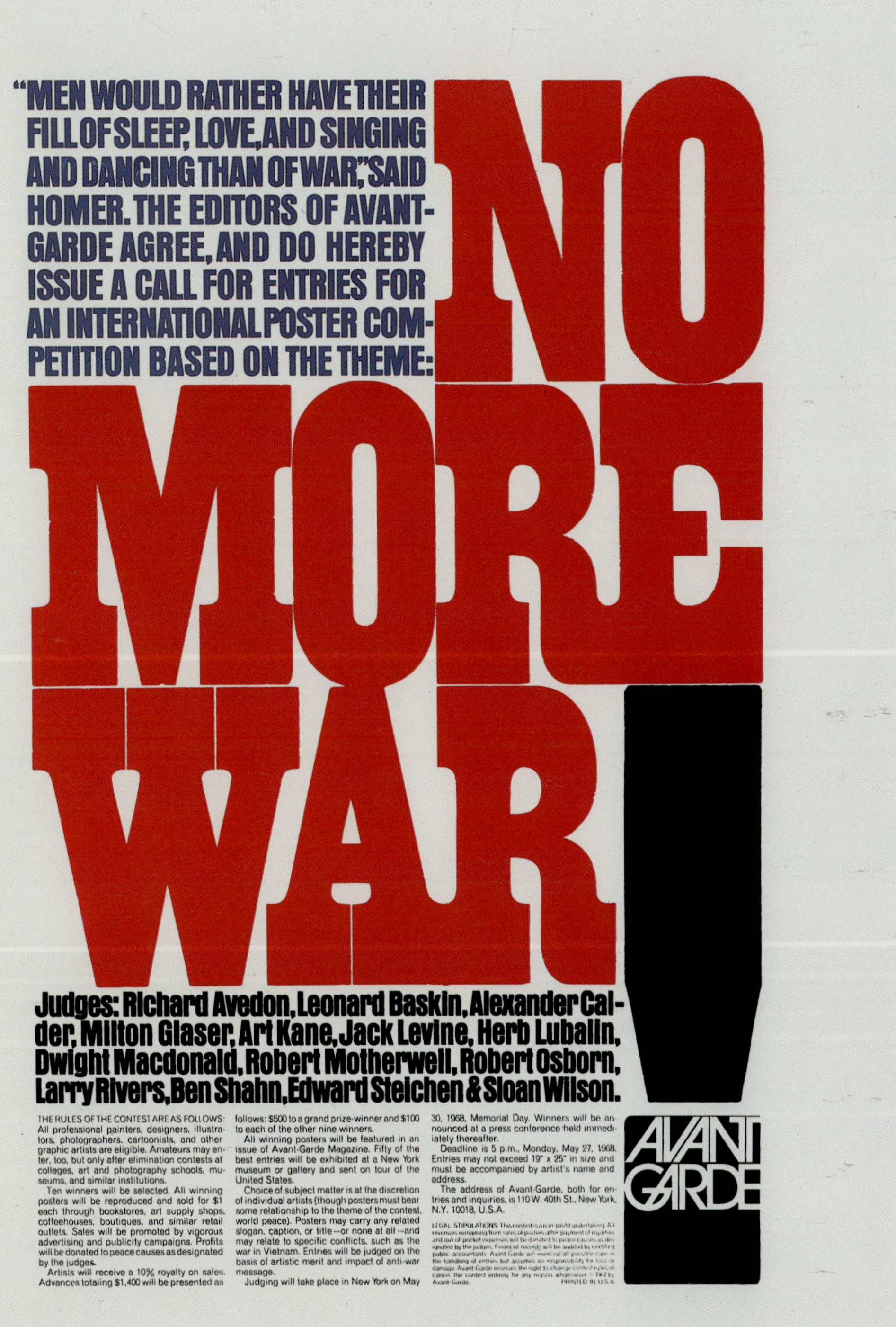

27.

UNDERSTANDING OF TYPE DEMANDS MORE THAN THE MERELY SUPERFICIAL KNOWLEDGE OF CERTAIN FACTS: ONE MUST RATHER PENETRATE INTO THE SIGNIFICANT BECOMING THAT STRETCHES BACK OVER CENTURIES AND MILLENIA—TYPES ARE A KEY TO THE GATE OF HUMAN UNDERSTANDING. IT IS THE INSTRUMENT WITH WHICH MAN OPENS FOR HIMSELF THE KNOWLEDGE OF NATURE AND OF HIMSELF. IT
OH?
IS LIKE A MIRROR WHICH, CAREFULLY REGARDED, CAN REVEAL THE COUNTENANCE OF THE TIMES AND THEIR CHANGING EXPRESSION. NO ADVANCE IS POSSIBLE WITHOUT THE PRINTED WORD. HOW MANY HOPES, HOW MANY DREAMS OF MANKIND HAS IT BROUGHT TO FULFILLMENT! PRINT IS THE LINK BETWEEN MAN AND MAN, BETWEEN OUR YESTERDAYS AND OUR MORROWS—HERMANN VIRL, STUTTGART.
A STAN MACK
B BARBARA NESSIM
C SEYMOUR CHWAST
D DICK HESS
E CHARLES SLACKMAN
F WILSON McLEAN
G MILTON GLASER
H BOB ALCORN
I GIL STONE
J DOUG JOHNSON
K GERRY GERSTEN
L JIM McMULLEN
M MARIE MICHAL
N NORMAN GREEN
O ROY CARRUTHERS
P FRANCOIS COLOS
Q ROGER HANE
R BOB GROSSMAN
S JIM SPANFELLER
T SIMMS TABACK
U MURRAY TINKELMAN
V HEATHER COOPER
W CHARLIE WHITE
X JEROME SNYDER
Y MARVIN MATTELSON
Z JAMES GRASHOW
ITC Center
THIS POSTER WAS DESIGNED BY HERB LUBALIN FOR INTERNATIONAL TYPEFACE CORPORATION ON THE OCCASION OF THE OPENING OF THE ITC CENTER, 2 HAMMARSKJOLD PLAZA, NEW YORK, APRIL 1980

28.

LOGOS

1.

2.

3.

festival'78

4.

5.

Lubalin was best known for his Spencerian script lettering, a style which is often incorrectly referred to as calligraphy. Although calligraphy really is hand lettering that begins in sketch form, its execution is a free single-stroke movement with a brush or pen.

Spencerian script is lettering that is developed in sketch form, and is very tightly drawn with a croquil pen.

When designing with letter forms, Lubalin would develop a series of sketches until the lettering was exactly as he wanted. Depending on the complexity of his design, this would take as few as one, two, or as many as eight to ten sketches.

For final execution, the sketches were turned over to John Pistilli, Tom Carnase or Tony Di Spigna, three of the finest hand-letterers in the world. It was in their hands that the nuance and grace of the final art occurred.

1. The Steelograph Company of New York does meticulous steel engraving. Lubalin created this distinctive logo, which suggests the fine quality of the company's work.

2. Logo for the package of a new, short, slim cigar. It was rejected by the client who felt it was too feminine.

3. Logo for the Shawmut Sterling Group, an insurance company.

4. Logo for the Public Broadcasting System. It was used to identify a week of special programming.

5. Logo for an exhibition of soft sculpture.

6. Logo for a Ralph Ginzburg publication on life styles.

7. Logo for the film, "The Agony and the Ecstasy."

8. Logo for the motion picture, "The Sound Of Music."

Better Living

6.

7.

8.

9a.

9b.

9c.

Part of the total design for a never-published magazine. This logo has won numerous awards, and is in the permanent collection of the Museum of Modern Art. Typographically, the logo not only states the name but graphically interprets the message. Lubalin felt that the suggestion of the fetus in the logo was one of his finest typography designs.

9a. In 1965, Lubalin's assistant, Alan Peckolick, developed this logo from tissues Lubalin had given him.

9b. Filling O's in words was a Lubalin specialty. Obligingly, Peckolick put the words "and child" in the O of Mother, and returned the tissue to Lubalin.

9c. This was the final logo developed by Lubalin and Tom Carnase.

HER

THE BIBLE

10.

11.

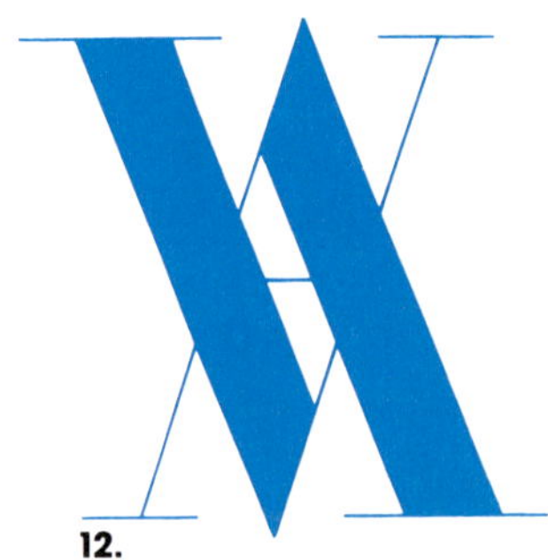

12.

13.

14.

15.

16.

10. Logo for the film, "The Bible."

11. A logo for the design division of Young & Rubicam derived from the Madison Avenue address of the agency.

12. Logo for photographer Ike Vernon, Vernon Associates.

13. Logo for Stevens Fabrics. The interlocking S's suggest woven cloth.

14. Logo for Ego, a computer which will generate page and format design.

15. Logo for the First National Bank of Dallas, playing on the fact that the bank was located at a First Place address. It was intended for use on all printed material, as well as for a street sculpture. It was rejected by the client.

16. Logo for Interior Planning & Design Services.

17. Logo for a French eyeglass manufacturing company. It is a good example of typographics. See page 50, #9.

18. Logo for the first advertising agency owned jointly by blacks and whites. The logo works in positive and negative.

19. Logo for New York's PBS station. Lubalin was adamant that the logo not use numerals.

20. Logo for the alumni newsletter for The Cooper Union for the Advancement of Science and Art.

21. Logo and cover design for a new graphic arts magazine from Germany. Because the budget was small, Lubalin suggested that the logo and cover work as a single design. His concept could be used for 10 covers by printing the number of each issue in a second color.

17.

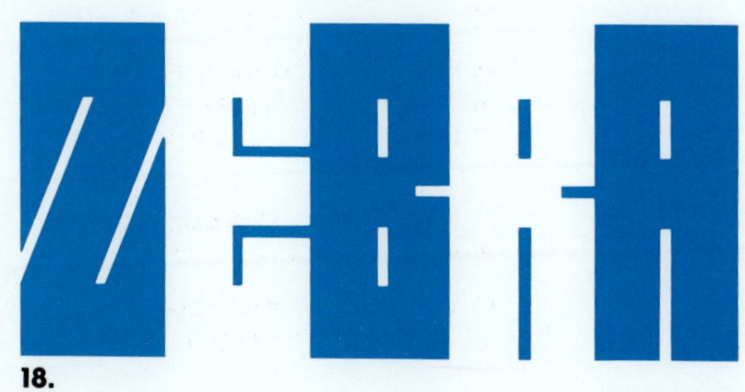

18.

19.

20.

21.

22.

22. Logo for Typographic Communication, Inc., typesetters.

23. Logo for Mel Simon Productions, film producers.

24. Corporate logo for Ladies Home Journal, Curtis Publications.

25. Logo for Finch-Pruyn, paper manufacturers.

23.

24.

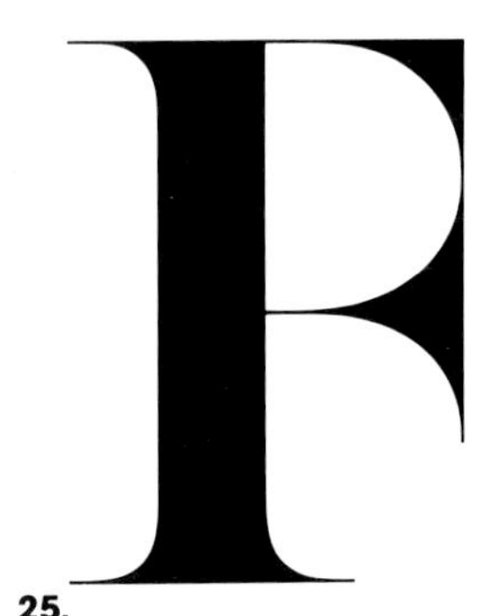
25.

26. Logo for Galeries Lafayette, a Paris department store. They wanted a contemporary logo that would work equally well with signage and packaging. Lubalin saw the Art Nouveau building that housed the Paris store, and consequently dissuaded his client from using too trendy a logo.

27. Logo for Moneysworth, a Ginzburg publication on consumer spending.

28. Masthead logo for a one-shot political newspaper. It was produced by designers and illustrators for McGovern.

29. Logo for a graphic arts quarterly. In this particular issue on good and bad typography, Lubalin opined, "the best typography never gets noticed."

26.

27.

McGraphic

28.

Typahgrrphy

29.

Logos usually are simple designs, using two or three letter forms and/or symbols. Most designers shy away from creating logos with many words. But not Lubalin. He was also an expert at using O's typographically. The ultimate in O-filling exercises is #33.

THE COOPER
UNION
SCHOOL
OF ART &
ARCHI-
TECTURE

30.

31.

30. Lubalin held a competition in his Cooper Union class, and asked his students to design a school logo. Not without ego, Lubalin entered the competition and lost.

31. Logo for the United Nations.

32. Logo for the Lincoln Center Repertory Theatre.

33. Logo for a committee that introduces young audiences to theatre and opera productions.

REPERTORY
THEATRE OF
THE LINCOLN
CENTER

32.

THE
NEW YORK
COMMITTEE
OF YOUNG
AUDIENCES
400 WEST
END AVENUE,
NEW YORK,
N.Y. 10024
212 874-5503

33.

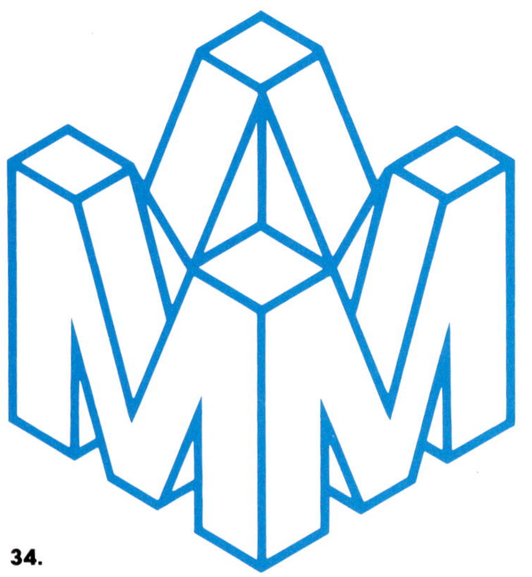
34.

35.

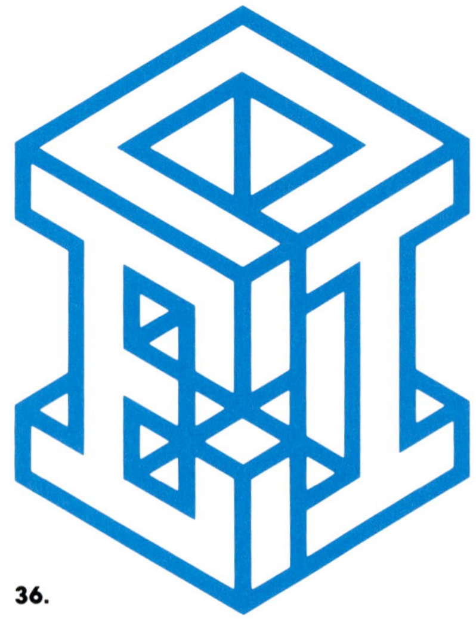
36.

This series of cubist designs has met with little or no enthusiasm in the market place. Except for the "Dimension" logo which is owned by CBS Radio, and has rarely been seen, all of the designs are for sale at bargain prices.

"Dimension" was created in the early '60's as a symbol for CBS' Dimensional Radio Programming. It received a warm reception from the client, bringing a modicum of self-respect to the designer, despite the fact that radio is not a visual medium.

A good friend in television approached Lubalin for a logotype needed for a three-network broadcast from President Johnson's office in the White House. Lubalin came up with a three-dimensional design solution: "CBS NBC ABC." It was unacceptable.

The Multicon Construction Corporation retained Lubalin to design a trademark. What does a designer do for a company that manufactures multi-construction, prefabricated housing? He digs up his old three-dimensional designs, and adapts them to a multi-constructed four-sided "M." It, too, was promptly rejected.

Éspace Interieur, a French company, was involved in the design and construction of interior office space. They wanted a logo. Lubalin borrowed from "M" to create "EI." In this case, the aesthetically astute Europeans at least gave the design some thought before the ultimate rejection.

Also in Europe, a Sears Roebuck type operation called Trois Suisse required a trademark representing the many-faceted nature of its business. Thus "3SSS". Once again, the design was rejected.

If you can't sell it, give it away. This design was finally accepted for a Christmas card by a friend of Lubalin's whose name began with "H."

At this point, good luck smiled on Lubalin. He was asked to design a logo for the motion picture, "The Longest Yard." His decision to use the cubist approach again was based on the amount of material in his reject file. Fortuitously, he created the ultimate solution to the problem, which inadvertently went unrecognized by the client.

This logo is available now, with a few modifications, on a first-come, first-serve basis to a land developer, or to somebody in the yard goods business.

Which leaves two to go. Perhaps an Eskimo in need of an ice cube. Or, maybe, YOU.

—**Herb Lubalin**

Excerpted from an article in U&lc/Vol. 1, No. 3, 1974.

34. Logo for Multicon Construction Company.

35. Logo for the radio division of the Columbia Broadcasting System.

36. Logo for Éspace Interieur.

37. Logo for PBS Festival '76, a special week of programming on public television.

38. Logo for the movie, "The Longest Yard." It was rejected because the design did not incorporate a photo of the film's star.

39. Logo for Trois Suisse.

40. Logo for a combined broadcast from three major networks.

41. Logo for Hedda Johnson, illustrator.

37.

38.

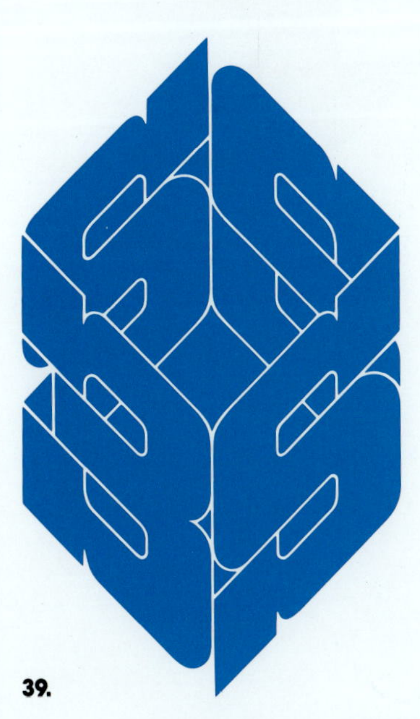

39.

40.

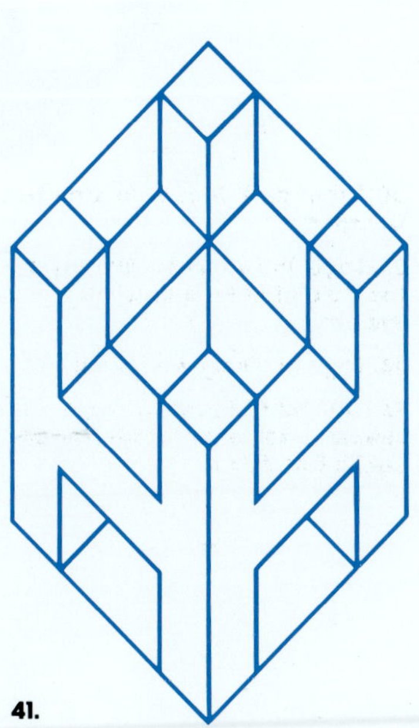

41.

42. Logo for a series of skyscrapers on the outskirts of Paris called Le Manhattan. The logo simulated the different heights of tall buildings in Manhattan.

43. Corporate design for the City of New York. Although the design was accepted, Lubalin saw it used only once, on a white sanitation truck.

42.

43.

EDITORIAL DESIGN

1.

Bertrand Russell considers *Time* magazine to be "scurrilous and utterly shameless in its willingness to distort." **Ralph Ingersoll:** "In ethics, integrity, and responsibility, *Time* is a monumental failure." **Irwin Shaw:** *Time* is "nastier than any other magazine of the day." **Sloan Wilson:** "Any enemy of *Time* is a friend of mine." **Igor Stravinsky:** "Every music column I have read in *Time* has been distorted and inaccurate." **Tallulah Bankhead:** "Dirt is too clean a word for *Time.*" **Mary McCarthy:** "*Time*'s falsifications are numerous." **Dwight Macdonald:** "The degree of credence one gives to *Time* is inverse to one's degree of knowledge of the situation being reported on." **David Merrick:** "There is not a single word of truth in *Time.*" **P.G. Wodehouse:** "*Time* is about the most inaccurate magazine in existence." **Rockwell Kent:** *Time* "is inclined to value smartness above truth." **Eugene Burdick:** *Time* employs "dishonest tactics." **Conrad Aiken:** "*Time* slants its news." **Howard Fast:** *Time* provides "distortions and inaccuracies by the bushel." **James Gould Cozzens:** "My knowledge of inaccuracies in *Time* is first-hand." **Walter Winchell:** "*Time*'s inaccuracies are a staple of my column." **John Osborne:** "*Time* is a vicious, dehumanizing institution." **Eric Bentley:** "More pervasive than *Time*'s outright errors is its misuse of truth." **Vincent Price:** "Fortunately, most people read *Time* for laughs and not for facts." **H. Allen Smith:** "*Time*'s inaccuracies are as numerous as the sands of the Sahara." **Taylor Caldwell:** "I could write a whole book about *Time* inaccuracies." **Sen. John McClellan:** "*Time* is prejudiced and unfair."

2.

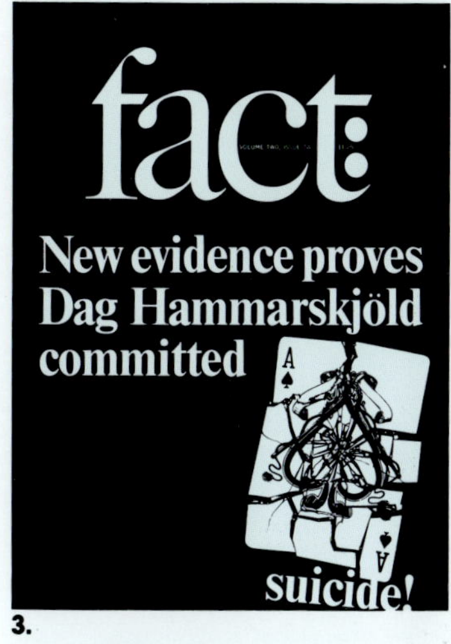

3.

4.

fact A professor of ophthalmology says, "Everybody who puts on contact lenses will experience eye damage, and in many cases the damage will be permanent."

5.

6.

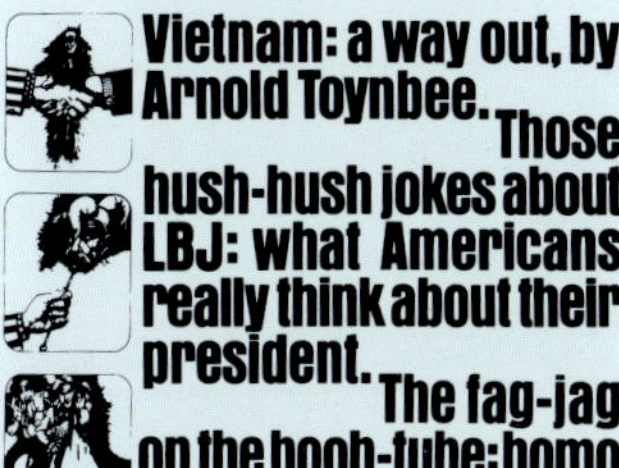

7.

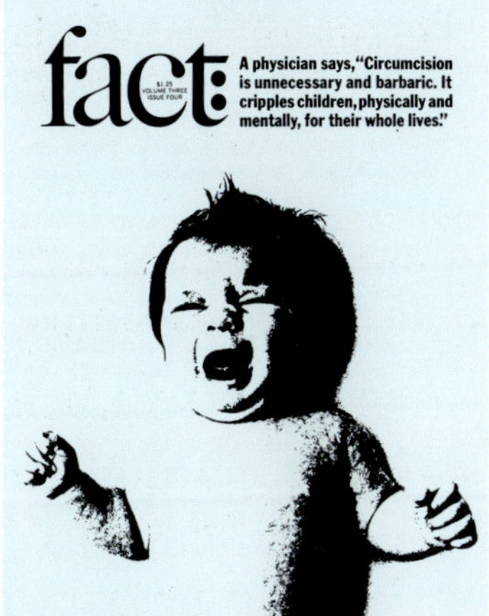

8.

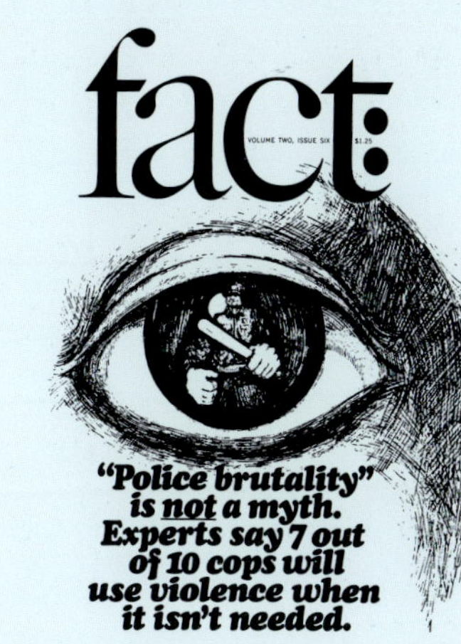

9.

10.

fact

This issue contains a portfolio of the most beautiful art from Eros together with the true story of how the magazine was suppressed

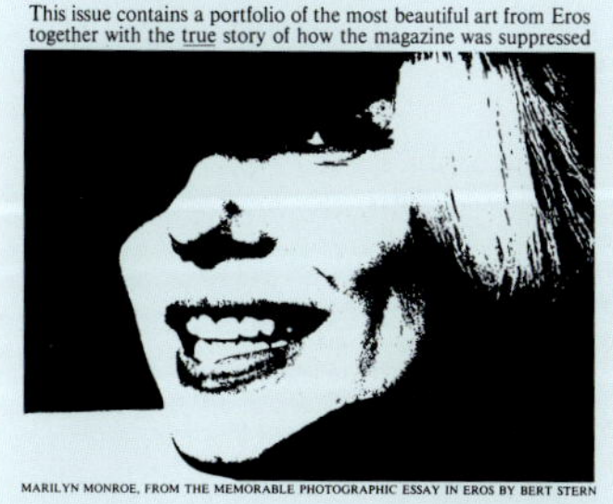

MARILYN MONROE, FROM THE MEMORABLE PHOTOGRAPHIC ESSAY IN EROS BY BERT STERN

11.

fact Dr. Spock says, "The Johnson administration is acting like a 1-year-old child having a prolonged temper-tantrum."

12.

13.

1. Families magazine, produced by Reader's Digest, lasted only a few issues. Tony Di Spigna relates: "Herb was getting nowhere with his design for the logo. He gave me the tissues to work on. I got nowhere, too. One morning, Herb phoned. All he said was, 'Dot the L!'".

Fact magazine was a Ginzburg publication with a low budget. It was printed on newsprint, occasionally with a two-color cover. Lubalin designed the format, and assigned entire issues to up-and-coming illustrators who were delighted to have a showcase for their talents.

2.-13. Covers from Fact magazine.

14.

Catholic Take-Over of Public Schools

By the Rev. Gaylord Briley

At least 200 schools in as many as 20 states are supported by general taxation but staffed by nuns and controlled by the Roman Catholic Church

Beyond doubt, 999 out of every 1000 Americans have never in their lives heard the phrase "captive school." It is a phrase never published in newspapers or magazines, never broadcast over the radio or TV. So it might be well to offer, right now, a definition:

***Captive school.* An American public school, supported by common taxation like any other public school, but controlled by the Roman Catholic Church and taught by nuns of the Roman Catholic Church.**

Defined as such, a captive school would make a laughing-stock out of the Constitution and the principle of church-state separation. Yet the unhappy fact is that *hundreds* of captive schools exist, and all over the United States.

In a typical captive school, the Mother Superior of the local convent is the principal; religious images hang from classroom walls; and all the students are taught the Baltimore (official) catechism. Most, or all, of the classes are conducted by nuns, robed in the distinctive garb of their calling and under the most solemn vows to advance the Roman Catholic religion in everything they do. And money supporting the school comes from the pockets of Protestants, Jews, and other non-Catholics.

Many captive schools follow the pattern of two in Conejos County, Colorado, near the New Mexico State line. During the Depression, the community of Antonito was getting so little revenue from impoverished taxpayers that the city fathers were about ready to close down the schools. But then the Benedictine sisters volunteered to operate the schools for the County, at low salaries. This they have been doing ever since—and with considerable benefit to their church.

In the 1962–1963 school year, the local paper listed "Sister Bernice" as superintendent of the Antonito public schools. That same year, 26 of the 37 teachers employed were Benedictine nuns. (Only one of the 11 lay teachers was *not* a member of the Catholic Church, though this is a minor point.) Salaries paid by taxpayers to the 26 nuns ranged between $80,000 and $100,000—and the nuns turned all of that straight back to their church. Not one penny in federal or state income taxes was deducted. Now, since the church allots these dedicated women about $600 each for annual living expenses, the church in Antonito gets a gross profit of $64,400 to $84,400 a year. And this is ample reason for the church fathers not to ship the entire convent to one of the many teacher-shy Catholic parishes in other parts of the country. In nearby Denver, for example, at least one parochial school stands empty for lack of nuns to staff it. The priest, Father Joseph Koontz of Notre Dame parish, told Denver *Post* reporters that it would be several years before

45

15.

A Cook's Tour of Travel Agents

By Onofrio Bruni

Go ahead and *ask* your travel agent–about his hidden mark-up, about getting an itemized bill, about justifiable refunds. But don't be surprised if he won't tell you

No one knows for sure, but it's estimated that 5 million Americans consult travel agents every year to make arrangements for their trips outside the country. In 1965, American tourists spent $1.3 billion on overseas transportation, and 75% of that total was handled through travel agents. Once outside the country, tourists spent $2.4 billion on lodgings, meals, local transportation, etc., and about a third of *that* total passed through the hands of the travel agents. On all these transactions, the agents got a certain percentage of the cut. So, obviously, these men are making a heck of a lot of money.

There's nothing wrong with making lots of loot, of course, and many travel agents perform a genuine service for their clients. On the other hand, many other travel agencies are also incompetent, unscrupulous, and irresponsible. And one reason they can get away with it is that the American public, by and large, is stupefyingly ignorant about travel agents. Those people who visit travel bureaus very possibly know less about what they are buying, and how much they are paying for it, than about any other retail product or service in the United States.

Now, it's true that many travel agencies, as we shall see, *want* to keep their clients ignorant. But another cause of this widespread public ignorance is the fact that the whole travel industry has grown so big so quickly–on account of greater wealth among Americans, increased leisure time, the quickened speed of travel, and so on. Five times as many Americans went abroad last year as in 1950. In 1940, the country had about 750 travel agents. In 1950, about 1100. Today there are over 7000 travel agencies–one in every city and almost every town in the U.S.A. And one result of this sudden and tremendous upsurge in traveling and travel agents is that the general public simply hasn't had a chance to get informed about travel agents–who they are, what they do, and how they get paid.

Who *are* they? The truth is that almost anyone can set himself up as a travel agent. To go into the business, an agent must:

- post a $10,000 bond (at a cost of about $150) in case he defaults on any travel tickets he sells;
- get the location of his office approved;
- have no record of business malpractice and give the impression of having solid finances;
- testify to his ability to make out a travel ticket.

Once he has done this, he will probably be "accredited" by the Air Transport Conference (so he can sell tickets on most domestic lines) and the International Air Transport Association (for most international airlines and ships).

Yet he can also hang out his shingle–without any authorization whatsoever–and peddle

15

14-19. Spreads from *Fact*.

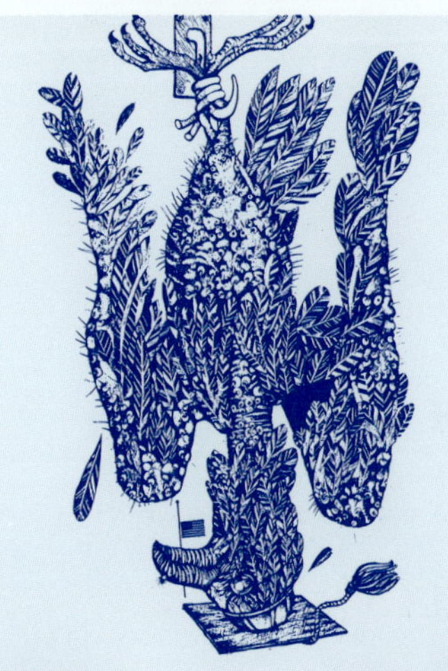

Is America a Dying Country?

Fact publishes the answers 41 well-known citizens gave to this provocative question

Something is radically wrong.

Throughout America people are strangely uneasy and fretful. They are, above all, tense, as if they had glimpsed flashes of lightning some time ago and were now waiting, not quite consciously, for the terrible thunderclaps. There has been much abstruse analysis of this eerie American malaise; much Fall of the Roman Empire talk. Only the dim-witted, or those insulated by self or circumstance, can have failed to notice it.

Our writers have noticed it. Bruce Jay Friedman says: "If you are alive today, and stick your head out of doors now and then, you know that there is a nervousness, a tempo, a near-hysterical new beat in the air, a punishing isolation and loneliness of a strange, frenzied kind." Nelson Algren writes: "Though ten thousand voices announce our national contentment coast to coast, every hour on the hour, through editorial, headline and the fashion magazines, actually we are living today in a laboratory of human suffering as vast and terrible as that in which Dickens and Dostoevsky wrote." Norman Mailer has written, simply, "The country is in disease."

Many others have remarked this strange new American malaise. "Living," says Karl Menninger, the psychiatrist, "in spite of all the multiplying mechanical aids, grows daily more difficult, complicated, and restrictive." Philosopher Charles Frankel maintains that anxiety has become our "way of life." James Reston, the New York *Times* writer, notes that "There is scarcely a philosopher in the nation or a serious historian who is not full of anxiety about the political or spiritual derangement of the free world" led by the United States. Before his death Adlai Stevenson wrote: "An air of disengagement and disinterest hangs over the most powerful and affluent society the world has ever known. Neither the turbulence of the world abroad nor the fatness and flatness of the world at home are moving us to more vital effort." The dean of the Harvard Divinity School, Samuel H. Miller, has said, "Make the rounds of people on any level. Something's wrong with America, they all say. In our work, we find no purpose. In our frenzy, there is no direction." Richard N. Goodwin, one of Johnson's aides, said last July that there is a "growing discontent with what we have, dissatisfaction with the life we have created, unhappiness and restlessness."

America, in short, seems to be on the verge of a nervous breakdown. Perhaps, as some say, the trouble is that our country lacks a goal, a common, elevating, national purpose; that—in this age of the anti-novel and the anti-hero and even anti-matter—America has only an anti-purpose, namely, fighting Communism.

51

16.

The Women's Army Corps: Life Among the Funny-Bunnies

By Gloria Dippolitino

An ex-WAC describes how her feelings about the Lesbians she met in the service changed from disgust and fear to genuine pity

In 1962 I was 18 years old, and had never been anywhere outside my small home town in the Midwest. Also, as the only daughter of a religious Catholic family, I had led a particularly sheltered life. That year, therefore, when a WAC recruiter came to our high school to talk to us seniors about careers in the U.S. Army, I was positively enthralled.

The recruiter's spiel was worthy of Madison Avenue. In a private interview, he told me that as a member of the Women's Army Corps I would be well-fed and properly housed and smartly clothed. I would meet brilliant women and fascinating men. And (the key to my heart) I would travel. All I had to do in return was serve my country for 3 years.

I was so enthusiastic that I spent hours in the public library reading up on the WACs. Among other things, I learned that while the WAVES (Women Accepted for Voluntary Emergency Service) have declined since World War II, and the SPARS are just about out of existence (they now have 9 officers and 34 enlisted women), the Women's Army Corps—as well as the WAFS (Women's Air Corps) and the Women Marines—are still thriving. An outgrowth of the Women's Army Auxiliary Corps of World War II, the WACS today have 3700 officers and 8625 enlisted women.

I was so eager to enter this new life that, with my parents' blessing, the day after I graduated I went to the nearest recruiting station. There I was informed that I would have to be interviewed by a psychiatrist. This made me a little nervous—none of my friends had ever been to a psychiatrist, and I didn't know what to expect. I certainly *didn't* expect to spend a mere 5 minutes explaining why I bite my nails and the way I feel about my parents to an unimpressive little man. On the other hand, I had to take a barrage of aptitude tests. The Army spends hours giving and marking aptitude tests, but only 5 minutes evaluating the mental health of its candidates.

Well, the Army decided I was mentally healthy. And within 2 hours after I'd said "I do" to Uncle Sam, I was whisked onto a train heading for a fort in Alabama.

Despite some misgivings, I was still so starry-eyed about my new life that I stayed awake throughout the whole 5-hour trainride imagining my future: my fashionable uniform, my important and glamorous job, the friends I would make, the places I would visit. At my destination, Fort McClellan, home of the Women's Army Corps Center and School, I was furnished a bed in a room with 40 other women, given linen, assigned a wall and foot locker, and told, "You're in the Army now!"

And so I was.

It was a letdown from the very beginning. I

41

17.

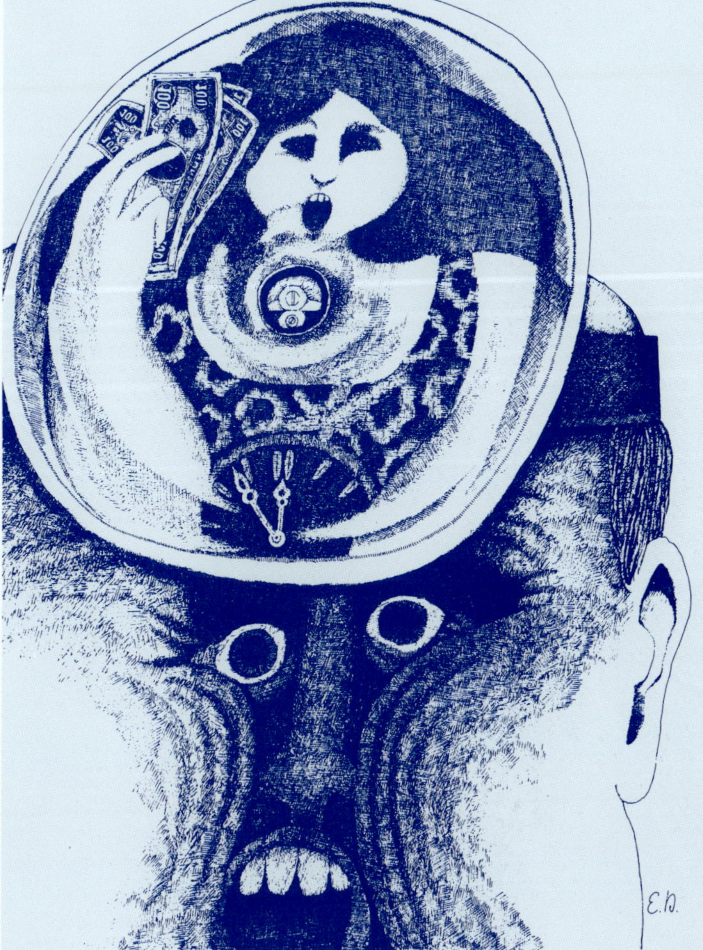

How a Middle-Class American Housewife Goes About Getting an Abortion

By Francesca Milano

The operation itself is a breeze. The nightmare lies in finding a decent abortionist

It takes an experienced doctor about half an hour to perform an abortion. The amount of pain involved varies from patient to patient, but the operation is roughly equivalent, in my experience, to a bad half-hour in a dentist's chair. For the woman who, for whatever reasons, dreads the alternative to abortion, the operation—in capable hands—is thus really not so bad after all. The nightmare, the horror, is finding a doctor.

I am a New York housewife with three children. Last winter I found myself expecting an unwanted fourth. My husband and I decided that the least unpleasant way out of our dilemma would be for me to have an abortion. Our decision was made when I was only a few weeks pregnant, so during the first part of our search for a doctor we managed to avoid the panic of fighting against the calendar. Plenty of time, we felt, to find someone safe, and perhaps someone whose fee would not be too exorbitant. There was no possibility of my leaving the country: We don't have that kind of money.

Our first problem was deciding where to begin looking, whom to ask. My obstetrician was out of the question. I knew his opinion in advance: immovably opposed to abortion on almost any grounds. So we went through a list of our friends, bypassing those who seemed too innocent of these matters on the one hand, and too sordidly experienced on the other. For we wanted something more than any abortionist. There were three conditions: we must find a qualified doctor, an M.D.; he must perform the operation nowhere but in his office; and he himself must perform the operation from beginning to end.

We also tried to avoid asking those friends who might be inclined to talk too freely. After all, I intended to participate in a criminal act. But at no time did I have any feelings of guilt: My main emotion was anger at the United States for *making* what I was trying to do a criminal act.

Well, at last we asked three people for information and from them we got seven names and seven telephone numbers. One emerged as the most promising. A friend knew of several women who had been to him and all were satisfied; he met our three conditions; his price was only $300; and, for a wonder, he was almost casual about that fee—"Pay me when you can," he reportedly told one girl. This man was the first I tried. And tried, and tried. Never an answer. The phone number was listed in the Manhattan directory, and I tried it at all hours of the day and evening and for nearly 2 weeks. Never an answer. Later I learned that there had been no answer for over a year. The second doctor was, according to his nurse, ill and unavailable for a month. The third was on Lenox Avenue, and while I had not the slightest objection to a doctor who was Negro, it was not a good year, it seemed to me, for a

61

18.

Bitch
JA

A Glossary of Homosexual Slang

By A. F. Niemoeller

A distinguished sexologist shows what queens are doing to the King's English

Though the bigots among us must hate being reminded of the fact, our American language has been enriched by all sorts of minority groups—Negroes and hobos, cops and robbers, pickpockets and prostitutes. The anti-Semite Gerald L. K. Smith probably uses expressions like "Who needs it?" and "What's with him?" totally unmindful of their Yiddish origin, just as Negro-phobe Governor Wallace must occasionally label somebody "chicken," serenely unaware that the source of that picturesque term is the American Negro community. And beyond any question when B. Goldwater was boasting that his Presidential campaign was "coming on like Gang Busters," he hadn't the foggiest idea that *that* particular expression is the pride and joy of America's homosexuals.

American homosexuals, as a matter of fact, are coming on like Gang Busters in the rate they are adding slang words to the general vocabulary. For homosexuals, and for other cultural subgroups, slang is a way of establishing a sense of identity and of streamlining intercommunication. Some of their favorite words and phrases, which I have assembled below, may fade away as quickly and as completely as rookies in spring training; others may catch on, hold on, and wind up in the Hall of Fame—eventually to become part of the daily vocabulary of the people who want to put all "perverts" in prison. Which goes to show that if there is one area of American life where liberty, equality, and fraternity really prevail, where drug addict and debutante can rub elbows and where the fag need have no fear of the fuzz, it is in our magnificent American language.

---

auntie *n.* An elderly homosexual.

bag *n.* A fellow homosexual. *Derogatory.*

basket *n.* The male genitals and region immediately surrounding.

basket days A period of mild weather that permits men to wear garments light enough to reveal the contours of their *baskets.*

beating the dummy Autoerotism.

beating the meat Autoerotism.

belle *n.* A fellow homosexual.

Bess A term applied to a fellow homosexual, usually preceding an admonition, as in "Listen here, Bess. . . ."

bi *n. & adj.* Bisexual.

bif *n.* A public restroom.

bitch *n.* A blatant homosexual. *Derogatory.*

blind *adj.* Uncircumcised.

bring out *v.* To acquaint with homosexual practices and traditions.

bull *n.* An elderly female homosexual.

bull-dagger *n.* Same as *bull-dike.*

bull-dike, bull-dyke *n.* A female homosexual who plays the male part.

PORTRAITS OF THE AMERICAN PEOPLE A MONUMENTAL PORTFOLIO OF PHOTOGRAPHS

20.

Avant Garde, another Ginzburg publication, came after the demise of Fact. It was more ambitious in design and production.

20. Cover from Avant Garde showing a good use of the Avant Garde typeface.

21.-35. Spreads and single pages from Avant Garde.

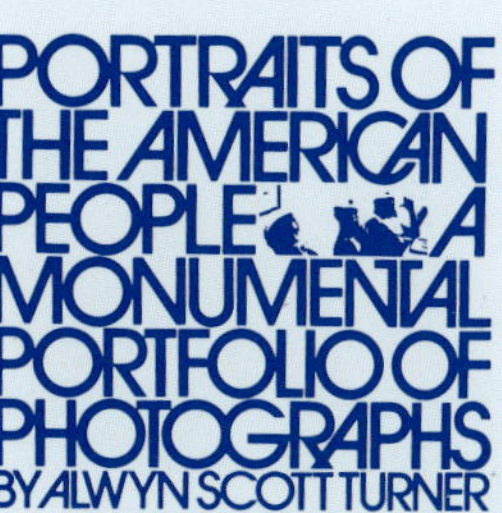

BY ALWYN SCOTT TURNER

"Most photographers are interested in the bizarre, the off-beat, the unpredictable," says Alwyn Scott Turner. "But for me the most fascinating subject is also the most obvious: the American people." And photographing them has been a 25-year obsession for Turner. Starting when he was a boy in Texas, then as a photojournalist in Detroit, and finally as a perpetual vagabond, Turner has crossed and criss-crossed the breadth of the land, photographing its people. "I figure I've photographed 50,000 individuals," says Turner, "and I'm not tired of my subject yet." Two months ago, Turner walked into the offices of Avant-Garde, deposited 2,000 of his most recent pictures, and invited us to devote an entire issue to publishing the best of them. After looking them over, we decided it wasn't a bad idea. Turner's pictures reveal not only glimpses of the lives of his subjects but also of his own. The Texas farmer who posed for him is a man for whom he used to pick cotton. The Detroit assembly-line worker is a man his father worked beside. And the mother and child seated before a typical American house are Turner's own wife and daughter. "When you ask someone to pose for a picture," says Turner, "they reveal themselves more completely than at any other time. Their pride, aspirations, longings, and anxieties become immediately apparent." The editors of Avant-Garde agree, and in presenting the photographs of Alwyn Scott Turner believe that they are preserving a view of not only the faces and features of the American people, but also their souls.

21.

BY WARREN BOROSON

LAST YEAR, THE WEST GERMAN RED CROSS WAS INVOLVED IN A SHOCKING SCANDAL—A SCANDAL THAT YOU CERTAINLY DIDN'T READ A WORD ABOUT, BECAUSE THE AMERICAN MASS MEDIA DECIDED TO HUSH THE WHOLE THING UP

22.

23.

PHOTOGRAPHS BY LEE KRAFT

Andy Warhol's "Factory," a silver-lined loft on East 47th Street in New York, has in the past few years become the Olympus and Parnassus of American avant-garde-dom. There it is that the mild but relentless presence, Warhol, has presided over the production of endless art works that have proved the joy and scandal of the world. There, too, since about 1963, has been the headquarters of the renowned—and joyous, and scandalous—Warhol film industry. Dozens of movies, including the fabled "Sleep," "Empire," "Harlot," "Vinyl," "The Chelsea Girls," "The Nude Restaurant," and "★★★★," have there been executed in the revolutionarily deadpan, laissez-faire Warhol style, a style that has given birth to a new kind of actress: the Superstar. The Superstar is given no set part to play. Warhol's directions consist mainly in yes's, no's, and the subtlest of suggestions. The Superstar plays, in effect, herself—her own personal emotions, anxieties, fantasies—in witty psychodramas, adding up to a vast Human Comedy of the underground before the camera's implacable eye. The Superstars past and present (and, being underpaid, their turnover is terrific) are beautiful, complex, extravagant, and haunted people whose lives on and off screen tend to merge and become one. Veterans include such prominent names as Baby Jane Holzer, Edie Sedgewick, Mary Woronov, Ingrid Superstar, and Nico. On the following pages Avant-Garde introduces, speaking for themselves, five of the newest, hottest female Superstars—the pride and flowering of the breed.

16

24.

"Andy taught me that everything that I ever thought before was right. My ego has gotten tired from being battered by so many people for so many years; it's a little frayed, like an old camel hair coat. Andy's never battered me, though. He's like a cool running brook....The best drug as an aphrodisiac is peyote; however, it's nauseating. Now I don't take drugs at all. I don't like drugs. I like wine and good conversation around a table. I used to like pot but then found when I used it I was actually coming down. And I don't take acid anymore, because I don't want to warp my chromosomes. Anyway, drugs are for weak people....The last time I took acid I did a dance for the sun on the roof. The man I was with didn't want to make love to me so he told me to go up on the roof—imagine! So I made love to the sun. Since then I haven't made it with many men except an occasional creature who had no place to stay. The sun is the greatest lover in the world. Men can't hold a candle to it....I would like to be Elizabeth Taylor because of all the children she has around her—and the dogs and the cats and the houses—and Richard Burton. A fantastic entourage! I'd like to have a lot of money. I guess I'll have to be a Superstar. Then I could say 'fuck you' to the world....I have a plan to protest the war. As soon as it gets a little warmer I'm going to Washington, and I'm going to ride naked on a black horse with a black saddle and carrying a black flag with the skull and crossbones on it. And my hair won't be long, either. But I guess I'll need some body guards.... In 50 years words will be extinct (and I was saying this before I even heard of Marshall McLuhan!). We'll communicate by ESP—vibrations. Vocal cords will be only for singing with. You might say I'm the last dying gasp of verbosity. I hate talking so much that I do it obsessively!"

VIVA

The Sins of Their Fathers

THE DOVISH CHILDREN OF 10 HAWKS IN THE NIXON ADMINISTRATION COMMENT ON THEIR FATHERS' ROLES IN THE WAR

COMPILED BY DIANE E. BENTE

All of us know how Vice-President Agnew's 14-year-old daughter feels about the war: she wanted to support one of the moratoria. The Vice-President censored her, and, flushed with victory, went on to try censoring the nation's news media, as well. But what about other high Administration officials —do they allow their children to express themselves about the war? And if so, exactly what do their children think? To find out, Avant-Garde asked various school-newspaper editors to interview 30 such youngsters. Twenty, including Tricia what's-her-name, refused to cooperate. (The Silenced Majority we call them.) As for the remainder, most struck us as surprisingly shrewd and sophisticated, and not just because so many of them forthrightly opposed the war. (An exception was a young man who compared America's intervention in Vietnam with Lafayette's helping America against the British. Up to that point, we hadn't been aware that the Marquis de Lafayette had murdered innocent American civilians.) All in all, we were quite favorably impressed with these young people, even if they did place filial piety above any moral outrage, and we hereby suggest that all ten of their fathers—well, nine of them—resign immediately and nominate their children as their successors.

David Laird, freshman, the Landon School, Bethesda, Maryland, son of Melvin R. Laird, Secretary of Defense. (Interviewed by Jim Sulzer, the Landon News.)

James Westmoreland, freshman, the Landon School, Bethesda, Maryland, son of Gen. Wm. C. Westmoreland, Chief of Staff, United States Army. (Interviewed by Jim Sulzer, the Landon News.)

25.

26.

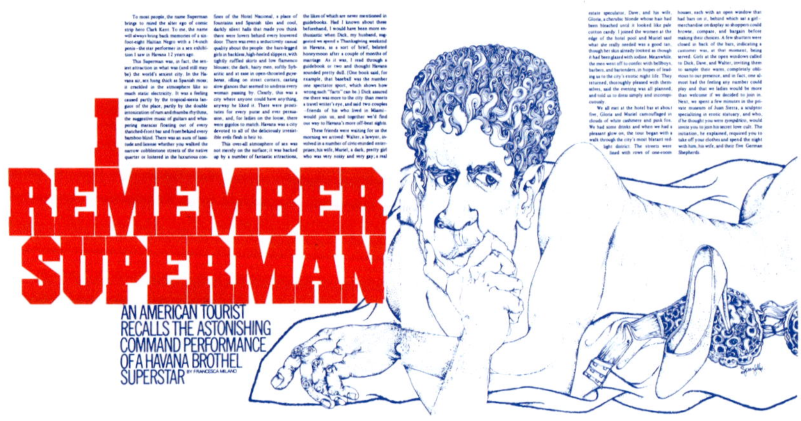

I REMEMBER SUPERMAN

AN AMERICAN TOURIST RECALLS THE ASTONISHING COMMAND PERFORMANCE OF A HAVANA BROTHEL SUPERSTAR BY FRANCESCA MILANO

27.

AN EDITORIAL STATEMENT BY NOBEL LAUREATE GEORGE WALD

AVANT GARDE

AMERICA IN DISTRESS

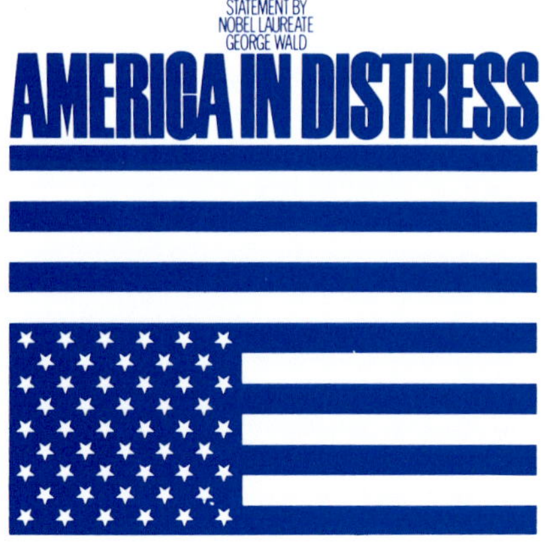

I am a teacher at Harvard. I have a class of about 360 students—men and women—most of them freshmen and sophomores. Over these past few years I have felt increasingly that something is terribly wrong—and this year ever so much more than last. Something has gone sour, in teaching and in learning. It's almost as though there were a widespread feeling that education has become irrelevant.

A lecture is much more of a dialogue than most people appreciate. As you lecture, you keep watching the faces, and information keeps coming back to you all the time. I began to feel, particularly this year, that I was missing much of what was coming back. I tried asking the students, but they didn't or couldn't help me very much.

But I think I know what's the matter, even a little better than they do. Some of them tell you that what's bothering them is the Vietnam War. I think the Vietnam War is the most shameful episode in the whole of American history. The concept of war crimes is an American invention. We've committed many war crimes in Vietnam; but I'll tell you something interesting about that. We were committing war crimes in World War II, even before Nuremberg trials were held and the principle of war crimes started. The saturation bombing of German cities was a war crime. Dropping atom bombs on Hiroshima and Nagasaki was a war crime. If we had lost the war, some of our leaders might have had to answer for those actions.

I've gone through all of that history lately, and I find that there's a gimmick in it. It isn't written out, but I think we established it by precedent. That gimmick is that if one can allege that one is repelling or retaliating for an *aggression*—after that everything goes. And you see we are living in a world in which all wars are wars of defense. All War Departments are now Defense Departments. This is all part of the double-talk of our time. The aggressor is always on the other side. And I suppose this is why our ex-Secretary of State, Dean Rusk—a man in whom repetition takes the place of reason, and stubbornness takes the place of character—went to such pains to insist, as he still insists, that in Vietnam we are repelling an aggression. And if that's what we are doing—so runs the doctrine—anything goes. If the concept of war crimes is ever to mean anything, these crimes will have to be defined as categories of acts, regardless of alleged provocation. But that isn't so now.

I think we've lost that war, as a lot of other people think, too. The Vietnamese have a secret weapon. It's their willingness to die beyond our willingness to kill. In effect they've been saying, "You can kill us, but you'll have to kill a lot of us, and you may have to kill all of us." And thank heavens, we are not yet ready to do that.

Yet we have come a long way—far enough to sicken many Americans, including our fighting men, far enough so that our national symbols have gone sour. How many of you can sing about "the rockets' red glare, the bombs bursting in air" without thinking, those are *our* bombs and *our* rockets bursting over South Vietnamese villages? When those words were written, we were a people struggling for freedom against oppression. Now we are supporting real or thinly disguised military dictatorships all over the world, helping them to control and repress peoples struggling for their freedom.

But the Vietnam War, shameful and terrible as it is, seems to me only an immediate incident in a much larger and more stubborn situation.

Part of my trouble with students is that almost all those I teach were born since World War II. Just after World War II, a series of new and abnormal procedures came into American life. We regarded them at the time as temporary aberrations. We thought we would get back to normal American life some day. But those procedures have stayed with us now for more than 20 years, and those students of mine have never known anything else. They think those things are normal. They think we've always had a Pentagon, that we have always had a big army, and that we always had a draft. But those are all new things in American life; and I think that they are incompatible with what America meant before.

How many people today realize that just before World War II the entire American army, including the air force, numbered 139,000 men? Then World War II started and it got to be eight million. And then World War II came to an end, and we prepared to go back to a peacetime army of the size it had been before. And indeed in 1950—you think about 1950, our international commitments, the Cold War, the Truman Doctrine, and all the rest of it—we got down to 600,000 men.

Now we have 3.5 million men under arms: about 600,000 in Vietnam, about 300,000 more in "support areas" elsewhere in the Pacific, about 250,000 in Germany. And there are a lot at home. Some months ago we were told that 300,000 National Guardsmen and 200,000 reservists—half a million men—had been specially trained for riot duty in the cities.

The Vietnam War is just an immediate incident because so long as we keep that big an army, it will always find things to do. If the Vietnam War stopped tomorrow, with that big a military establishment, chances are that we would be in another military adventure before long.

As for the draft: Don't reform the draft—*get rid of it!*

28.

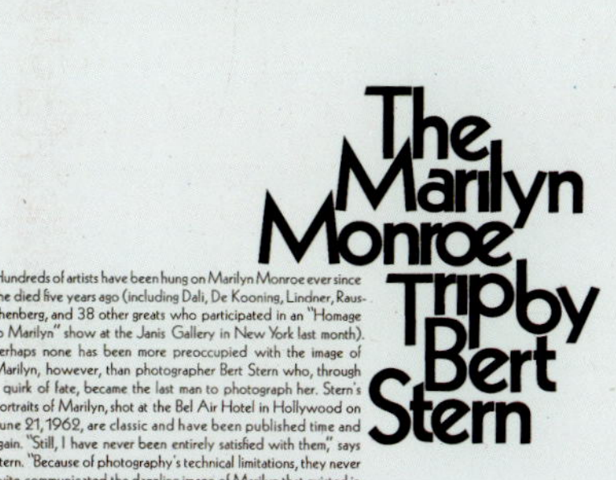

The Marilyn Monroe Trip by Bert Stern

Hundreds of artists have been hung on Marilyn Monroe ever since she died five years ago (including Dali, De Kooning, Lindner, Rauschenberg, and 38 other greats who participated in an "Homage to Marilyn" show at the Janis Gallery in New York last month). Perhaps none has been more preoccupied with the image of Marilyn, however, than photographer Bert Stern who, through a quirk of fate, became the last man to photograph her. Stern's portraits of Marilyn, shot at the Bel Air Hotel in Hollywood on June 21, 1962, are classic and have been published time and again. "Still, I have never been entirely satisfied with them," says Stern. "Because of photography's technical limitations, they never quite communicated the dazzling image of Marilyn that existed in my mind's eye at the time I photographed her." As a result, over the past five years Stern has been experimenting with various new techniques that would enable him to capture and preserve the image of Marilyn he saw at the time he photographed her. Just this past fall he hit upon the answer: an amalgam of the dramatic technique of serigraphy and the blazing colors of Day-Glo ink. On the next 12 pages the editors of Avant-Garde are pleased to present Bert Stern's phantasmagoric vision of Marilyn Monroe.

29.

30.

GEORGE TOOKER

31.

PHOTOGRAPH BY ART KANE

BREAKING OUT: A BLACK MANIFESTO BY DICK GREGORY

George Wallace was half right when he said, "Gregory's not funny any more." The whole truth is that Dick Gregory is far from merely funny these days. His years of immersion in the caldron of our racial strife have transmuted the master comic into a wise, eloquent, and lacerating spokesman for black aspiration, a one-man hot-line from the heart of the ghetto to the conscience of White America. Speaking at rallies and on college campuses across the country, running for President, publishing an insightful book (Write Me In!), Gregory has spread the word of black liberation with wit and passion. Now that Malcolm X and Martin Luther King are gone, Gregory's is one of the few truth-telling voices left in the land; and, for all its jokes, it leaves no bitter truth untold. Turn this page to find out why it makes George Wallace squirm.

32.

FUGS ED SANDERS, KEN WEAVER, AND TULI KUPFERBERG, PHOTOGRAPHED BY PETER HUJAR

The Fugs: Nextness is Godlier than Cleanliness.

33.

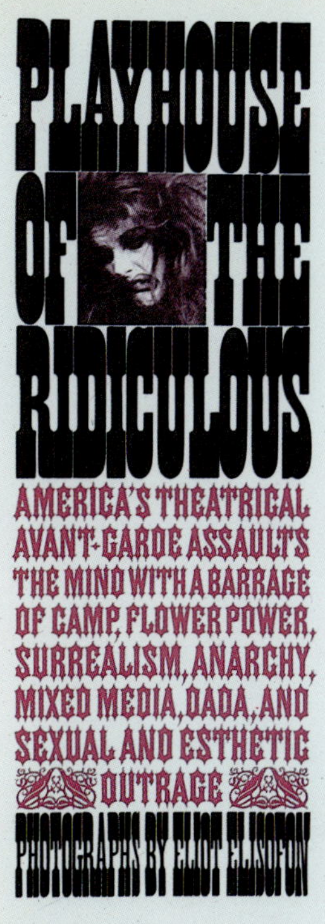

PLAYHOUSE OF THE RIDICULOUS

AMERICA'S THEATRICAL AVANT-GARDE ASSAULTS THE MIND WITH A BARRAGE OF CAMP, FLOWER POWER, SURREALISM, ANARCHY, MIXED MEDIA, DADA, AND SEXUAL AND ESTHETIC OUTRAGE

PHOTOGRAPHS BY ELIOT ELISOFON

Down on New York's ill-famed Bowery, amidst all manner of dirt and squalor, noise and decay, stands a lovely, white-columned old bank building, now converted into a playhouse called the Bouwerie Lane. The anomaly is striking enough, but it's nothing compared to what's inside, namely, one of the wildest, most brilliant—and most "perverse"—experiments in American theater history: The Playhouse of the Ridiculous. This three-year-old congregation of eccentric genius represents the acme of the New York super-Underground, Off-Off-Broadway avant-garde. It has, by the way, but little relation to the European "Theater of the Absurd"; it is as American as John Birch and the blue movie, a volatile emulsion of camp, flower-power, surrealism, anarchy, mixed media, Dada, world literature, and sexual and esthetic outrage. If the art of the theater is indeed (as people have been saying) dead, this is a flush on the corpse bright enough to light up the sky.

The Playhouse of the Ridiculous materialized out of the random chaos of the Underground via a lucky combination of several unique (to say the least) talents. Foremost at the beginning were the incredible wit and savvy of Playwright Ronald Tavel, whose style might be described as mixing Brecht and Beckett with Hellzapoppin, and the directorial fireworks of John Vaccaro, whose background included academic training and first-hand experience of Japanese puppet theater. At the time (July, 1965), Tavel was making a series of movies with Andy Warhol, on the order of a political spoof entitled The Life of Juanita Castro (in which Fidel, Che, et al., played by girls, berate Juanita, played by a boy). Eventually dissatisfied with the vagaries of Warhol's Superstars, he teamed up with Vaccaro, marshaled his own actors, and opened what was to be a one-shot production of Juanita and a new ("psychedelic") play, Shower, at a gallery on the Lower East Side. The success of this enterprise, while not exactly stupendous, was so gratifying that the neophyte company reformed itself as a "theater club," moved into a playhouse on 17th Street, and started putting on full-length Tavel plays, of which the first was The Life of Lady Godiva, and the second, Indira Gandhi's Daring Device.

Indira Gandhi brought PHOTR its first widespread recognition, though from somewhat unexpected quarters—two major governments, the Mayor of New York, and the FBI. The plot of the drama, such as it is, is typical PHOTR hijinks: Indira is in love with an Untouchable, whom she allows to have at her with a mammoth dildo (the "Device"). An Indian student who chanced to view this diversion was not edified. He told the Indian Embassy about it, they had a look for them-

12

34.

VOODOO LIVES!

Many people probably still think of Voodoo as something Tarzan's native friends indulged in—all mumbo-jumbo and skulking around—later to be set straight by stern white missionaries. Now, however, what with the resurgence in America of African culture and traditions, the evangelism may soon be working in reverse, bringing to a "civilized" society that prefers to lock the mysteries of life and death up in churches a message of primitive directness and power. As manifested in this ritual dance, called "Obeah," by young Valda Cadogan, of Barbados, Voodoo is an abandonment to primal feelings undreamed of in our philosophy.

35.

36.

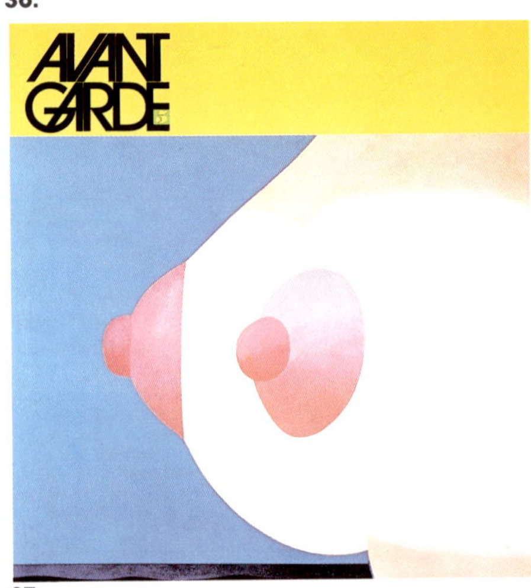

37.

38.

36.-48. Covers from <u>Avant Garde</u>.

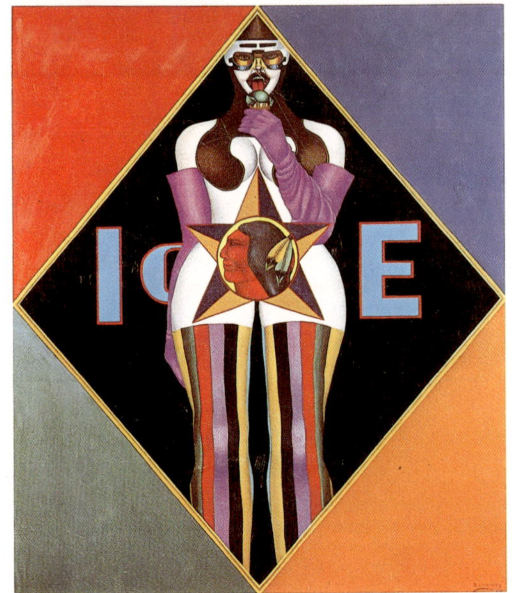

39.

40. 41. 42.

43. 44. 45.

46. 47. 48.

In 1961, Lubalin was asked to redesign The Saturday Evening Post. His assignment included a new logo and total revamp of the interior.

49.-50. Two covers of the newly designed Saturday Evening Post. The publisher suggested to the illustrator, Norman Rockwell, that the first cover be its designer at work.

51.-53. Interior spreads from The Saturday Evening Post.

49.

51.

52.

50.

53.

In 1972, Lubalin was asked to redesign the magazine again. The object was to bolster readership.

53-55. First cover and internal pages of the new Saturday Evening Post. The magazine folded several issues later.

JUNE 15, 1968
The Saturday Evening Post 35c

HAIR: BROADWAY'S ROCK REVOLUTION

MAJOR BOOK ON: **WALLACE** "LET THEM CALL ME RACIST"

THINKING MAN'S SWINGER: **JOHN KENNETH GALBRAITH**

54.

55.

56.

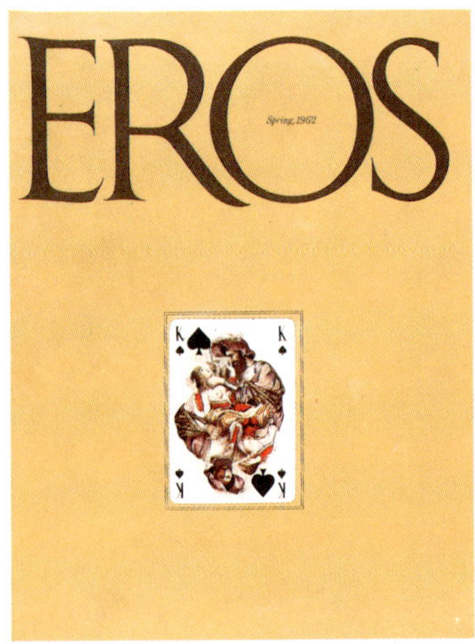

57.

58.

Eros, a Ginzberg publication, was the first magazine with a mature approach to love and sex. Its landmark design was a major step in establishing Lubalin's reputation as an editorial designer. There were, however, only four issues published.

57.-60. Covers from the four issues of Eros.

61.-78. Spreads and single pages from Eros.

59.

60.

"Le Florentin" Playing Cards de Luxe

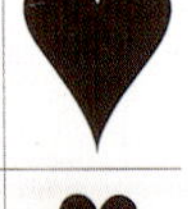
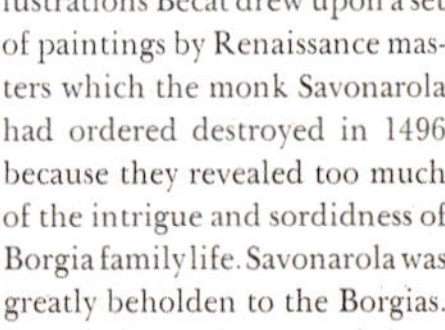

In 1951 the famous Parisian playing card manufacturer Éditions Philibert commissioned the French artist Paul-Emile Bécat to paint a set of miniatures depicting Florentine life during the Renaissance. The miniatures were to be used as illustrations for a deck of playing cards that Philibert planned to produce in a limited edition of twelve thousand decks. Bécat took four years to prepare the pictures. Finally, in 1955, the cards were manufactured. The twelve thousand decks, which were widely distributed in Europe, sold out almost immediately. The few hundred that reached this country now sell for several times their original price of $17.50 a set. For many of his illustrations Bécat drew upon a set of paintings by Renaissance masters which the monk Savonarola had ordered destroyed in 1496 because they revealed too much of the intrigue and sordidness of Borgia family life. Savonarola was greatly beholden to the Borgias. Detailed descriptions of these paintings had been preserved, however, and it was from them that Bécat was able to paint a number of his miniatures. The balance of his pictures he based on other Florentine themes. On the following pages are reproduced the aces, kings, queens and jacks of Bécat's "Le Florentin" deck, with the artist's own titles.

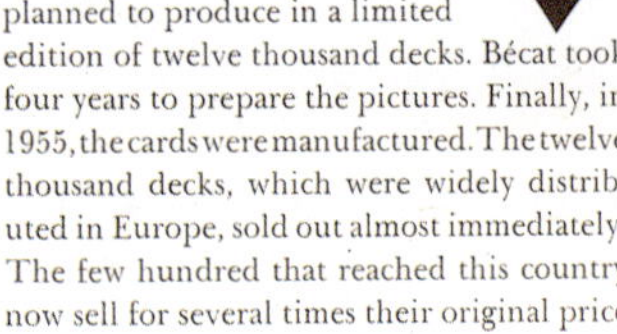

24

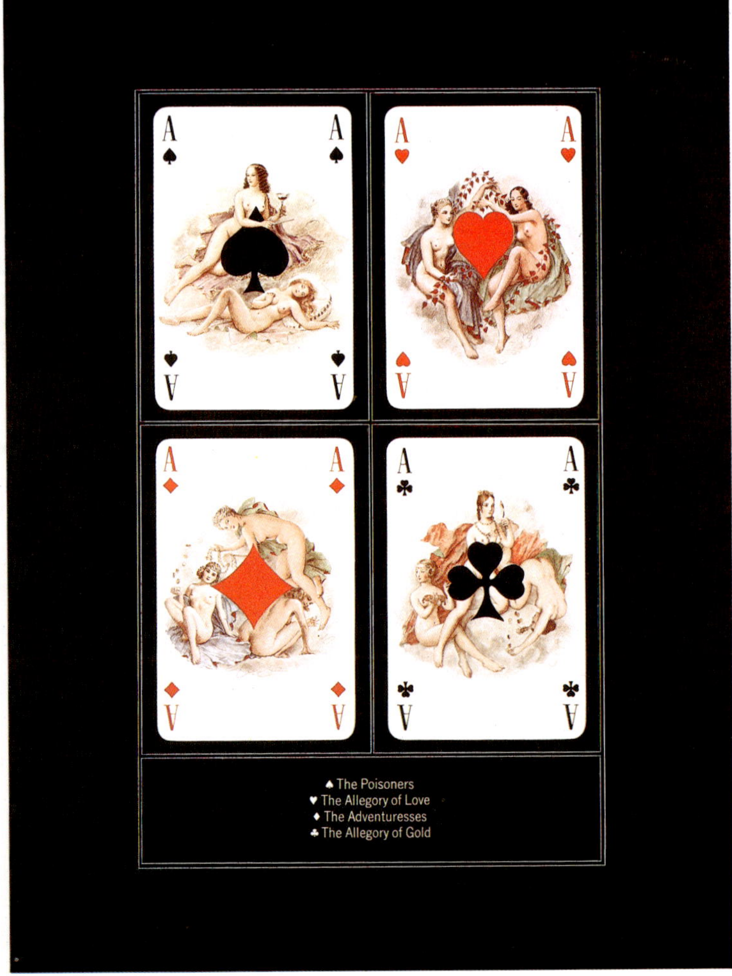

61.

Amores
Liber Primus
Elegia 5

In summer's heat, and mid-time of the day,
To rest my limbs, upon a bed I lay;
One window shut, the other open stood,
Which gave such light as twinkles in a wood,
Like twilight glimpse at setting of the sun,
Or night being past and yet not day begun.
Such light to shamefaced maidens must be shown
Where they may sport and seem to be unknown:
Then came Corinna in her long loose gown,
Her white neck hid with tresses hanging down,
Resembling fair Semiramis going to bed,
Or Lais of a thousand wooers sped.
I snatched her gown being thin,
the harm was small;
Yet strived she to be covered therewithal,
And striving thus as one that would be cast,
Betrayed herself and yielded at the last.
Stark naked as she stood before mine eye,
Not one wen in her body could I spy.
What arms and shoulders did I touch and see,
How apt her breasts were to be pressed by me.
How smooth a belly under her waist saw I,
How large a leg, and what a lusty thigh!
To leave the rest, all liked me passing well;
I clinged her naked body, down she fell:
Judge you the rest, being tired she bade me kiss.
Jove send me more such afternoons as this!

Ovid

Ovid, the greatest of classical love poets, dedicated not only his work but also his life to the exaltation of passion. Born outside Rome in 43 B.C., he forsook a life of aristocratic leisure to devote himself to the elegizing of love. His poems were an instantaneous success; his *Loves, Heroines, Art of Love* and *Love Cures* were the delirium of his day. The power of his muse brought Rome's most desirable women to his feet, and from all accounts it is evident that he exploited their admiration to the fullest. Ovid was three times married and innumerable times scandalized. In the end, it was love which led to his downfall. Emperor Augustus, enraged by a scandal in which his granddaughter's name was linked with that of the aging poet, banished Ovid to an outpost on the Black Sea. There, embittered, he died in 18 A.D. Ovid's influence over succeeding centuries of literature and art is unparalleled. Shakespeare, Spenser, Cervantes, Milton, Swift, Goethe, Rodin, Picasso, T. S. Eliot are among those who have acknowledged their debt to Ovid. The finest English translations of Ovid were done by Christopher Marlowe. Unfortunately these translations are not widely read, mainly because timorous educators deem them too erotic for their students. As a result, generations of readers, particularly in the United States, have come to know Ovid more by his name than by his works. EROS is pleased to present on these five pages several of the Marlowe translations of Ovid's earliest and most passionate poems, *Loves*. These alone prove the aptness of the title conferred upon Ovid by Chaucer in the *Canterbury Tales:* "Venus' clerk."

76

62.

FRANK HARRIS: HIS LIFE & LOVES!
WARREN BOROSON

63.

64.

black & white in color

A PHOTOGRAPHIC TONE POEM BY RALPH M. HATTERSLEY JR.

On the following eight pages, EROS proudly presents a photographic tone poem on the subject of interracial love. This is presented with the conviction that love between a man and a woman, no matter what their races, is beautiful. Interracial couples of today bear the indignity of having to defend their love to a questioning world. Tomorrow these couples will be recognized as the pioneers of an enlightened age in which prejudice will be dead and the only race will be the human race.

65.

66.

67.

68.

From bare-breasted Indian maidens on earliest handbills to present day catchphrases such as "Should a gentleman offer a Tiparillo to a lady?", sex has always been used to sell tobacco. For psychologists, the connection between smoking and sex is as obvious as a nipple on a breast. Smoking has its roots in the oral erotic pleasure derived from infantile sucking and so does much of sex play. Nineteenth Century tobacco advertising linked sex and tobacco perhaps more beautifully (and naively) than any advertising before or since. It is from that period that we present the cigar box labels on the following eight pages.
THE CIGAR BOX SIRENS
ECSTACY
17

69.

HOLD THE FORT
LA BELLE HELENE
YOUTH
THE OLD FOOL
SMAX
ODALISQUE
NEPTUNE'S RACKET
TRYST
SWEET COMFORT
TRUE LOVE
PRETTY COUSIN

70.

PATIENCE
PAY TOLL
BELLA VISTA
INTRODUCTION
OCEAN FAIRY
SWEET INNOCENCE
HOME PLEASURES
LOVE MATCH
20

MONEY
LOVE
WOLFF'S CHOICE
21

71.

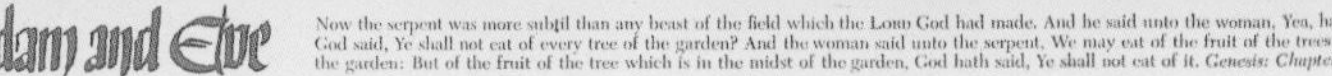

Adam and Eve

Now the serpent was more subtil than any beast of the field which the LORD God had made. And he said unto the woman, Yea, hath God said, Ye shall not eat of every tree of the garden? And the woman said unto the serpent, We may eat of the fruit of the trees of the garden: But of the fruit of the tree which is in the midst of the garden, God hath said, Ye shall not eat of it. *Genesis: Chapter 3*

Love in the Bible

In 1895, John B. Wise of Clay Center, Kansas, was convicted of sending obscene material through the mail—material that consisted entirely of excerpts from the King James version of the Holy Bible.

At his trial, it must have struck Wise as ironic that *Exhibit A* in the case against him was also the book upon which the accusing postal authorities swore their oaths. Wise was hardly the first to discover this irony. At least twice before in American history, obscenity prosecutions had been based upon the Holy Bible, once in Maryland and once in New York.

So the Bible is obscene?

By the moral and social standards of postal officials in nineteenth century America, the answer is yes. For those postal officials, the Bible's countless descriptions of rape, incest, sexual sadism, fetishism, homosexuality, masturbation, castration, adultery, prostitution, and phallic worship were too much to take. What is more, these acts are seldom deplored in the Bible—they are in most cases related without comment.

In the Bible, sex begins in the Beginning. Adam seeks a mate in the animal kingdom (Genesis 2:20) and only when he fails to find one does God create Eve from Adam's rib. That the man "gives birth" to the woman here, contrary to both natural law and to the mythology patterns of most other cultures, is a reflection of one of the most interesting psychological phenomena in the Bible, the superinflated importance of the male role in life—a function no doubt of the strong patriarchal influence in ancient Hebrew life. Obviously, the incident implies, the more important sex came first. We shall see further examples of this strong patriarchal point of view as we proceed.

That the rib in this story is a phallic symbol is apparent to mythologists as well as to psychologists. Aphrodite, in a less inhibited Greek version of this same story, was created from the cut-off

3

72.

MM62162

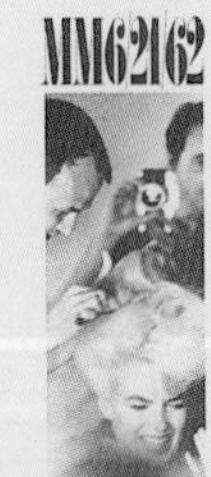

Photographs by Bert Stern

Editor's Note: The scratches and orange crosses on many of the photographs on the cover and following pages are not defects. They were made by Marilyn Monroe herself, her own reactions to various shots that showed a strand of hair out of place or a pose she felt was somehow awkward. We thought her markings were so interesting that we decided to leave them in. (We might add that Marilyn was delighted by the set as a whole.)

On June 21, photographer Bert Stern began to take the last studio pictures ever made of the woman who had become, as much as any woman ever had, the sex symbol for the world. Six weeks after the memorable photographs on these pages were taken, Marilyn Monroe was dead.

Stern set out to photograph Marilyn as no one ever had before—as a fashion model for Vogue. She was fascinated by the idea; it was a challenge, and she loved a challenge. Stern was also able to talk Marilyn into posing for the first time with no make-up, other than a little eye shadow. Despite the fact that Marilyn was wearing strange clothes by a strange designer, and although the photographer was new to her, Marilyn became a fantastic model right before Stern's eyes. She would work until two and three in the morning, playing her favorite Frank Sinatra records to help her react before the camera, while the improvised studio at the Bel Air Hotel in Los Angeles became littered with rolls of film, lights, trays of food, and bottles of champagne.

Then, one night, Marilyn seemed to tire of posing in all the chic clothes from New York. She grabbed a flimsy bed jacket and whisked it away to the bedroom. When she emerged, she was a different woman. While she laughed and relaxed and had a marvelous time, Stern went on to take the pictures that appear in this issue.

"She was so beautiful and untouched," Bert Stern told Eros. "It was as though she were just beginning."

73.

"The passing of time is making it clear that the peak of Marilyn Monroe's tragedy was that she never knew how much people everywhere loved her." **Richard Watts Jr.**, *critic.*

74.

75.

"She was one of the most unappreciated people in the world."
Joshua Logan, director.

15

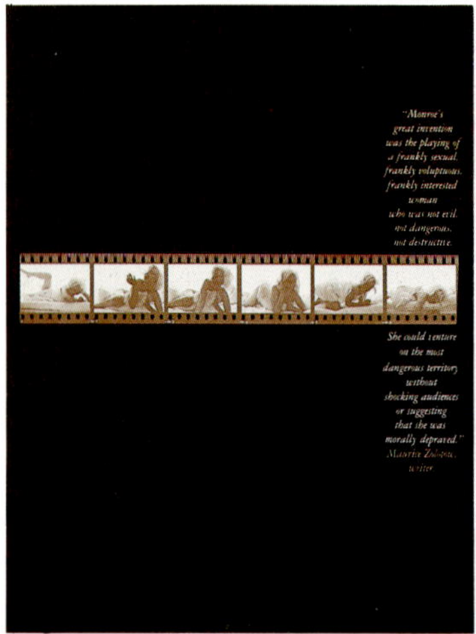

76.

77.

"1601" is perhaps the most hilarious piece of wit ever produced by America's greatest humorist. In it, Mark Twain has gathered together a number of eminent Tudor figures and drawn them into an imaginary conversation concerning a fart. The dignitaries include William Shakespeare, Sir Walter Raleigh, Ben Jonson and Francis Bacon. The setting of the conversation is the fireside of Queen Elizabeth I. The time is the year 1601, from which the piece takes its title. Twain's aim in writing "1601" was to poke fun at the overblown language and overstuffed morals of his own 19th century America. Twain was not attempting to parody Elizabethan England; open and frank discussion of such topics as flatulence was not taboo then. Rather, Twain was comparing the foolish restrictions of 19th century America with the hearty boisterousness of the Elizabethan period.

Unfortunately, Twain's contemporaries were never allowed to read "1601." The same conventions and proprieties that Twain was ridiculing prevented publication of this ribald work. It was not until recently that "1601" became freely available in the United States. (Ironically, "1601" has always been Twain's best-loved and most widely read piece in most of Europe and the Far East.)

Twain wrote "1601" in 1876 as he was finishing *Tom Sawyer* and about to begin *Huckleberry Finn*. He included the original draft in a freehand letter to his lifelong friend, the Reverend Joseph Twichell, of Hartford, Connecticut. Twichell had officiated at Twain's marriage and had baptized all of Twain's children. In 1882, at the insistence of Twichell, Twain consented to the printing of four copies of "1601." They were run off, unlikely enough, on the presses of the United States Military Academy at West Point. Since then, 44 editions of "1601" have been published in the United States, almost all of them strictly limited and surreptitious, due to fear of prosecution on the part of their printers.

If America has reacted ambivalently to "1601," so did Twain himself. Though he frequently took pleasure in candid and unashamed discussion of the work, and though many of his most literate friends proclaimed "1601" to be his satiric *tour de force*, still Twain hesitated to admit publicly to authorship. However, late in life his reason prevailed and he condoned the work with the statement, "It is not the word that is the sin, it is the spirit back of the word."

Clearly, Twain's laughter and skill in "1601" are as vital today as when the work was first conceived. On the following two pages EROS publishes for the first time in a periodical the complete "1601" text. It is followed by a psychoanalytical treatise on "What Mark Twain Reveals About Himself In '1601.'" We hope that you will enjoy "1601" for, as Twain himself once said, "Between you and me, the thing *is* dreadfully funny."

Conversation, as it was by the Social Fireside, in the Time of the Tudors. [Date, 1601.]

[MEM.—The following is supposed to be an extract from the diary of the Pepys of that day, the same being Queen Elizabeth's cup-bearer. It is supposed that he is of ancient and noble lineage; that he despises these literary canaille; that his soul consumes with wrath to see the queen stooping to talk with such; and that the old man feels that his nobility is defiled by contact with Shakespeare, etc., and yet he has *got* to stay there till her Majesty chooses to dismiss him.]

43

78.

UPPER & LOWER CASE

UPPER AND LOWER CASE, THE INTERNATIONAL JOURNAL OF TYPOGRAPHICS

PUBLISHED BY INTERNATIONAL TYPEFACE CORPORATION, VOLUME SIX, NUMBER THREE, SEPT 1979

The marvelous typographic portrait of Pablo Picasso was sent to us by Paul Siemsen in response to our "Put your best face forward" request. We thought so much of the design that we decided to use it as our cover for this issue. The idea was conceived, designed, researched, and written by Siemsen as a promotion poster for The Graphic Corporation, a studio-print house in Des Moines, Iowa. It uses four different size/weight combinations of ITC Korinna. It is now available in poster form, silk-screened on rag paper, and is signed by the designer. If you're interested, write to Paul Siemsen, The Word/Form Corporation, 130 Main Street, Box 508, Ames, Iowa 50010. Thanks, Paul, for certainly putting ***your*** *best face forward.*

When the name Picasso falls upon the eye, a portrait of a legend comes to mind. It's the legend in the world of art which surrounds a man who possessed and expressed many of the highest ideals of mankind. The popular legend is of the outward attributes: seclusion and gregariousness; wealth and love; abundance of works and extraordinary versatility in all facets of his field. It has been estimated that Picasso created over fifty thousand works of art. Pablo Ruiz Picasso was born into a family of art, so he naturally had a very early beginning in his creations. His life was long, ninety-one years, but when we do the arithmetic we still find that he averaged throughout his creative years almost two pieces of art per day. Considering the physical size and the conceptual scope of many of his works, these numbers bespeak a remarkable feat. How is it that a man could be so one pointed and inventive that he would become, as one author describes him, "the most prolific artist of all times?" Picasso's own words may reveal the answer: "Painting is stronger than I am; also, "painting makes me do what it wants." Another of the components of the popular legend is that of his departure from tradition. Picasso is known by many as having been instrumental in founding and energizing two new movements in art, cubism and surrealism; and to have inspired other movements including abstract art and pop art. His departure into cubism, which has become perhaps his best known realm, was met at the time with ridicule and contempt. The general attitude of those who saw this new trend was, at best, closer to endurement than to endearment. A very few had any awareness that in Picasso painting was giving birth to truly significant modes of seeing and expression. These few, and Picasso himself, might have argued that his seemingly radical forms were logical outcomes or extensions of the traditions of painting thus far, or at least, of the spirit of painting. That same unbounded energy of art that had explored so many obvious and subtle ways of seeing was, in this twentieth century Spaniard, continuing its exploration. The world has indeed marveled that so much of that energy was concentrated through the eye hand of this one man. Those who have known Picasso and have written of him begin to reveal the inner, mystical legend when they independently ascribe this superconductivity to his unceasing wonderment-a wonderment born of innocence and openness that had no need to look through the tinted glasses of dogma. Indeed, as his own cubist movement became intellectually structured and dogmatic, he left its mainstream. In doing this, he kept himself in the main evolutionary stream of art itself, which adheres to principles of a more general and interaccommodative nature. Picasso was thus free to draw upon the principles he had discovered in several specific modes of painting to achieve an even more comprehensive vision. One needs to be careful not to think that he mixed some of this style and some of that to achieve something new. His art grew from within and manifested itself in the appearance of mixture. He elaborated, "Art is not the application of a canon of beauty, but what the instinct and the brain can conceive independently of that canon. When you love a woman you don't take instruments to measure her body, you love her with your desires." His ability to create independently of the numerous canons of beauty was witnessed by Gertrude Stein, one of his earliest patrons, who said, "He alone among painters did not set himself the problem of expressing truths which all the world can see but the truth which only he can see." This internal truth must have been operative when Picasso painted his well-known portrait of Gertrude Stein, for without something of an inner vision his reflections on the portrait would seem absolutely baffling. As the story goes, he made Miss Stein sit eighty times for the portrait, and then he wiped out her face and substituted a face with mask-like qualities. There were criticisms which he dismissed with "Everybody thinks that the portrait is not like her, but never mind, in the end she will look like the portrait." Such a statement might seem impertinent, but it is hard to question his integrity, for his commitment to his work was absolute. Every work was born of desire and in deep concentration. Every work was also born living its own life. A painting or sculpture or lithograph or whatever, would begin in impulse, in vague idea, in spirit. Then as art "made him do what it wanted" it would evolve through the brush of its creator. Each stroke and each picture was an end, a breathing universe itself. Picasso seldom signed his works and never named them. He also customarily refused to explain them. It is perceived that such acts might have put too definitive boundaries on the pieces, limiting the potential that continues to exist within them. A father gives his child his own autonomy, never acknowledging the moment he becomes adult and never saying to him this is the kind of person you are or that is the kind of influence you have, because the child may become much more or may be seen to be much more. For similar reasons, one hesitates to write of the legend of Pablo Picasso, [illegible] for fear of severely limiting its fullness. Yet, even as the legend itself is found within the depths of the viewer's consciousness, so are these words found looking out of a piece of paper.

1.

1. Cover for U&lc, using computer-generated typography to create a portrait.

2.-11. Sometimes U&lc covers featured the table of contents; other times they highlighted an article from within.

12.-14. Design using quotes on typography and printing.

U&lc.

Aa Bb Cc Dd Ee Ff Gg Hh Ii Jj Kk Ll Mm Nn Oo Pp Qq Rr Ss Tt Uu Vv Ww Xx Yy Zz 1234567890&ÆŒ$$¢£%!?()[]

UPPER AND LOWER CASE, THE INTERNATIONAL JOURNAL OF TYPOGRAPHICS PUBLISHED BY INTERNATIONAL TYPEFACE CORPORATION, VOLUME THREE, NUMBER TWO, JULY 1976

1776 1976

The Sad State of the Union
A satirical comment by Geoffrey Moss on our highly revered American way of life, our institutions, our systems, and the folks in charge. **Pg 2**

The Publick Printer
The first in a new series by **U&lc** tracing the remarkable history of printing in America beginning, naturally enough, with the beginnings. **Pg 6**

U&lc's Presidential "Primary"
Handsomely-engraved portraits of each of our 37 presidents, taken from the Ralph Ginzburg Collection, wherein we are inviting our readers to select their primary choice of the one president they believe would be most suited to lift the country out of its doldrums. **Pg 8**

Sam Fink's Typographic Paintings
Whoever said there was nothing new under the sun obviously hadn't seen the art of Sam Fink. Blending words and illustrations is a highly specialized skill, as evidenced from the stunning examples within. **Pg 10**

The Fifty-Six Who Signed
Sam Fink seems to have a monopoly on this issue, but he's worth it. This time around, he shows us his uncanny perceptive portrait of all the signers of the Declaration of Independence, with an incisive profile of each. **Pg 14**

Erté: The Artist and his Coterie of Female Characters
Four pages in full color of the famed Alphabet and Numerals of America's foremost fashion illustrator. **Pg 18**

Our Bicentennial Turkey
Following a lengthy discussion with Ben Franklin, Vikki Romaine – designer of toys for adults – has created, especially for this issue, a new symbol for America. **Pg 22**

What's New from ITC?
Under special license from D. Stempel AG, ITC offers a redesigned and smartly updated version of Rudolph Koch's original Kabel, created in the early 1920s and now available from ITC Subscribers as ITC Kabel. **Pg 24**

Someone for Everybody
The space, customarily devoted to our regular features "Something for Everybody" and "Famous Ampersands" is devoted instead to Jerome Snyder, whose death was such an unexpected shock to everyone who knew him and such a severe loss to us all. **Pg 26**

2.

U&lc.

Aa Bb Cc Dd Ee Ff Gg Hh Ii Jj Kk Ll Mm Nn Oo Pp Qq Rr Ss Tt Uu Vv Ww Xx Yy Zz 1234567890&ÆŒ$$¢£%!?()[]

UPPER AND LOWER CASE THE INTERNATIONAL JOURNAL OF TYPOGRAPHICS PUBLISHED BY INTERNATIONAL TYPEFACE CORPORATION. VOLUME SIX, NUMBER ONE, MAR. 1979

Jim Spanfeller's Fantastic Airplane

What has a fabulous drawing of a fabulous airplane got to do with the state of the typographic arts? The answer is fairly simple. In recent issues of U&lc we have attempted to create exciting formats, reproduced in color, to display as effectively as we know how, our latest featured typefaces. The devices we have employed stray considerably from the purely typographic. In one case we resurrected some old posters to show how they could look—and possibly be improved—with the use of contemporary ITC typefaces. Our issue on ITC Cheltenham included significant commentary on typography by famous literary figures. Our attempt there was to indicate that some very important people, not associated with letterforms, had written astutely on the subject. At the same time we tried to show that good writing and good typography are highly synergistic. Our last issue, featuring the ITC Benguiat Condensed series, sent us scurrying through every page of an unabridged dictionary to select what we thought were the eight most exciting looking words in the English language when set in ITC Benguiat Condensed. All of which brings us back to the answer to the long forgotten question at the beginning of this article.

3.

U&lc.

Aa Bb Cc Dd Ee Ff Gg Hh Ii Jj Kk Ll Mm Nn Oo Pp Qq Rr Ss Tt Uu Vv Ww Xx Yy Zz 1234567890&ÆŒ$$¢£%!?()[]

UPPER AND LOWER CASE THE INTERNATIONAL JOURNAL OF TYPOGRAPHICS PUBLISHED BY INTERNATIONAL TYPEFACE CORPORATION. VOLUME SEVEN, NUMBER THREE, SEPT 1980

Something for Everybody...

Z is the most neglected character in the English language. E is by far the most popular. For each Z used in the formation of words the following proportions have been fairly accurately established for the usage frequency of the other 25 letters.

E-60, T-45, A-42.5, I, N, O, & S-40, H-32, R-31, D-22, L-20, U-17, C & M-15, F-12.5, W & Y-10, G & P-8.5, B-8, V-6, K-4, Q-2.5, J & X-2 & Z-1.

E for Enigma:

The beginning of eternity, The end of time & space, The beginning of every end, The end of every place.

Reading from left to right and from top to bottom this word square was worked out by an anonymous puzzlist. The degree of difficulty increases with the size of the square. Try it sometime.

NESTLES
ENTRANT
STRANGE
TRAITOR
LANTERN
ENGORGE
STERNER

TO WIDOWERS AND SINGLE GENTLEMEN

WANTED

BY A LADY, A SITUATION TO SUPERINTEND THE HOUSEHOLD AND PRESIDE AT THE TABLE. SHE IS: AGREEABLE, BECOMING, CAREFUL, DESIRABLE, ENGLISH, FACETIOUS, GENEROUS, HONEST, INDUSTRIOUS, JUDICIOUS, KEEN, LIVELY, MERRY, NATTY, OBEDIENT, PHILOSOPHIC, QUIET, REGULAR, SOCIABLE, TASTEFUL, USEFUL, VIVACIOUS, WOMANISH, XANTIPPISH, YOUTHFUL, ZEALOUS. ADDRESS ALL INQUIRIES TO: XYZ, SIMMONS LIBRARY, EDGEWARE ROAD, LONDON

LONDON TIMES, 1842

A
VILE
Young lady on
EVIL
Bent, Lowered her
VEIL
With sly intent,
"LEVI"
She said, "It's time to play. What shall we do to
LIVE
Today?"
"My Dear," said he, "Do as you please. I'm going to eat some
IVEL*
Cheese."

*This cheese is presumed to have been made in the valley of the Ivel River.

4.

U&lc.

Aa Bb Cc Dd Ee Ff Gg Hh Ii Jj Kk Ll Mm Nn Oo Pp Qq Rr Ss Tt Uu Vv Ww Xx Yy Zz 1234567890&ÆŒ$$¢£%!?()[]

UPPER AND LOWER CASE. THE INTERNATIONAL JOURNAL OF TYPOGRAPHICS

PUBLISHED BY INTERNATIONAL TYPEFACE CORPORATION, VOLUME TWO, NUMBER THREE SEPT., 1975

In This Issue:

Word Processing, Typography, and the gigo Principle
Paul Doebler provides U&lc readers with a broad spectrum analysis of exactly how the new office word processing technology may reshape the graphic communications industry of the future, and cautions against the **gigo** principle—"**g**arbage **i**n, **g**arbage **o**ut."

Typ.ah.grr.phy
The dazzling wave of new hardware is producing a fistful of naive misconceptions like "Now my secretary can give us all the typography we need right on her own keyboard! Right?" Wrong. Aaron Burns draws a clear-cut line from input to output, essential for typographic excellence by creative users of the new technologies.

Self-Promotion
Does Macy's tell Gimbel's? In this instance, yes. U&lc herein presents the self-promotional efforts of twelve of the competition—twelve outstanding designs by creative groups that heeded the old adage: "Promote Thyself!"

The Big Apple
There's nothing you can say about New York that somehow, somewhere, someplace, isn't true. Illustrator Diana Bryan captures the whole look and life of it with a few perceptive strokes of her remarkable razor blade.

Jean Larcher's '75
Give a young French designer-typographer-calligrapher a number and see how he runs with it. The number is this year's, and what he's done with it will excite number freaks from Maine to St. Jean de Luz.

Ms. Gun Larson Brunsbo
The striking selection of samples depicted on our Ms. page this issue is the work of the above-mentioned lady: a Gun that's Swedish, modest, and loaded—with talent!

Famous Ampersands
Ampersands have been with us all the way from Adam & Eve to Lox & Bagels. Written and illustrated by Jerome Snyder are eight of the world's most fantastic ampersands, with many many more to come in subsequent issues.

SVA:PAS
A group of students at the School of Visual Arts—turned off by what they felt was an overly materialistic orientation of advertising—originated the Public Advertising System as an opportunity to use their creative skills in making ads for clients with philanthropic causes.

My Best With Letters
Hermann Zapf, Wim Crouwel, Reba Sochis, and Will Sandberg are this issue's contributors.

The shortest distance between two points?
A straight line, according to Webster, is used where no confusion with curve is possible. With this in mind, the editors invited a number of leading graphic artists to draw us their own versions.

Something From Everybody For U&lc
Last issue when Herb Lubalin made the bald statement that the word "theater" was the only seven-letter word in the English language containing nine words in sequence, he didn't know what he was getting into. A flood of readers fairly inundated us with seven, as well as four, letter words.

Something For Everybody From U&lc
Fascinating trivia from here, there, and everywhere—whimsically designed to amuse, inform, and stimulate the curious mind.

What's New From ITC?
The latest in new typefaces from ITC which licensed subscribers are authorized to reproduce, manufacture, and offer for sale: ITC Bauhaus; ITC Century Ultra with Book; ITC Cheltenham Ultra with Book: and ITC Garamond Ultra with Book.

ah grr
PAGE 4

TradeMarks
PAGE 8

PAGE 10

PAGE 12

May
PAGE 13

&
PAGE 14

SVA PAS
PAGE 18

Word Processing, Typography, and the gigo Principle

The good old typewriter "ain't what she used to be"—and neither is the copy coming from it for typesetting.

The reason is technology—the same kinds of computer electronics that have been upsetting traditions in the typesetting field. Except that in the offices of America, it's being called "word processing," and not computerized composition, or computer-based editing and revision, or other such buzz words more familiar to the typesetting trade.

Word processing is the youngest of the automation movements to hit the ancient process of preparing copy. The concept, an outgrowth actually of copy preparation techniques embodied in the IBM MT/SC strike-on composition system, was first introduced to the office less than a decade ago and was publicly named "word processing" less than five years ago. But already word processing systems are feeding new kinds of copy input into phototypesetting machines in offices and composing rooms across the country.

With all the offices of the nation as its potential base of operations, word processing can muster an awesome presence in the consciousness of commerce and industry—a presence that typesetting has never approached. At the peak of technological ferment in typesetting machinery a few years ago, when Wall Street was agog with the potential, typesetting technology won a few columns in a back-of-the-book department in **Business Week.** Word processing, however, was just recently lavished in that same publication with a 40-page special report.

Perhaps, however, this status of specially-anointed growth market should not be surprising. After all, those two giant suppliers of office equipment, IBM and Xerox, are the leading forces driving toward the word processing revolution in office operations—and just incidentally toward what is regarded as potentially phenomenal sales of new office equipment and systems. Behind them follows an impressive list of Fortune 500 names also seeking a piece of a pie that dwarfs the graphic arts many times over.

With all this prestigious weight behind them, the most impassioned word processing zealots foresee their movement sweeping through all corners of corporate organization—encompassing not only typesetting but printing, binding, mailroom, and the like, in one unified corporate communications system. Others, with personal stakes elsewhere in the corporate hierarchy, are, of course, less sanguine about this vision. But even if the vision never quite materializes, challenges resulting from it already are—one of which is the sweeping claim that with word processing equipment, "You can now get your typography directly from your secretary's typewriter keyboard!"

5.

MECHANIMALS

I LOVE MACHINERY. I LOVE DRAWINGS, PHOTOGRAPHS AND DIAGRAMS OF MACHINERY. PARTICULARLY DIAGRAMS. THEY LOOK IMPORTANT. THEY DEMAND RESPECT AND THEY INSPIRE CONFIDENCE. HOW DARE ANYONE DOUBT THAT THOSE DOTTED LINES, THOSE BEAUTIFUL ARROWS AND THE MYSTICALLY PLACED LITTLE UPPERCASE LETTERS INDICATE SOMETHING OF GREAT BUT OBSCURE SIGNIFICANCE? ✱ THE BLUEPRINT ALSO IS A FORM OF VISUAL TYRANNY. IT IS YET ANOTHER KIND OF ICON TO BE REVERED BY THE MECHANICALLY SOPHISTICATED, AND LOOKED UPON WITH AWE BY THE MECHANICALLY ILLITERATE, SUCH AS MYSELF. ✱ THESE DRAWINGS ARE MY SEMI-RESPECTFUL HOMAGE TO ALL THE MODEL AIRPLANES THAT I ALMOST COMPLETED, EVERY PRINTED-IN-JAPAN SET OF INSTRUCTIONS THAT LED ME ASTRAY. BUT MOST OF ALL TO THOSE PASSIONATELY STERILE DRAWINGS AND ENGRAVINGS THAT GRACED THE PAGES OF THE DICTIONARIES AND ENCYCLOPEDIAS OF MY YOUTH. ✱ AS FAR AS I AM CONCERNED, A STEAM-DRIVEN CHAMELEON, A TRACTOR-TREADED RHINOCEROS, A DIESEL-DRIVEN GUPPY, AND A PROPELLER-POWERED BASS ARE AT LEAST AS VALID AS ALL THAT OTHER STUFF. THESE, TOO, ARE REAL. IF YOU DON'T BELIEVE HOW REAL THEY REALLY ARE, JUST FOLLOW THE DOTTED LINES AND ARROWS AND THE VERBAL DESCRIPTIONS ON THESE PAGES.

6.

7.

8.

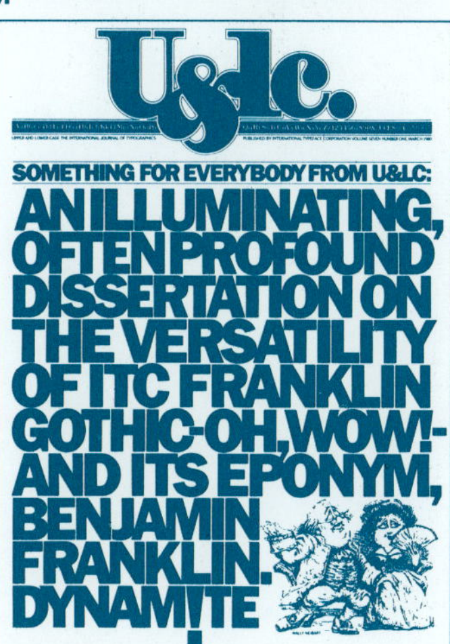

9.

10.

11.

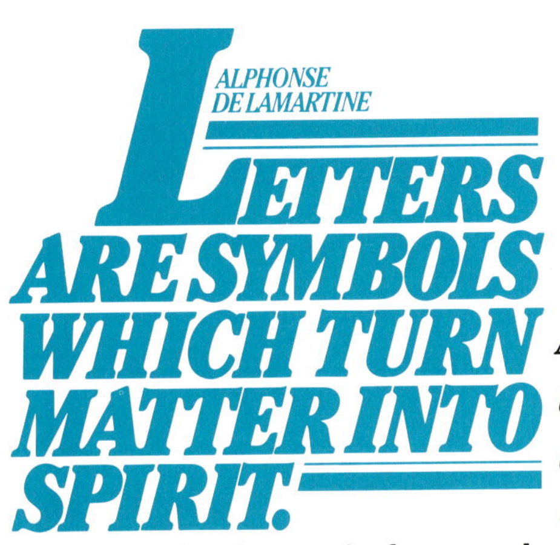

Architecture began like all scripts. First there was the alphabet. A stone was laid and that was a letter, and each letter was a hieroglyph, and on each hieroglyph there rested a group of ideas, like the capital on a column. Thus, until Gutenberg architecture is the chief and universal "writing." This granite book, begun in the East, continued by the Greeks and Romans–its last page was written by the Middle Ages. Until the fifteenth century, architecture was the great exponent and recorder of mankind. In the 15th century everything changed. Human thought discovered a means of perpetuating itself which was not only more lasting and resilient than architecture, but also simpler and more straightforward. Architecture is superseded. The stone letters of Orpheus have been succeeded by the leaden ones of Gutenberg. The book will destroy the edifice. The invention of printing is the greatest event in history. It is the fundamental revolution. Under the printing form, thought becomes more imperishable than ever; it is volatile, elusive and indestructible. It mingles with the very air. Thought derives new life from this concrete form. It passes from a life-span into immortality. One can destroy something concrete, but who can eradicate what is omnipresent? VICTOR HUGO

Whence did the wondrous, mystic art arise of painting speech, and speaking to the eyes? That we, by tracing magic lines are taught how to embody, and to colour thought?

WILLIAM MASSEY

THE TRADITION OF TYPE MUST BE CONSIDERED THE MOST ENDURING, QUIET AND EFFECTIVE INSTITUTION OF DIVINE GRACE, INFLUENCING ALL NATIONS THROUGH THE CENTURIES, AND PERHAPS IN TIME FORGING A CHAIN TO LINK ALL MANKIND IN BROTHERHOOD

JOHANN GOTTFRIED HERDER

12.

A LOVE OF LETTERS IS THE BEGINNING OF TYPOGRAPHICAL WISDOM. THAT IS, THE LOVE OF LETTERS AS LITERATURE AND THE LOVE OF LETTERS AS PHYSICAL ENTITIES, HAVING ABSTRACT BEAUTY OF THEIR OWN, APART FROM THE IDEAS THEY MAY EXPRESS OR THE EMOTIONS THEY MAY EVOKE.

JOHN R. BIGGS

Geometry can produce legible letters, but art alone makes them beautiful. Art begins where geometry ends, and imparts to letters a character transcending mere measurement.

LETTERS ARE THE KEY TO OUR CULTURE, THEY CAN ALSO BE A PICKLOCK TO OUR HEART.

BROR ZACHRISSON

Civilization and letters are two homogeneous, inseparable concepts; just as the development of civilization is unthinkable without the medium of letters, so it was the progress of civilization which gave the letter its full value as the bearer of thought, and raised it to universal importance. MAX CAFLISCH

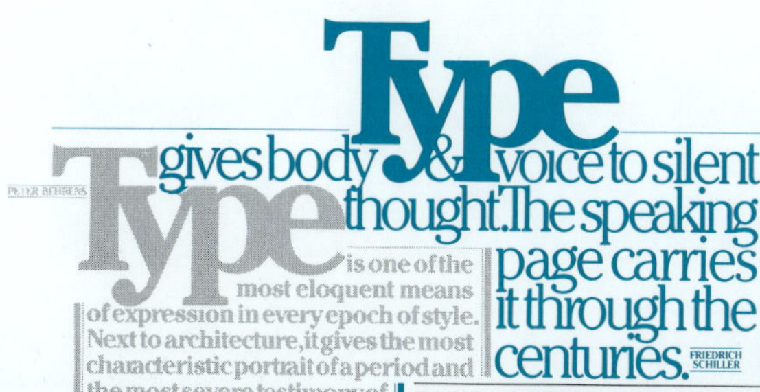

Type gives body & voice to silent thought. The speaking page carries it through the centuries.

FRIEDRICH SCHILLER

Type is one of the most eloquent means of expression in every epoch of style. Next to architecture, it gives the most characteristic portrait of a period and the most severe testimony of a nation's intellectual status.

PETER BEHRENS

Type which can be treated like an ornament,-and the clear-cut and even shape of a letter is a decorative means of monumental form-should fulfill two properties, namely to transmit, through the image of the word, thoughts & moods, knowledge and directions, and also to affect the senses thru its form, and lend visible grace to the contents.

HUGO LAGERSTRÖM

IT CAN BE CONSIDERED A SPECIAL MERIT OF OUR TIME THAT CREATIVE FORCES ARE AGAIN CONCERNED WITH THE PROBLEM OF TYPE DESIGN –A PROBLEM WHICH HAS BEEN FACED BY THE BEST ARTISTS OF EVERY AGE. TYPE & LETTERS HAVE ALWAYS BEEN THE IMMEDIATE EXPRESSION OF A NATION'S ARTISTIC FEELING, & IN OUR CONTEMPORARY DESIGNS ALSO, THE LEVEL OF OUR CREATIVENESS IS PERHAPS MORE FORCIBLE & LASTINGLY REPRESENTED THAN IN OTHER REALMS OF ART.

WALTER TIEMANN

Words remain impalpable abstract entities for most people, but for the lover and student of typography they can achieve a more or less perfect realization in the shape of letters. For him it becomes a constant need to delve into the prolific realm of type and through familiarity with that world he grows increasingly receptive to the myriad shades of meaning that can be expressed. It is only when he has succeeded in finding the most perfect embodiment for a particular line of thought, that his quest is over.

GOTTHARD DE BEAUCLAIR

13.

ALDOUS HUXLEY Machines exist; let us then exploit them to create beauty–a modern beauty, while we are about it. For we live in the twentieth century; let us frankly admit it and not pretend that we live in the fifteenth. The work of the backward-looking hand-printers may be excellent in its way; but its way is not the contemporary way. Their books are often beautiful, but with a borrowed beauty expressive of nothing in the world in which we happen to live.

JOHANN GOETHE GOD BLESS COPPER, PRINTING, AND ALL OTHER REPRODUCTIVE PROCESSES, WHICH ENSURE THAT ANY GOOD THING THAT EXISTS CAN NEVER BE WIPED OUT.

CHARLES DICKENS The printer is the friend of intelligence, of thought; he is the friend of liberty, of freedom, of law; indeed, the printer is the friend of every man who is the friend of order–the friend of every man who can read. Of all the inventions, of all the discoveries in science or art, of all the great results in the wonderful progress of mechanical energy and skill, the printer is the only product of civilization necessary to the existence of free man.

Now this is what I call workmanship. There is nothing on earth more exquisite than a bonny book, with well-placed columns of rich black writing in beautiful borders, and illuminated pictures cunningly inset. But nowadays, instead of looking at books, people read them. **GEORGE B. SHAW**

FINE TYPOGRAPHY PRESENTS A KIND OF CHALLENGE TO WHICH WRITERS CAN SCARCELY HELP RESPONDING. I FEEL IT IS BOUND TO EVOKE IN WRITERS THE WISH TO WRITE REALLY WELL THAT IS LATENT AND SOMETIMES FORGOTTEN BUT UNQUENCHABLE IN MOST OF THEM. FINE TYPOGRAPHY HAS A CURIOUS CHARM FOR THE LITERARY MIND–PERHAPS A LITTLE LIKE THE CHARM IN THE AIR OF VIENNA THAT HAYDN FELT OR THE AIR OF THE OLD SALONS OF PARIS THAT MADE WRITERS EXACTING. **VAN WYCK BROOKS**

We learn to read, in various languages, in various sciences; we learn the alphabet and letters of all manner of Books. But the place where we are to get knowledge, even theoretic knowledge, is the Books themselves!..The true University of these days is a Collection of Books. **THOMAS CARLYLE**

S.H. DE ROOS

Apart from technical and practical factors, it is especially the style of a period, the dominant expression of form, which is reflected in the character of a type, filling it with the changing and fascinating aspect of country and period.

TYPOGRAPHY IS A SERVANT-THE SERVANT OF THOUGHT & LANGUAGE TO WHICH IT GIVES VISIBLE EXISTENCE.

T. M. CLELAND

In all the alphabets yet created there lies a wealth, an abundance, of possible creative interpretations which we only perceive as we give them more intensive study. The letter was formed, and to form implies creation. This is a divine process even when it takes place within the four walls of a humble workshop. Once, there was someone working at each letter who felt the joy of creation pulsing in his veins. Whoever looks at letters with a receptive eye will therefore sense the miracle which occurs whenever individual signs composing a group become the image of a language, and he will discover a meaningful life in this allegedly dead matter.

ALFRED J. LUDWIG

MAURICE AUDIN

The triumph of the alphabet gave the true impetus to our Western civilization; it allowed a swift dissemination of the humanistic spirit, which was followed by works on theology, philosophy and mathematics, as well as a revival of scientific and literary learning. The alphabet made it possible to transmit all-embracing concepts and truths to humanity.

In the sense in which Architecture is an art, Typography is an art. That is, they both come under the head of "making or doing intentionally with skill".... Every work of Architecture, every work of Typography, depends for its success upon the clear conveyance of intentions, in words and otherwise, from one human mind to others: from the man who is supposed to know how the finished thing should look and function, to a concert of specialists who are responsible not only to master-designer but also to the public.

BEATRICE WARDE

14.

A bunch of characters in alphabetical order.

SCULPTURES BY RHODA SPARBER
LIMERICKS BY HERB LUBALIN
PHOTOGRAPHED BY CARL FISCHER

THE RESURGENCE OF INTEREST in the opulent remains of the great Pharaoh Tutankhamen has turned archaeological attention to the third and fourth lines of an ancient limerick found on a mutilated wall of his tomb, roughly translated:

She had for her clients
Both pygmies and giants

which some of the more enterprising among you might care to reconstruct in its entirety (four-letter words permissible), based on your own experiences and relationships with those whose accounts are responsible for your bread and butter, your ulcers, your migraines, and your general feelings of malaise.

THE LIMERICK HAILS, of course, from the sleepy Irish town of that name. In actuality, Limerick—little more than a wide place along an Irish road—gave but its name to this most pervasive of all verse forms: an arrangement, often nonsensical, of five anapestic lines. It was popularized by that famous "nonsense" gentleman Edward Lear, in his celebrated **Book of Nonsense** (1846), and became an entertaining subject for improvisation at convivial parties. Limericks gained their worldwide popularity with such thought-provoking observations as:

A wonderful bird is the pelican
His bill will hold more than his belican;
He can take in his beak
Food enough for a week,
And I'm damned if I see how the helican.

SOME OTHER MEANINGFUL DITTIES in our repertoire are more appropriate to stag parties than to the pages of **U&lc**. Let's change the subject to papier-mâché.

THE DICTIONARY DESCRIBES this sculptural medium as "chewed paper." A hard and strong substance made of paper pulp mixed with size, glue, rosin, and—in the case of Rhoda Sparber—patience, imagination, dexterity, ingenuity, and a sense of humor.

AND...INSPIRATION! The kind of inspiration supplied by the venerable bunch of characters shown, in alphabetical order, on the next eight pages.

RHODA AND I WERE SITTING around one evening chewing the fat (not paper). She was busily involved in a 3-dimensional doodle which, to my surprise, turned out to be yours-truly spewing myriads of letterforms from a mouth concealed within a gray beard. I must say I was fascinated by her incisive interpretation of my professional character, in spite of the fact that vanity reared its ugly head and I complained bitterly of the years she had added to my youthful countenance.

FROM AN EVENING'S congenial companion I was immediately transformed into the intrepid editor of **U&lc**. Wheels turned. Horns blared. Bells rang, and lights blinked on and off. I propositioned Ms. Sparber, the deal being this: if she could do to Saul Bass, Lou Dorfsman, Gene Federico, Milton Glaser, George Lois, Cipe Pineles and Henry Wolf what she had done to me, I would chew all the newsprint necessary to accomplish this mammoth undertaking and would give her a small stipend, on the side, to tide her over. Essential to the assignment, of course, was my role: to provide tasteful tidbits, intimate insights, as it were, into the professional (and otherwise) lives of this esteemed group.

AS I EXTOLLED the innumerable virtues of these graphic giants, Rhoda was caught up in a frenzy of creativity. The temptation to contribute my own resources to translating her visual images into verbal forms—to complete the picture, one might say—became irresistible.

SO, DRAWING UPON my long and fruitful relationships with the above-mentioned personalities to cull their most innate distinguishing characteristics, I proceeded to write the words set on the next eight pages in ITC Benguiat Gothic Book, Medium, and Bold.

I WANT TO THANK Carl Fischer for capturing the essence of these sculptures photographically, and Pioneer-Moss for the fine color separations.

SO MUCH FOR LIMERICKS. So much for papier-mâché. So much for the synergistic results. H.L.

COLOR SEPARATIONS BY PIONEER-MOSS

SAUL BASS

There is a big fish named Bass;
In his school he's head of the class;
The name of his game:
To design, frame by frame,
Film titles for Hollywood brass.

Another great claim to fame
For this man with a fishy name:
The design of a bell
For American Tel.
Which has brought him no end of acclaim.

This Bass whose first name is Saul
Has a lot more than this on the ball;
Erudite and quite bright,
His words tend to delight
One and all with his Bronxian drawl.

15.

HERB LUBALIN

An avid alphabetical freak
Herb likes to take type that's oblique;
And fill up the o's
With buttons and bows—
Or whatever makes sense out of Greek.

In school where they go by the book
His passion for o's was mistook;
Words like fool, stool, and spool
Had caused him to drool—
So they thought he was some kind of kook.

Although o's are the name of his game
There never ever were o's in his name;
For this only regret
Which shall remain ever stet—
He has his father and mother to blame.

CIPE PINELES

A designer whose talents are vast,
Cipe got to the top very fast;
At Vogue she was fired,
At Seventeen was rehired—
Alas! Your hard luck, Condé Nast.

Ma-a-a-ahvelous, her favorite word
Emanates from her mouth like a bird;
Fa-a-a-a-abulous, too
Another word she can coo—
To be believed, these words must be heard.

Pineles, a name we can't rhyme
Is bandied about all the time;
By both student and pro
And others who know
That Cipe hasn't yet reached her prime.

16.

15.-16. These limericks by Herb Lubalin about eminent designers were a spin-off on papiér-mache sculptures by Rhoda Sparber.

17. Introduction to an article on Benjamin Franklin.

17.

A French Postcard...is a French Postcard...is a French Postcard?

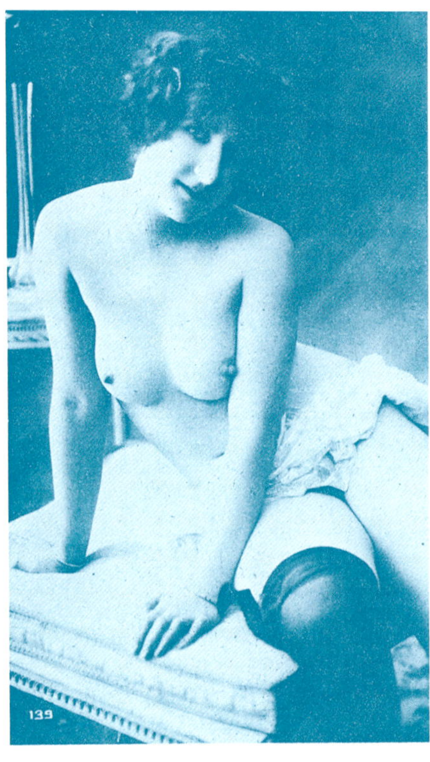

Picture yourself walking through the streets of Montmartre, looking up at teary, wide-eyed Keane children peering disconsolately out of gallery windows, breaking your heart, when a sleazy character slithers up to you wearing a beret, a black leather trenchcoat, dark shades, a cigarette dangling jauntily from under a majestic moustache. He hands you a packet wrapped in a plain brown wrapper, with tobacco-stained yellow fingers. He says: "Voulez vous acheter les French Postcards?"

Right away, your sexual fantasies run amok and you begin to visualize lascivious, 19th-century French femmes, lying indiscreetly, on ornate chaises, undraped, with pubic hair judiciously retouched out. Tempering these fantasies is the suspicion that what you're really going to get are pictures of the Eiffel Tower, the Arc de Triomphe, Notre Dame, Les Bateaux Mouche, etc.

Your fantasies overcome your suspicions, as you say to yourself, "What the hell, it's only six francs ($1.50)." You hand him l'argent, he hands you les cartes postales, and you slink off to the privacy of your hotel room, tear open the brown wrapper in a frenzy of sexual excitement and anticipation and, lo and behold, revealed before you are twenty-six of the most luscious titillating characters you have ever laid eyes on.

Typographic characters. A complete array of fantastic art nouveau letterforms, from A to Z. You indulge yourself in a veritable visual orgy, forgetting completely your oft-quoted statement that type forms sink into obscurity when compared to the human female form.

18.

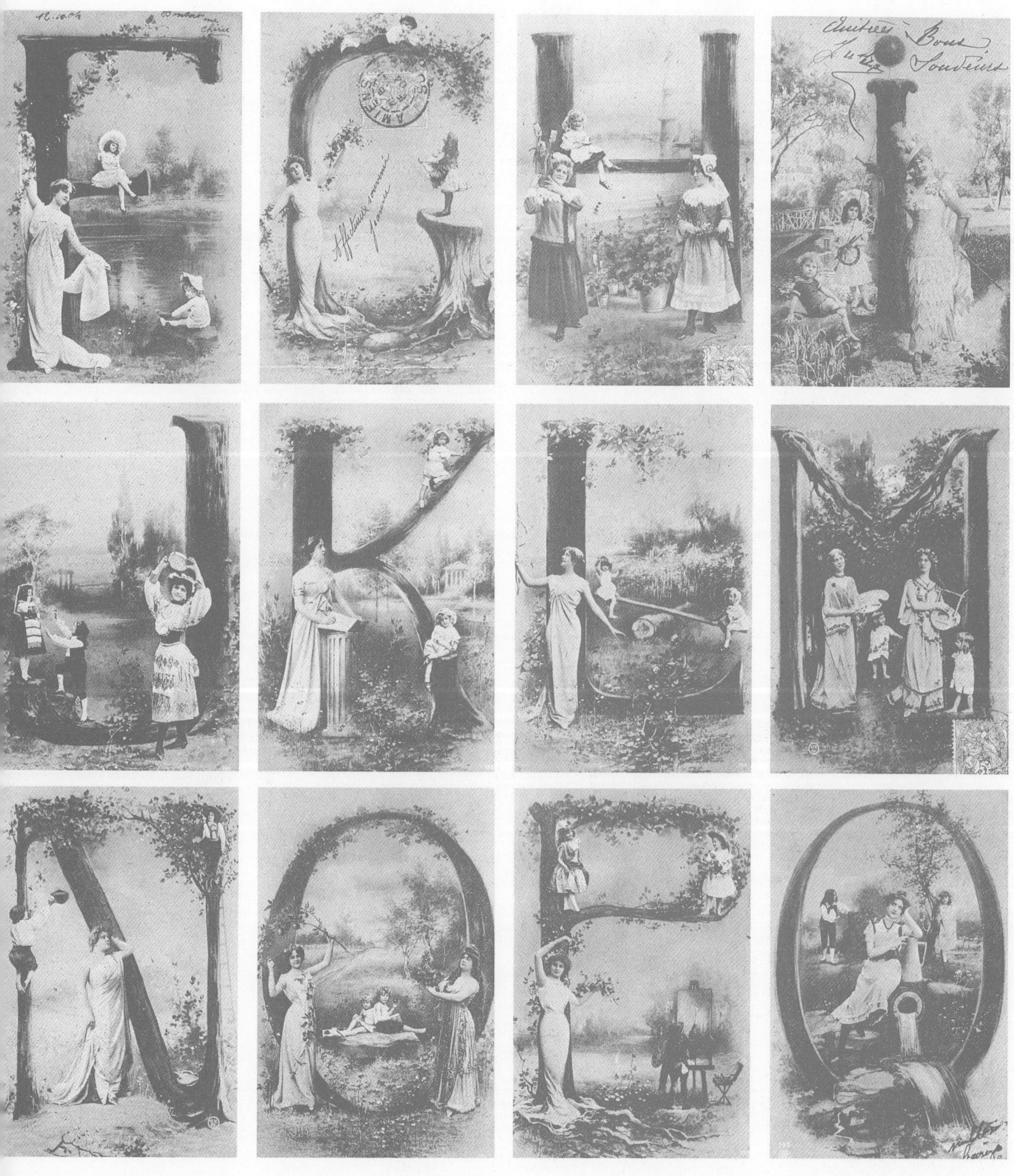

Take His Word For It

If this page looks like a word processor in panic, look again, friends. These are all 100% guaranteed recognized, if not recognizable, words. (Or at least so our correspondent, Karel Treebus, a typographic designer in The Netherlands, assures us. A devoted and appreciative reader, Treebus responded to an article in our December 1978 issue which featured a 70-letter German word. Not to be outdone, he sent us his own collection of jawbreakers. Although we've had this list stored away in our files for more than a year, the delay in publishing turns out to be an unplanned stroke of genius. In this issue, we can unveil them along with our new, highly readable ITC Century typeface, to give you every advantage in making sense out of what appears to be nonsense.

Hottentottensoldaten-tententententoons-tellingstenten?

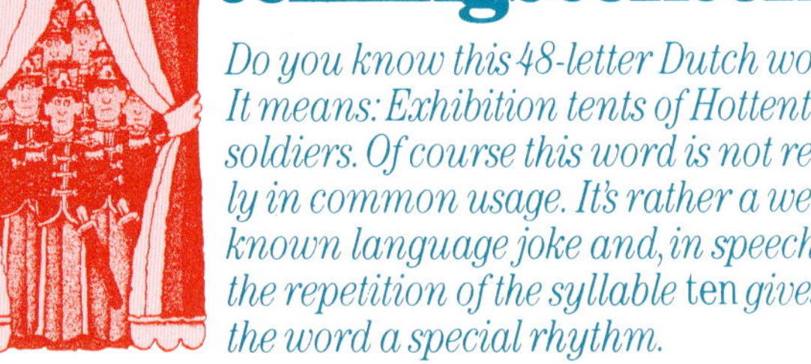

Do you know this 48-letter Dutch word? It means: Exhibition tents of Hottentot soldiers. Of course this word is not really in common usage. It's rather a well known language joke and, in speech, the repetition of the syllable ten *gives the word a special rhythm.*

Guinness to the contrary, this word has 41 characters and translates, "roc accident damage insurance system. However, it is possible in the Netherlands to create new and longer worc if one has a mind to, by combining two or more other words and addin them onto an established word, as in German.

Verkeersong-evalsschade-verzekeringssysteem?

Rijksluchtvaar-tdienstweersch-epenpersoneel?

According to the Dutch issue of the "Guinness Book of Records" this is the longest word in use. It has 40 characters according to the Dutch; 41 as we count them. The combination ij *is one character in Dutch. The meaning of this word is "weather ship personnel of the governmental aviation service."*

Talebuamaineiilikena-mainavalenivei-vakabulaima-kulalakeba?

By the way, speaking of long words, are you familiar with this name of a well known Fijian cricket player? How would you like to be the sportscaster with the responsibility of pronouncing this correctly?

Taumatawhakatangakoauaua-tamateapokaiwhenuakitanan-tahuwhakatamahangakoa...?

A village in New Zealand sports this name. It must be a constant frustration to the Welsh, who take pride in the ownership of some of the world's longest town and village names. This mouthful translates: "Hill crest where the traveller Tamatea piped on his nose flute for his beloved one." It contains 70 characters.

19.

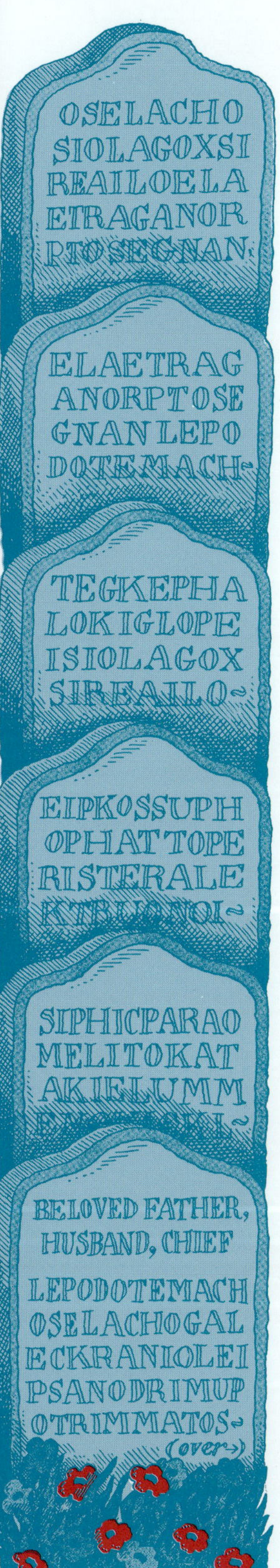

Lepodotemachosel-
achogaleckraniole-
ipsanodrimupotri-
mmatossiphicpar-
aomelitokatakielu-
mmenokickleipko-
ssuphophattoperis-
teralektruonoitegk-
ephalokiglopeisiol-
agoxsireailoelaetr-
aganorptosegnan?

Right here in the good old USA, an Indian chief died in Wisconsin in 1866. His heirs needed six tombstones to record his complete name. It contains 182 letters and it is believed to be a cryptogram.

Tiruvaly-anguidi Vijayara-ghavach-arya?

This one is a family name in India. The meaning of the first name is "village of prosperous rice fields"; the second name breaks down into a synonym for the god Rama and the name of a religious leader in the 14th century. The Fijian cricket player and this Indian family name were gleaned from "The Story of Language," by Mario Pei.

scar'ab 1. A large black, or nearly black, dung beetle of the countries bordering on the Mediterranean, which was regarded by the ancient Egyptians as symbolic of resurrection and immortality. 2. A conventionalized representation of a beetle commonly in stone, usually having an inscription on the flat underside; also a gem cut in this representation. It is the symbol of the sun-god Khepera.
SCARAB SCARABÉE DER SCARÄBAUS
abject abrupt adagio adapt adept adipyl adjoin adjust adlay adopt adrift Aeaea afflux affray aghast agleaf agley aglint albify aleph
alfaje alfalfa alforja algate algedo algid algist algoid alight alkyd allay alloy allyl alpha alphol alpist aphid aphtha aplomb apoplexy
appall apply aptly artful atopic atopy aught
badge baffle baffy baft bagpi baggit baggy Bailey bajada baldy balky bally

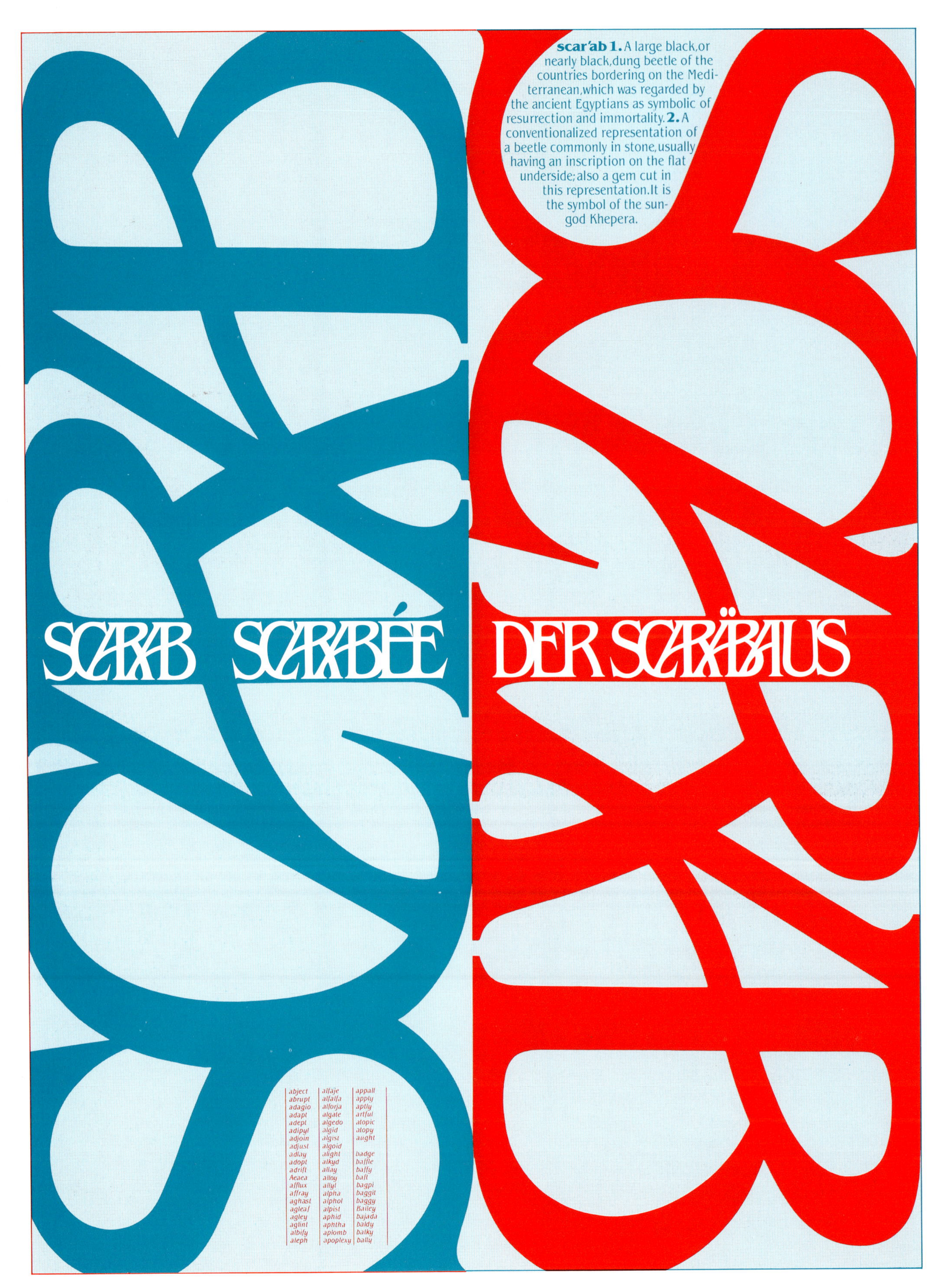

20.

18. A spread from an article on old French postcards.

19. Lubalin's love for words and the challenge of designing with them was the impetus for this article on long words in many languages.

20.-23. From the article, "My favorite 5,6,7,8,9-letter words."

24. Lubalin also designed an article on the longest sentences.

21.

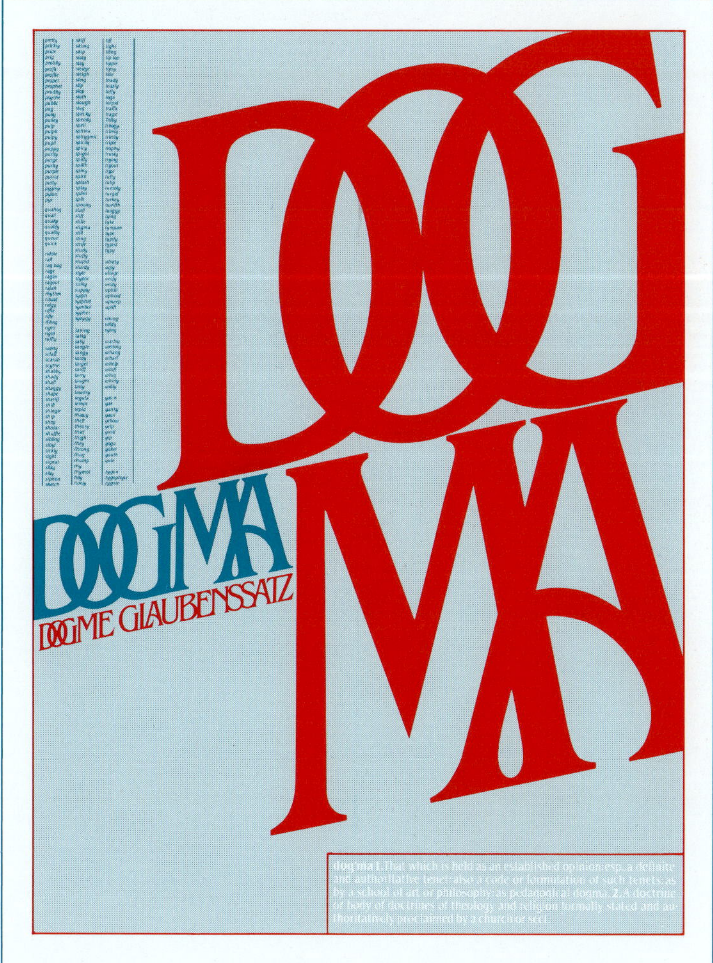

22.

23.

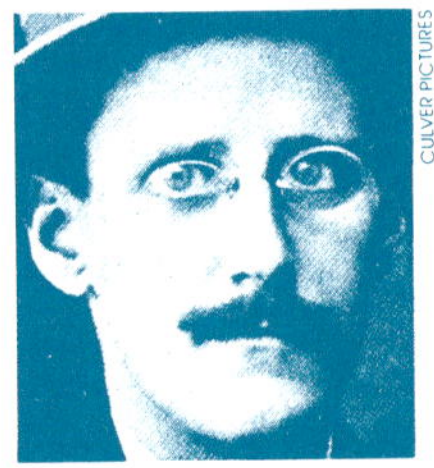

CULVER PICTURES

YES

Whose is longer, Victor Hugo's or James Joyce's?

Up to 1921, the longest sentence ever to appear in literature was to be found in Victor Hugo's famous Les Miserables. This sentence, three pages long, contains 823 words, 93 commas, 51 semicolons, and 4 dashes. Then came 1921 and the great James Joyce stream-of-consciousness novel, Ulysses. In the notorious and splendid last chapter, beginning on page 738 and running straight through 783, there are two continuous sentences with no punctuation at all. The first is 21 pages long. The second is 23, which makes these the longest sentences in all literature. Isn't that fantastic?

24.

kind of eye in it theyre all Buttons men down the middle on the wrong side of them Molly darling he called me what was his name Jack Joe Harry Mulvey was it yes I think a lieutenant he was rather fair he had a laughing kind of a voice so I went around to the whatyoucallit everything was whatyoucallit moustache had he he said hed come back Lord its just like yesterday to me and if I was married hed do it to me and I promised him yes faithfully Id let him block me now flying perhaps hes dead or killed or a Captain or admiral its nearly 20 years if I said firtree cove he would if he came up behind me and put his hands over my eyes to guess who I might recognise him hes young still about 40 perhaps hes married some girl on the black water and is quite changed they all do they havent half the character a woman has she little knows what I did with her beloved husband before he ever dreamt of her in broad daylight too in the sight of the whole world you might say they could have put an article about it in the Chronicle I was a bit wild after when I blew out the old bag the biscuits were in from Benady Bros and exploded it Lord what a bang all the woodcocks and pigeons screaming coming back the same way that we went over middle hill round by the old guardhouse and the jews burial place pretending to read out the Hebrew on them I wanted to fire his pistol he said he hadnt one he didnt know what to make of me with his peaked cap on that

25.-27. Lubalin liked a portfolio of etchings by Stephen Alcorn, and designed an eight-page article to display them.

28. A thematic crossword puzzle.

STEPHEN ALCORN'S RITRATTI DEGLI ARTISTI PIU CELEBRI

We recently became intrigued with a portfolio of prints—31 portraits of famous artists. There was something about these prints—not just the archaic look of them—but the sentimental idea of them, like somebody's collection of rock stars or sports heroes, that completely disarmed us. In this day and age of sophisticated technology, of cleverness, of oblique references and obscure meanings in art, what prompts a contemporary printmaker to get wrapped up in such a quaint idea as a portrait gallery of great artists?

To begin with, if you are Stephen Alcorn, son of the illustrator John Alcorn, you were born into an art-conscious, art-appreciating home. Then if you were carted off to live in Florence during your impressionable years, if you went to school there and absorbed the Renaissance right through your American jeans and T-shirts, you would understand the impetus for this project. As Steve puts it, "going to school in Florence, you couldn't help but feel that the Renaissance was still part of everyday life." The architecture of the school reminded you; it had arched ceilings like the cathedral. Instead of Palmer-method alphabet placards around the schoolrooms, he stared at marble blocks incised with the names of the great Renaissance poets, artists and writers. In the very rooms of the school building, workers were pouring plaster casts of Renaissance sculpture. The Renaissance was still alive in Florence, and going strong.

Back home in the United States, Steve is now a Fine Arts Major in Printmaking and Painting at SUNY at Purchase, New York. Partly out of nostalgia, partly in homage to the memory of Florence, he conceived of rendering a series of portraits of the Italian Renaissance masters. His inspiration for the series came, surprisingly, not from the high art of the Uffizi and the Pitti Palace, but from the little known Italian Folk Art of the Renaissance and the two centuries following. The work, turned out by local artisans, took the form of woodcuts illustrating proverbs, fables and religious themes, for the most part. Like most folk art, they were straightforward, ingenuous and full of inventive decorative motifs.

It was the spirit of these woodcuts that Steve tried to absorb and translate into his own linoleum cuts. Actually, portraits were rarely done in that period of Italian Folk Art, so he had to imagine how the local artisans of Umbria or Campania might have rendered them. Once he completed the Italian masters, there was no stopping him. He went on to include the Renaissance Masters of the North...the "greats" of the Middle Ages...and all his favorites from Cimabue to Picasso. For his references, he had to rely on already existing portraits of the older artists, and photographs of more recent ones. So far, there are 31 portraits in his gallery. The original blocks are 10" x 13," printed on 15" x 22" sheets of "Goyu" Japanese rice paper, in black ink. The name block beneath each portrait is printed in red.

We are reproducing 16 of Steve's prints, because we not only admire his unabashed hero-worship and the deep sentiment behind the project, but we are completely bowled over by his artistry.

We also recognized that this feature was a perfect foil for demonstrating our new Roman typeface designed by Dick Isbell and Jerry Campbell. This is an elegant, sophisticated face, but you can see how well it complements the straightforward, unaffected character of the artwork. ITC Isbell has grace. It's spirited. It has beautiful forms. It is classic and contemporary at the same time. Like all great art forms, it will stand up to the whims of fashion, in the same way that the works of master artists never look "dated." MARION MULLER

25.

1475-1564

Any artist who has suffered rejection at the hands of a client should take comfort from the fact that Michelangelo was not always an instant hit with his patrons either. His David, one of the most revered sculptures in all the world, got a thumbs-down review from the general public when it was first unveiled. ❧ In 1501, the citizens of Florence decided to erect a monument to commemorate the ousting of the tyrannical Medicis from power, and the establishment of a benevolent republic. Michelangelo won the commission with his plan to create an image of the shepherd David. It would be a symbol of the small and meek triumphing over the ignoble giant. He went to work on a piece of marble that was abandoned 40 years earlier by a sculptor who found it too long and narrow for his purposes. Michelangelo chipped away at the awkward, skinny block for about 3 years. What emerged was not the locals' vision of the little shepherd boy they knew from their bibles. For starters, they couldn't deal with a 13-year-old boy that was 13 feet tall. And instead of their image of an innocent youth, still damp behind the ears, they were faced with the formidable physique of a Greek warrior. They quibbled that the right hand was too large...the nose too long. But worst of all, this not-so-little David stood stark naked! ❧ Nevertheless, cool heads prevailed over the objections of the townspeople. A committee of artists and citizens, including Botticelli and Leonardo voted unanimously to accept the sculpture, and it was erected in the Piazza della Signoria, the political heart of Florence.

MICHELANGELO

TIZIANO

1485-1576

TITIAN! WHAT ROMANTIC IMAGES THE NAME CONJURES UP...PEACHY-SKINNED BEAUTIES LOLLING ABOUT, WITH HAIR THAT ALL THE GENIUS OF ALL OUR LEADING COIFFEURS COMBINED CAN'T MATCH. IT MAY SEEM HARD TO IMAGINE, BUT THIS SENSUOUS PAINTER, WHO TOOK GREAT PLEASURE IN RENDERING FLESH BY THE POUND, HAIR BY THE STRAND AND VELVET BY THE YARD, WAS AS ASSIDUOUS ABOUT BOOKKEEPING AS HE WAS ABOUT HIS AESTHETICS. ❧ HE PAINTED HIS WAY ACROSS EUROPE, LEAVING PORTRAITS IN EVERY NOOK AND CRANNY OF EVERY CASTLE THAT COUNTED. HE ALSO KEPT A VERY SHARP EYE ON HIS ACCOUNTS RECEIVABLE, NEVER MAKING CONCESSIONS TO DEFAULTING CLIENTS, AND EVEN DUNNING ROYALTY WHEN THEY FELL BEHIND IN THEIR PAYMENTS. IN ADDITION, HE CULTIVATED POTENTIAL CUSTOMERS BY ENTERTAINING A STEADY STREAM OF GUESTS AT HIS HOME, WHEELING AND DEALING ALONG WITH MANY OF THE BEST MERCHANTS IN VENICE. ASIDE FROM HIS INCOME FROM PAINTING, TITIAN MADE A LITTLE EXTRA ON THE SIDE AS AN ART DEALER, AND FROM A SAWMILL HE OWNED IN THE HINTERLANDS. HE WAS ALSO FINANCIALLY ASTUTE ENOUGH TO KNOW HOW TO FALSIFY HIS INCOME TAX, TAKE ADVANTAGE OF TAX SHELTERS AND LOOPHOLES IN THE LAW, AND TO INCLUDE, IN CONTRACTS WITH HIS CLIENTS, SUCH LITTLE EXTRAS AS PENSIONS AND ANNUITIES FOR HIMSELF AND HIS CHILDREN. ❧ BUT THIS EXTREMELY VERSATILE MAN WAS, ABOVE ALL, A FABULOUS PAINTER WHO MANIPULATED OIL PAINTS—WITH GLAZES, TEXTURES AND A NEW STYLE OF BRUSHWORK THAT STARTED A UNIQUE FORM AND STYLE OF EXPRESSION IN PAINTING.

1518-1594

JACOPO ROBUSTI WAS HIS REAL NAME, BUT THIS GIANT OF A PAINTER, WHO DREW LIKE MICHELANGELO AND USED COLOR LIKE TITIAN, WAS STUCK WITH THE DEMEANING LABEL "TINTORETTO" BECAUSE HIS FATHER WAS A DYER. ❧ STILL, THE NAME WAS NO HANDICAP. HE WAS HIGHLY SUCCESSFUL IN WINNING COMMISSIONS, NOT ONLY BECAUSE HE WAS SO GOOD, BUT HE WAS FAST—PROBABLY THE FASTEST BRUSH IN VENICE AT THE TIME—AND A GREAT PAIN TO HIS COMPETITORS BECAUSE HE SWALLOWED UP ALL THE WORK IN TOWN. HIS APPETITE AND HIS ENERGY IN THAT RESPECT WERE ENORMOUS. HE DIDN'T MAKE THINGS EASY FOR HIMSELF EITHER. HE COMPOSED PICTURES WITH MULTITUDES OF CHARACTERS IN THE FOREGROUND, SO NOTHING COULD BE FUDGED. HE THRUST HIS FIGURES INTO OBLIQUE POSTURES, CREATING MIND-BOGGLING FORESHORTENINGS, AND HE WORKED TO ENORMOUS SCALE. HIS LARGEST WORKS ARE LOCATED IN THE DOGE'S PALACE IN VENICE, WHERE TINTORETTO HAD A HAND IN DECORATING THE CEILINGS AND WALLS. IN THE TRIBUNAL ROOM, THE LARGEST ROOM IN THE PALACE, WHERE A THOUSAND MEN SAT TO APPROVE LAWS AND ELECT THE DOGE, TINTORETTO'S PAINTING OF PARADISE FILLS THE ENTIRE WALL BEHIND THE THRONES. IT IS REPUTED TO BE THE LARGEST PAINTING (FRESCOES ASIDE) IN THE WORLD, 7 X 22 METERS. ❧ IT MUST BE MENTIONED THAT, IN SPITE OF HIS FINANCIALLY SUCCESSFUL CAREER, TINTORETTO LIVED MODESTLY, WAS A GOOD HUSBAND AND FATHER, AND, TO HIS EVERLASTING CREDIT, INVITED HIS DAUGHTERS AS WELL AS THE BOYS TO ASSIST HIM IN HIS SUCCESSFUL STUDIO. TINTORETTO, A NICE MAN!

TINTORETTO

BRVEGEL

1525-1569

On the surface, the paintings of Pieter Brueghel, The Elder, look a lot like charming bucolic landscapes. But in essence they are really symbolic, moralizing religious pictures in a "pop" setting. Although, like every other serious painter of his time, Brueghel made the obligatory trip to Italy to see the masters of the Renaissance, he rejected their heroics—their grandiose religious and historic themes in Roman settings. The people of Brueghel's Lowlands were in a Protestant rebellion against Spanish and High Church domination at that time. Though Brueghel himself was not a member of any radical religious sect, he was a religious painter in another sense. He identified man with nature, and nature with God. Instead of pictures of the Holy Family, he painted whole communities of village people. Instead of a Last Supper, he painted a peasant Wedding Feast. He painted people at work, in towns and in the fields. He painted God at work, in a series depicting the seasons of the year. He illustrated proverbs and adages to underscore moral lessons. He was a constant observer and commentator on the human condition, though it was obvious that his point of view changed with time. In his youth, he was disparaging about the stupidity of human beings. In his later works he showed empathy for their folly and their irremediable poverty and misery. ❧ His voyage to Italy did influence his point of view in the literal sense of the word. Coming from the Lowlands, where every road shoots straight as an arrow toward the horizon, the trip over the Alps was an eye-opener for Brueghel. The panoramic vistas he experienced were incorporated into his paintings. His birds-eye view of village scenes and landscapes gave his paintings a spaciousness and spiritual grandeur that lifted them above their mundane subject matter.

26.

1853-1890

His whole life story is one of clashes—with parents, employers, neighbors—and of unrequited love affairs and unsuccessful jobs. He couldn't please his parents, so he tried fanatically to please God. His services as a lay minister to a flock of Belgian miners were just another disaster. He never felt saintly enough, and his overzealous behavior, his fasting, his self-deprivations, made him sick and everyone else, tired. ❧ Fortunately, in Millet's paintings and Rembrandt's etchings, he finally discovered the empathy for poor, wretched little people that he craved to express himself. It gave him license to pursue his religious fervor through art instead of the pulpit. He started to draw and paint peasants in the fields, in their thatched huts, at their meals. He made studies of their muddy boots, their looms and their farm tools—all in suitable dark and somber tones. But on a visit to France, he discovered the Impressionists. The ascetic demons in him gave way to the aesthetic ones. His new paintings blazed with color—emerald green, vermilion, Prussian blue and dazzling yellow. Instead of dreary peasant pictures, he painted rolling verdant farmlands, orchards in bloom, voluptuous flower bouquets, still life objects and portraits. That his frenzy transferred from religion to art was obvious from his output: in 15 months, he turned out over 200 canvases. It was also at this time, in an argument with Gauguin over form—not faith—that Van Gogh cut off his ear. ❧ A hundred years earlier, he might have been "exorcised" of his demons. A hundred years later, he would have been psychoanalyzed. But Van Gogh solved his anguish by putting a bullet in his head when he realized that his pathological personality had been interfering with his painting.

1859-1891

WHEN WE HEAR THE NAME SEURAT, WE SEE SPOTS BEFORE OUR EYES. IT'S THE NAME WE MOST CLOSELY ASSOCIATE WITH THE TECHNIQUE OF PAINTING IN TINY DOTS OF COLOR. ❧ IN THE LATE 1800's, SEVERAL NEW SCIENTIFIC TREATISES SURFACED DEALING WITH THE OPTICS AND PHYSICS OF COLOR. GEORGES SEURAT WAS FASCINATED. MANY OF THE OBSERVATIONS, OLD-HAT TO US NOW, WERE REVELATIONS THEN. FOR INSTANCE: DOTS OF DIFFERENT COLOR, MIXED OPTICALLY, LOOK BRIGHTER THAN THE SAME COLORS MIXED ON A PALETTE! COLORS APPEAR BRIGHTEST NEXT TO THEIR COMPLEMENTS! COLORS REFLECT EACH OTHER! (RED APPLES ON A YELLOW CLOTH THROW TINGES OF RED ON THE CLOTH AND PICK UP TINGES OF YELLOW, IN TURN. AND SO ON.) ❧ SEURAT, AND A FEW OTHERS, COMBINED ALL THE NEW COLOR IDEAS WITH CLASSIC CONVICTIONS ABOUT STRUCTURE, LINE AND POSITION. THEIR NEW STYLE OF PAINTING WAS CALLED POINTILLISM... SOMETIMES, DIVISIONISM. IT IS MOST COMMONLY KNOWN AS NEO-IMPRESSIONISM BECAUSE OF THEIR SIMILAR DABS OF COLOR. BUT IT WAS AS DIFFERENT FROM IMPRESSIONISM AS NIGHT FROM DAY. THE IMPRESSIONISTS WORKED OUTDOORS, IN THE BLAZING SUN OR A BLINDING SNOWSTORM, IN A FRENZY TO FINISH THEIR PICTURES BEFORE THE LIGHT CHANGED. COMPOSITION DID NOT MATTER; FORMS DIDN'T MATTER EITHER. REMEMBER, THEIR CHAOTIC DABS OF COLOR WERE STRICTLY USED FOR ACHIEVING ATMOSPHERIC EFFECTS. SEURAT'S DOTS, ON THE OTHER HAND, WERE ALL SCIENTIFIC AND CONTROLLED. HE ALSO SKETCHED OUTSIDE, BUT THE MAJOR WORK WAS DONE IN HIS STUDIO, WHERE HE SPENT MONTHS ANALYZING THE ARRANGEMENT OF COLORS, SO THAT EVERY FORM EMERGED SOLIDLY...NOT A LEAF STIRRED OUT OF LINE...AND THE COLORS INTEGRATED AND VIBRATED ACCORDING TO HIS SCHEME, NOT NATURE'S WHIMS.

27.

No. 8 in a series of Very Graphic Crossword Puzzles by Al McGinley and Don McKechnie

It's a lazy evening forty years ago. The family is gathered around the most imposing piece of furniture in the house, a big Stromberg-Carlson console radio. It was a time for laughter, tears, suspense, mystery, and a free-wheeling imagination.

"Curtain going up!" hailed another installment of "Mr. First Nighter." The locomotive roared and clanged into "Grand Central Station." The thundering hoofbeats of the great horse Silver made the old West live again. Edwin C. Hill gave us "the human side of the news." Time marched on the cathedral tones of Westbrook Van Voorhis. The Old Maestro, Ben Bernie, soothed us with a heartfelt "Yowsah, yowsah." Phil Baker granted the astounding sum of $64 for the right answer to a simple question. Fred Allen delighted us with the country's most irreverent wit.

Remember the incredible crash and clatter when Fibber McGee opened the closet door? The eerie greeting from Raymond, your host on "Inner Sanctum"? The funniest moment of silence ever—while Jack Benny considered a thief's demand for "your money or your life"? And there were the inevitable soap operas: Young Doctor Malone, Our Gal Sunday, When a Girl Marries, Pepper Young's Family.

Sadly, that golden age of entertainment will never again be ours to treasure. "Good night, Mrs. Calabash, wherever you are."

Radio introduced Will Rogers' homespun philosophy and biting political observations to millions.

"...the little bastards for another night."
—Uncle Don, unwittingly

The Jack Benny-Fred Allen feud (they were really good friends) drew some of radio's largest audiences. Left to right: Portland Hoffa, Benny, Allen, Mary Livingstone.

ACROSS

1. "There's good ______"
10. Conversational zinger
14. Santa quote
15. Food Fish
16. "Suits me to ______"
17. Comedian Bob
18. "The Romance of ______"
20. French instance
21. M.D. org.
23. Re is one
25. The Shadow
31. Half a string toy
32. They keep falling on my head
35. Seymour for short
36. "Fee, ______ fo, fum."
38. Goose eggs
39. Raw materials for paper
41. ______ be or not...
42. Drug dosage
44. Radio's Major
46. Ms Russell
48. German district
50. Decree
51. Ma and ______ Kettle
52. "Woe is ______"
53. Follows a star (3 words)
54. He owned a Maxwell
56. Old-time cutting tool
58. Radio's George
59. Actress Joanne
60. Not an E.M.
62. "______ and Sade."
63. I've been working on it (abbr.)
65. Ending for Superintend or refer
66. Morning, for short
67. Old radio crime show
73. The Shadow's girl friend
75. Old French coin
76. Bird prefix
77. In the year of the reign (Lat. abbr.)
79. Dines
82. "______ Doctor Malone"
83. Half a goodbye
84. Radio network
86. Hasten
88. Preposition
89. Joel Kupperman was one of them
90. As to
91. Ruby ______
92. Shoe width
94. Poetic word
95. Of an arena
98. Tonto's steed
100. Jack of Hudson High
103. Body Covering
104. "______'n Abner"
105. He said 1. across
106. Unearth

DOWN

1. Negative
2. Classic Abbot and Costello routine
3. Soak up
4. Radio's "The Little ______" (4 words)
5. Scoreboard numbers
6. Slang for diamonds
7. Coagulate
8. Holy Roman Empire monogram
9. 2000 pounds
10. Soap or saloon
11. Sun god
12. Marriages end here
13. Girl friend of 100 across
17. Emoter
18. "America's Ace of the Airways"
19. Super-athlete Jim
20. "______ ______ top this?"
22. 1100 in Rome
24. Lots and lots of time
26. Help for the problem drinker
27. Goddess (var.)
28. One who pries
29. It's worth 6 points
30. Entre ______
33. Plural (abbr.)
34. Margarine or ranch
35. A kind of vote
37. "Old McDonald had a farm... E.I.E. ______"
40. "Be it ever ______ humble..."
43. ______ Farrow
45. Joe Penner's line
47. Radio's Pitts
49. Familiar greeting
54. Flames
55. Maritime Prov. (abbr.)
57. Medical man
58. Bikini part
60. Nurse
61. Ocean (abbr.)
62. Johnson or Heflin
64. College degree
65. Growing out
68. Proceed
69. He rode 98 across
70. Thus
71. Britain's fleet (abbr.)
72. Transportation for the Lone Ranger
74. "______ Tavern"
78. Egyptian sun god
80. Greek letter
81. ______ up (assess)
85. To exist
87. Scrape by
89. Condition
90. Gun an engine
91. Virginia's Virginia
93. Actor Paul
96. A degree
97. Mauna ______
98. Russia's Georgia
99. Suffix meaning like or resembling
101. New Testament (abbr.)
102. ______ Brt.
104. Lutetium (sym.)

ANSWERS ON PAGE 77

Groucho Marx made many unforgettable radio appearances, but never succeeded with a regular show of his own until "You Bet Your Life."

Franklin D. Roosevelt began his fireside chats eight days after his inauguration. Never before had the American people been spoken to simply and directly by their president.

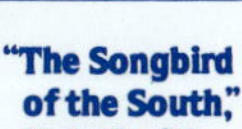

"The Songbird of the South," Kate Smith.

Freeman Gosden and Charles Correll created "Amos 'n Andy" and made it one of the most popular radio comedy shows of all time.

29.

29.-33. Lubalin designed these pages, using ITC typefaces, for an article on American jazz.

34. This calendar shows the passing of the seasons through the growth of a vine on a brick wall in Paris.

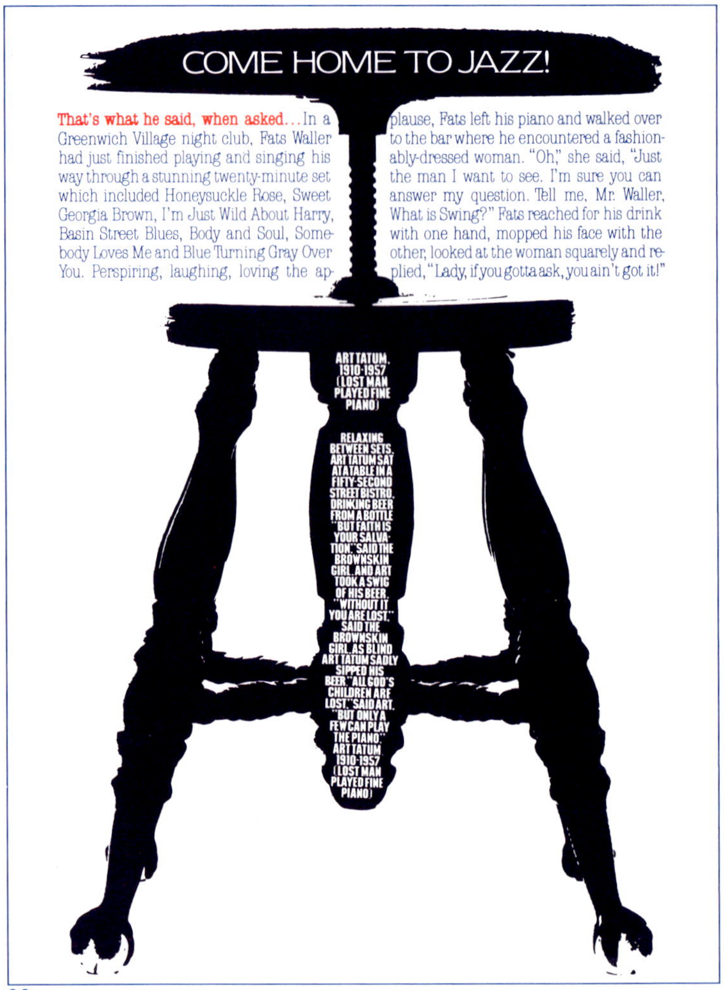

COME HOME TO JAZZ!

That's what he said, when asked... In a Greenwich Village night club, Fats Waller had just finished playing and singing his way through a stunning twenty-minute set which included Honeysuckle Rose, Sweet Georgia Brown, I'm Just Wild About Harry, Basin Street Blues, Body and Soul, Somebody Loves Me and Blue Turning Gray Over You. Perspiring, laughing, loving the applause, Fats left his piano and walked over to the bar where he encountered a fashionably-dressed woman. "Oh," she said, "Just the man I want to see. I'm sure you can answer my question. Tell me, Mr. Waller, What is Swing?" Fats reached for his drink with one hand, mopped his face with the other, looked at the woman squarely and replied, "Lady, if you gotta ask, you ain't got it!"

ART TATUM, 1910-1957 (LOST MAN PLAYED FINE PIANO)

RELAXING BETWEEN SETS, ART TATUM SAT AT A TABLE IN A FIFTY-SECOND STREET BISTRO, DRINKING BEER FROM A BOTTLE. "BUT FAITH IS YOUR SALVATION," SAID THE BROWNSKIN GIRL, AND ART TOOK A SWIG OF HIS BEER. "WITHOUT IT YOU ARE LOST," SAID THE BROWNSKIN GIRL AS BLIND ART TATUM SADLY SIPPED HIS BEER. "ALL GOD'S CHILDREN ARE LOST," SAID ART. "BUT ONLY A FEW CAN PLAY THE PIANO." ART TATUM 1910-1957 (LOST MAN PLAYED FINE PIANO)

30.

He blow; he don't worry... There's this cat he knows. Wingy from way back. But he's a sadistic and a square, not that it matter to Wingy Manone, he got only one arm. He blow; he don't worry. Each year this guy send Wingy Manone his Christmas present in a fancy box: 1 cuff link.

PARABOLIC BORE:

OLD JAZZ NEED NOT BE BEST BUT STILL IT'S TRUE THAT SAXOPHONES WERE FEW AND FAR BETWEEN IN GOOD KING PORTER'S MERRY TIMES. THOSE WHO DO NOT LOVE THE SOUND THAT ISSUES FROM THE BLEND OF BRASS BENT HORN WITH WOODEN REED ARE THREATENED IN THESE PARTS, BUT THEY'RE AROUND!

Trumpet: *I am a busy puppy with a loud voice. If I am tired, I never show it. In fact, I never know it.*

Trombone: I play the solo part in a composition titled "Shaving Mug." I sleep in the musty cellar of an old house. I can sing under water. I am very fond of sunflowers, yams and barreled beer.

Clarinet: *Sober-sing, I'd rather. Will not sweet-talk you one way or t'other. Know more than I tell. Smooth me, I'll be your friend.*

31.

Über die Philosophie der Kunst.

An evening in the year of 1935. Huebner's garden restaurant in the Stadtpark, Vienna.

It's Spring, 2 American young men are seated at a table drinking Kaffee mit Schlag. The band is playing the Saint James Infirmary Blues.

1ST AMER: NOT BAD.
2ND AMER: NOT GOOD, EITHER.
1ST AMER: GIVE THEM A CHANCE; THEY'LL GET IT.
2ND AMER: THE DRUMMER KNOWS THE TRICKS. HE MUST HAVE STUDIED.
1ST AMER: YOU'VE GOT TO STUDY.
2ND AMER: AND YOU'VE GOT TO FORGET YOU STUDIED. JAZZ DRUMMER LIKE BABY DODDS, CHICK WEBB, COZY COLE, HE GIVES YOU THAT MOVE-ALONG FEELING.
1ST AMER: I GUESS THAT'S IT; THAT MOVE-ALONG FEELING.
2ND AMER: THAT'S NOT ALL; YOU'VE GOT TO PASS THE TEST.
1ST AMER: WHAT IS THE TEST?
2ND AMER: THE TEST OF A JAZZ DRUMMER IS: CAN HE MAKE A FAT MAN FALL DOWN A WHOLE FLIGHT OF STAIRS WITHOUT HURTING HIMSELF.

32.

"CHECK YOU AT LINGA LONGA."

We made it over the Jefferson Davis Highway in a Model-T some 200 miles south of Richmond, Virginia in the State of North Carolina, a couple of 18-year-old kids. The back of the open touring car was loaded with ponchos, pup tents, army blankets and cans of Van Camp's pork and beans. I had a pen knife that was an arsenal in the pocket: two cutting blades, a can-opener, a bottle-opener and a corkscrew. I'd never before in my life been south of Philadelphia nor heard of Brunswick stew. The girls walking along Fayetville Street were unbelievable. Corn silk, they made me think of. I could not take my eyes off them. Were these the southern belles I had read about? That night, we saw Norma Talmadge, Conway Tearle and Wallace Beery in "Ashes of Vengeance" at the Superba Theatre, college kids in the audience, hissing the villain. The next day was Saturday and in the afternoon my Carolina cousin Fed (short for Confederate), two of his school friends and the two of us piled into the Ford and went checkin.' Checkin' was riding up and down the wide street bordering the campus as the girls either sat on the lawn or promenaded within limits. On Saturday afternoon, everybody went checkin' mainly to arrange for more checkin' later on. "Check you at Linga Longa," one of the boys called out to a honey blonde. Linga Longa, seemed to be the place. That's what they kept saying: Linga Longa. Saturday night, we put on our white pants and blue blazers and drove through cotton fields and scrub pine to Linga Longa. But the sign said Linger Longer. Southern talk had thrown me. Linger Longer was a kind of lake resort featuring an out-door dance pavilion in a pine grove. The floor was jammed with dancers and boys cutting in, the first I ever saw of that practice. Band was a piano, trumpet, trombone, clarinet, banjo, drums—Negro musicians. "Ja Da," familiar since World War One, was the old-shoe favorite: Ja da, Ja da, jada jada jing, jing, jing…a strain, really, like so many great jazz vehicles. Then "Sister Kate" did her shimmy, "Wang Wang Blues" cut out, followed by "Indiana" and "Everybody Loves My Baby but My Baby Loves Nobody but Me." Six of us on the way home in the Model-T, and checkin' achieved its objective of neckin.' At eighteen, we'd already won the grand prize: full possession of the hour. Did I dream all this?

LASTING LESSONS TAUGHT IN RHYTHM

…OF HEAVEN: SO HIGH, CAN'T GET OVER IT; SO LOW, CAN'T GET UNDER IT; SO WIDE, CAN'T GET AROUND IT; YOU MUST COME IN AT THE DOOR.

…OF EARTH: NOBODY WANTS YOU WHEN YOU'RE DOWN AND OUT!

…OF MAMIE'S SINS AND SORROWS: IF YOU CAN'T GIVE A DOLLAR, GIVE ME A LOUSY DIME. I WANNA FEED THAT HUNGRY MAN OF MINE.

33.

The Four

PHOTOGRAPHED BY DEIDI VON SCHAEWEN

WINTER

SPRING

Jan. Feb. Mar. Apr. May June

S		6	13	20	27	3	10	17	24	2	9	16	23	30
M		7	14	21	28	4	11	18	25	3	10	17	24	31
T	JAN.	8	15	22	29	5	12	19	26	4	11	18	25	
W	2	9	16	23	30	6	13	20	27	5	12	19	26	
T	3	10	17	24	31	7	14	21	28	6	13	20	27	
F	4	11	18	25	FEB.	8	15	22	29	7	14	21	28	
S	5	12	19	26	2	9	16	23	MAR.	8	15	22	29	

S		6	13	20	27	4	11	18	25	JUNE	8	15	22	29
M		7	14	21	28	5	12	19	26	2	9	16	23	30
T	APR.	8	15	22	29	6	13	20	27	3	10	17	24	
W	2	9	16	23	30	7	14	21	28	4	11	18	25	
T	3	10	17	24	MAY	8	15	22	29	5	12	19	26	
F	4	11	18	25	2	9	16	23	30	6	13	20	27	
S	5	12	19	26	3	10	17	24	31	7	14	21	28	

Seasons

SUMMER

FALL

July. Aug. Sept. Oct. Nov. Dec.

	6	13	20	27	3	10	17	24	31	7	14	21	28
	7	14	21	28	4	11	18	25	SEPT.	8	15	22	29
JULY	8	15	22	29	5	12	19	26	2	9	16	23	30
2	9	16	23	30	6	13	20	27	3	10	17	24	
3	10	17	24	31	7	14	21	28	4	11	18	25	
4	11	18	25	AUG.	8	15	22	29	5	12	19	26	
5	12	19	26	2	9	16	23	30	6	13	20	27	

	5	12	19	26	2	9	16	23	30	7	14	21	28
	6	13	20	27	3	10	17	24	DEC.	8	15	22	29
	7	14	21	28	4	11	18	25	2	9	16	23	30
OCT.	8	15	22	29	5	12	19	26	3	10	17	24	31
2	9	16	23	30	6	13	20	27	4	11	18	25	
3	10	17	24	31	7	14	21	28	5	12	19	26	
4	11	18	25	NOV.	8	15	22	29	6	13	20	27	

35. An ad announcing the first issue of U&lc.

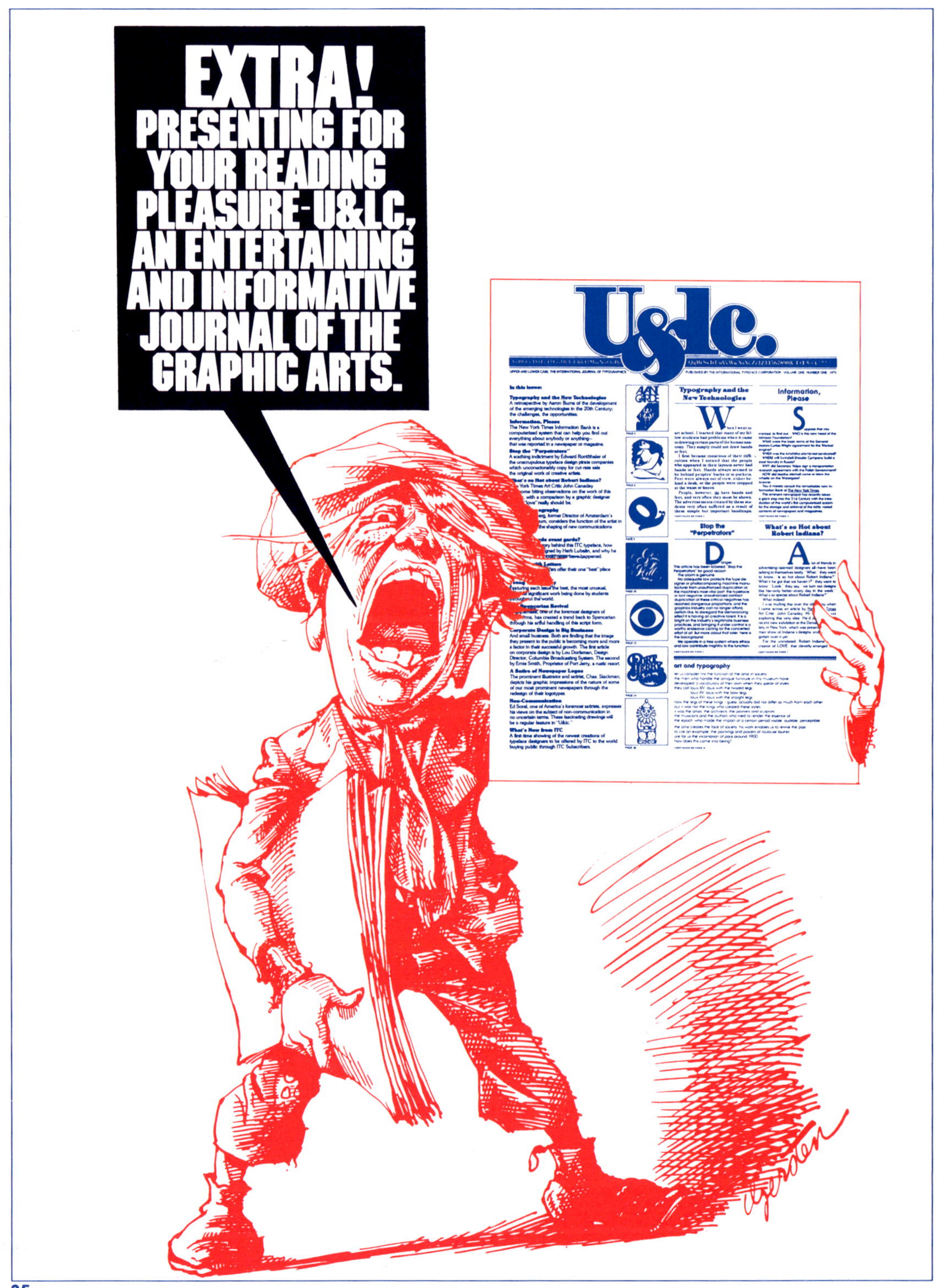

35.

ANNUAL REPORTS

Richton International Corporation Annual Report 1978

Jewelry Group:
CORO, VENDOME, COROCRAFT, VÉRITÉ

Active Sportswear Group:
ASPEN SKIWEAR, RICHTON SPORTSWEAR, GOLDEN BREED, HANG TEN

Accessories Group:
KAPS, CHIC MAID, BOND STREET, CORET, RONAY, LE SAC

R

Lubalin would approach an annual report much as he would an editorial design. He maintained the sophistication of "big corporate graphics," and added a warmer, more human quality.

1. Richton International Corporation, a holding company for several fashion and jewelry businesses.

2.-5. Schlumberger Limited, a French-American company involved in the exploration of gas and oil.

6.-9. Touche-Ross, an accounting and management firm. Their annual report focused on the many professions Touche-Ross represented and how they managed business transactions for such a diverse clientele.

10.-11. Avnet Corporation, electronics.

Schlumberger Annual Report 1973

2.

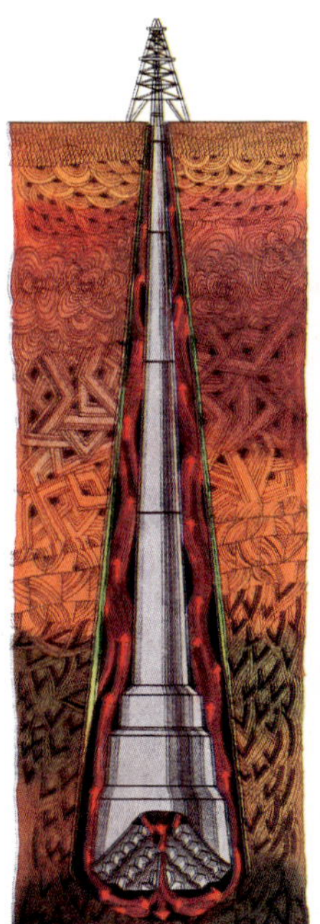

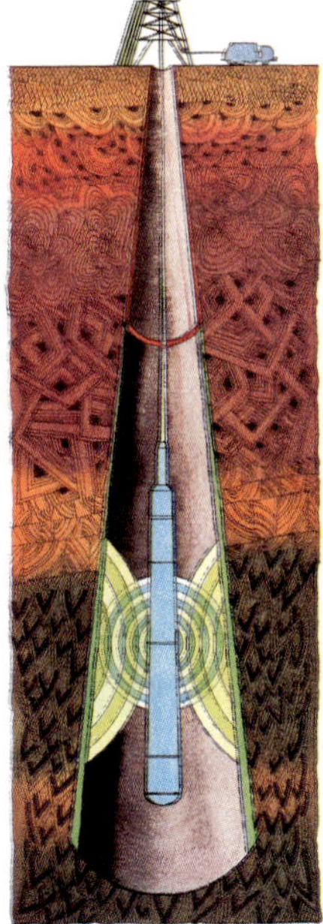

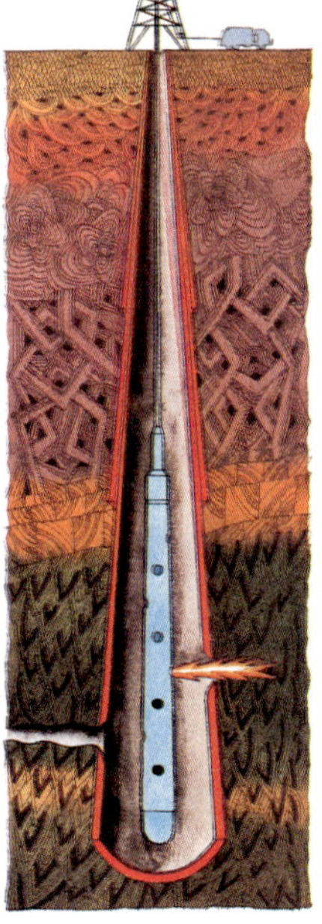

14

Schlumberger Wireline Services

Ever since I joined Schlumberger, quite often friends, stockholders, even relatives, say, "You work for a fine company, but what does Schlumberger really do?" Answering, invariably the words "logging," "wireline services" come up. These few pages explain for our 50,000 stockholders what Schlumberger's original business is and why our logging services are indispensable in the search for oil and gas. —JEAN RIBOUD

Three phases in the search for oil:

Drilling (left)—*The drill bit rotates breaking the formation—drilling mud, forced down the drill pipe and up the well, lubricates the drill bit and carries up cuttings.*

Wireline logging (center)—*A Schlumberger down-hole instrument at the end of a wireline is used to measure physical properties of underground formations, such as electrical resistance, sonic, or nuclear properties.*

Completion (right)—*A Schlumberger perforating gun is lowered to the level of the oil reservoir and explosive charges are fired through the steel casing, permitting oil to flow into the well bore.*

Schlumberger wireline services are provided to the oil industry in more than seventy countries. These services have become as vital to the exploration and production of oil and gas as the x-ray is to the practice of medicine.

It is generally accepted that oil and gas are formed from the residue of plant and animal life and are accumulated in porous rocks such as sandstone and limestone. Some of these geological formations contain reservoirs of petroleum in commercial quantities.

To find these reservoirs, it is first necessary to locate geological areas where oil-bearing formations may be present. Seismic testing (shock waves) gives preliminary indications of structures which may contain oil but there is no reliable way to precisely measure these subsurface structures without drilling.

Even when a well is drilled, very little information is available to the geologist standing at the top of a hole which is several thousand feet deep and only a few inches in diameter. Often there is no evidence at the surface that the drill has penetrated an oil or gas reservoir.

To get this essential information, the drilling is interrupted periodically so that a Schlumberger mobile laboratory can lower various measuring instruments to the bottom of the drill hole on a line of wire-wrapped electrical cable—hence the term "wireline." As each instrument is pulled out of the hole, it measures the depth and physical properties of the various formations it passes. These measurements are transmitted on the wireline to a recorder in the mobile laboratory. The recorder in turn produces a graph, called a "log"; it shows a complete picture of subsurface formations—how deep, how thick, how porous and the oil and gas content. This log is essential to the determination of oil reserves—location and quantity. Also, wireline logging services are indispensable for evaluating the production potential of a well and establishing the location of future wells.

Once oil has been located, a steel

15

3.

tion" devices to measure direction and angle.

Other wireline services include taking samples of formations and downhole fluids—permitting surface measurement of downhole pressures; placing mechanical seals to isolate zones for testing and production; measuring fluid flows; and perforation of well casing with explosives to allow oil or gas to flow.

It is not enough to accumulate data; expert interpretation is required. A quick review of the log at the well site is made by both the customer and the Schlumberger engineer. Often this results in the immediate running of another, more specialized log to pinpoint a promising zone.

Various logs run on the same well must be interpreted in combination. This is often done with the aid of a computer. When speed is essential, while the log is being run, data is imprinted on magnetic tape and sent by telecommunications to a Schlumberger computer center for immediate computer processing and analysis. On occasion, data has been sent between continents by satellite.

Dipmeter sonde—During logging the four arms are opened to press against the well bore. Electrical signals from the arms and other sensors in the body of the sonde are recorded to compute the direction and angle of dip of underground formations. The tool is also used to measure the deviation from vertical of the bore-hole. This information is useful in the location of other wells.

Tools Built for Tough Environments

Oilfield wireline equipment must withstand the shock and vibration of transport by land, sea or air, the salt spray offshore, and temperatures ranging from the hot jungle to the frozen arctic. Downhole tools must withstand the "pressure-cooker" environment of the well, where the operating temperature may be over 500°F and pressure may be as high as 20,000 pounds per square inch. Under these conditions, normal electronic components and insulators fail, plastic materials melt or burn. Also, downhole tools often encounter corrosive conditions which weaken the hardest metals. The wireline itself must withstand corrosion and the stress of both weight and winch tension with minimum stretching, otherwise the depth measurement on the log would be inaccurate.

Schlumberger downhole tools contain the most sophisticated electronic components available. It is the equivalent of squeezing a high-precision oscilloscope into a four-inch pipe, then expecting it to work perfectly while banging it with a hammer and boiling it in acid.

Such equipment cannot be bought off the shelf; Schlumberger must design and manufacture it in-house. In 1974 the company will spend $60 million to produce wireline service equipment.

Most of this equipment is manufactured at two plants—one in Houston, Texas and the other in Clamart, a suburb of Paris. Both plants build downhole tools and surface instruments; both plants have assembly lines for the construction of surface laboratories. Only the truck chassis used for land-based mobile units and power units are bought from outside suppliers; all technical equipment is Schlumberger-designed and built.

Schlumberger wireline cable is manufactured either by a subsidiary in Houston or by outside suppliers to our specifications.

Each laboratory, whether truck-mounted for land use or skid-mounted for use on offshore platforms, is self-contained. It has a motor-generator, electronic control panels for the engineer in charge, winch controls for the operator and a small photographic dark room to develop the film on which log data is recorded.

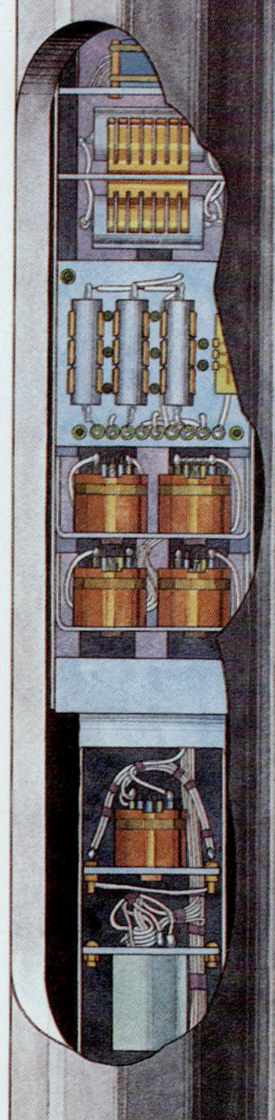

This Year—$20 Million for Research

A continuous research program spanning 50 years has played a fundamental part in Schlumberger leadership in wireline services. In 1974, $20 million will be spent on wireline research alone—this has doubled in five years. Altogether 620 persons, including 250 engineers and scientists take part in wireline research and development. Basic studies at the Schlumberger Doll Research Center in Ridgefield, Connecticut are supplemented and extended by development and engineering in Houston and Clamart. Research and development money is spent for invention of new logging tools, for improving the precision and reliability of existing tools every year, for the creation of new interpretation techniques.

It may be years between a laboratory concept and the introduction of a new tool to customers. Prototype development is followed by extensive testing, both in Schlumberger test wells and in the oilfields. Often, significant changes must be made to meet various environmental conditions. Too, there is extensive feedback from field engineers with valuable suggestions for improvement.

The computer is used more and more in research to improve log interpretation.

Cutaway view shows a portion of the electronic section of a Dual Laterolog down-hole instrument. The thick steel casing is needed to protect circuitry from pressures to 20,000 psi. The electrical circuits must withstand temperatures of 350°F or higher.

18

19

4.

Four typical well-logging instruments (from left to right).

Sonic Instrument—*Measures sound velocity in the formation along the borehole, indicating porosity.*

Compensated Neutron Instrument—*Neutrons radiated from the tool measure hydrogen content of formations and give another porosity reading.*

Compensated Density Instrument—*Gamma-rays radiated from a nuclear source in the tool measure the density of the formation.*

Dual-Laterolog/Micro Spherically Focused Combination Instrument—*Electrical current sent into the formation measures resistivity, a key factor in determining hydrocarbon content.*

Above, are actual examples of logs recorded at identical depth in the same borehole.

In simple terms, we have defined the terminology used and have explained the technology involved in providing wireline services to the oil industry.

There are many other essential features to wireline operations—quality of service, integrity in handling confidential information, the field engineer, the operators, their continuous training, all essential to a highly technical service business—but this is another story for another time.

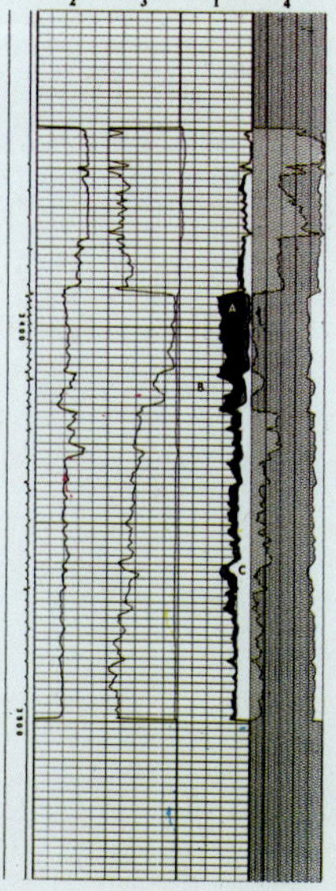

Data from the four logging instruments on the opposite page were merged by computer to produce a Computer Processed Interpretation, 220 feet of computed log as the client would receive it. The figure on the left shows the depth in feet—each division corresponds to two feet.

Section 1 shows the percentage by volume of—rock (B), hydrocarbons (A), and water (C).

Sections 2, 3, and 4 show physical characteristics of the rocks, the amount of water in the formation compared to hydrocarbons, and the porosity and types of rocks.

20

21

5.

"Mankind is then divided into those who are still what they were, and those who have changed: into the men of the present age and the men of the past."

JOHN STUART MILL

TOUCHE ROSS

6.

LETTER FROM THE MANAGING DIRECTOR

As I look at the firm's accomplishments in 1977, I am struck by two different feelings. I am at once delighted by our past success—1977 was the best year yet for Touche Ross—and I am also filled with a sense of anticipation. Everywhere, there is a new spirit, a new commitment to growth and professional excellence, and I believe that we are poised on the threshold of the most challenging and exciting era in the history of our firm.

The highlight of 1977 was our merger with J. K. Lasser & Company, the largest merger ever to take place in the accounting profession. It places us solidly in the middle of the Big Eight accounting firms. Almost as impressive in the long run, however, is our record of steady internal growth in revenues and earnings—1977 was the firm's most profitable year thus far. Worldwide revenues exceeded $350 million. In the United States, net services reached $185 million, an increase of 12 percent over 1976, and domestically net worth stood at $65 million. (These figures do not reflect the Lasser merger.) We achieved strong *real* growth, as well, increasing our chargeable hours by more than 7 percent. We have made changes in our organizational structure, which have resulted in better lines of communication, an expanded emphasis on client service, and an even stronger program of resource development. Our Washington Service Center continues to expand, providing better service to our clients in their dealings with the various Federal agencies. We have admitted 100 new partners worldwide and have brought partners from outside the firm to add significant experience in selected areas of need. Professionally, we continue to take strong leadership. The work of the FAF Structure Committee, in which we participated, will help keep the setting of accounting standards in the private sector. Our first peer review, recently completed by Price Waterhouse, was highly favorable, and our public image has never been better. Internationally, we have continued to make significant progress, bringing over 90 percent of our worldwide volume into the global partnership of Touche Ross International.

Individually, then, each member of the firm can take pride in our accomplishments this year. I believe, however, that this report should provide us with more than merely an opportunity for listing the year's highlights or for congratulating ourselves on a job well done. This year, we are taking the title, *Progress and Perspectives*, more literally than we have in past issues. Certainly our report will outline the progress the firm has made during 1977. But it will also challenge us to pause for a moment, to stand back from the tremendous demands of our professional lives and gain a broader perspective on the place of Touche Ross in both the profession and society.

The actual structure of *Progress and Perspectives* reflects this approach. Immediately following this letter, we will outline the changes that have taken place within the firm during 1977, emphasizing growth, innovation, and our continuing commitment to the highest professional standards. The next section will examine some of the issues facing the profession itself, and will outline our firm's leadership and response. Finally, because the "outside" world has a much greater influence than ever before on our profession, we have asked leaders from other professions and disciplines to comment on the ways in which they are responding to a changing world environment. Indeed, "meeting the challenge of change" can stand as the theme of this year's *Progress and Perspectives*.

It is not a new or even original theme. Three years ago, in the first issue of *Progress and Perspectives*, I opened my letter by noting that "the accounting profession has changed dramatically in recent years." If anything, the change in our professional world has accelerated during the intervening time. Many of the factors responsible in 1975 for these ongoing changes are still with us. The worldwide concern about inflation has not abated. Credit crises are still commonplace. There is widespread concern about capital depletion, and in the Touche Ross Survey on Tax Reform, an opinion study based on interviews with chief executive officers of major U.S. corporations, 49 percent of the sample of *Fortune* 500 CEOs specifically singled out capital formation as one of the most serious problems facing the U.S. economy. The recent fluctuation of the dollar raises the question, still once again, of the volatile nature of currency relationships. Tightening credit, the stock market's performance and a host of other economic developments and pressures are exerting a profound influence on our business climate.

Throughout the world, society has increased its demands on the institutions that serve it. In the U.S. we have witnessed growing governmental interest in how our profession conducts itself. This past year, for example, the Metcalf committee broadly criticized the accounting profession. Both the

7.

MEDICINE

The College of Physicians and Surgeons of Columbia University is one of the oldest medical schools in America. It was founded in 1767 as the medical faculty of King's College—renamed Columbia College after the American Revolution—and it was the first institution in the North American colonies to confer the degree of Doctor of Medicine. Since 1891, the College of Physicians and Surgeons has been an integral part of Columbia University. It is affiliated as well with a number of major teaching hospitals, including the Presbyterian Hospital, Harlem Hospital Center, and St. Luke's Hospital. Dr. Donald F. Tapley, a Canadian-born endocrinologist, became the Dean of the College of Physicians and Surgeons in 1974. During his tenure he has actively supported educational reforms that humanize and improve health care services at the source—in medical school itself.

American medicine has changed tremendously since the First World War, but it seems clear that we are on the verge of even more far-reaching transformations. To take the vantage point of a medical school dean does not qualify one as a soothsayer, but it does offer a close view of trends in medical education, and it is these that signal where medicine is going, and even where society would like it to go.

The transformation that coincided approximately with the First World War resulted, in the United States, in the belief that medicine is a science whose teaching must meet university standards. This view had long gone unchallenged in Europe, and even in such American centers as the Johns Hopkins University. But in most of the United States this was the era of diploma mills, which required of students as their main credential the ability to pay the fee. Abraham Flexner, the great educator who documented the shortcomings of this era and catalyzed the reform that was to follow, found that a person seeking care was more likely to meet a charlatan than a scientifically trained physician.

Flexner's suggestions for improving medical education were concrete: shut down the inferior schools; insist that every remaining school offer a basic science curriculum taught by full-time faculty, followed by clinical training in a hospital; and require that clinical education and research be linked.

The reforms that Flexner instigated set into motion a train of developments which has probably made American medicine second to none. The thirty years since the Second World War, in particular, are probably without parallel in the history of medicine. The activities of the National Institutes of Health, supported by massive federal funding, have made possible a seemingly unending series of triumphs in which one after another of mankind's ancient scourges has fallen by

8.

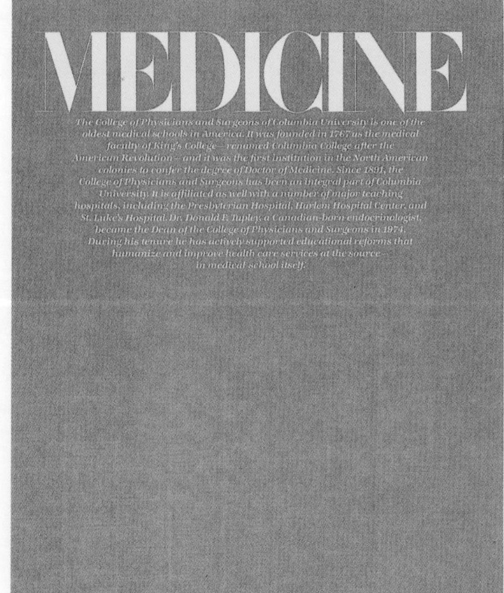

A CHANGING WORLD

In an issue of *Progress and Perspectives* dedicated to looking at change, we have concentrated thus far on changes at Touche Ross and within the accounting profession, mentioning only briefly some of the broader trends in business, government and the professions.

In any human activity, day-to-day pressures tend to create a limited view of the world. Those of us in accounting or in management services may work intimately with many different disciplines and businesses in the course of our careers. We may audit or advise engineering firms, investment houses, or manufacturers. We may see many specific elements with great clarity, sometimes seeing the larger issues only vaguely. We may be painfully aware that medical costs are high, for example, but we may not know about developments in the medical profession or that some medical schools are taking a fresh look at the ways in which they educate the doctors of the future. We certainly know that Congress is under increasing pressure to reform itself; yet we may be confused about the practical steps that can be taken to meet the public demand for greater responsibility. We may know that the legal profession is itself going through a period of self-examination; we may not really be aware of the issues at stake.

This section of *Progress and Perspectives* gives us an opportunity to hear directly from leaders in the professions, government, and business about change in their particular worlds. More importantly, in the essays contributed by these leaders, we will learn how they are responding positively to the challenge of perpetual change.

9.

1979

AVNET ANNUAL REPORT, FISCAL YEAR JUNE 30. A HISTORY OF GROWTH IN THE SEVENTIES.

1978
1977
1976
1975
1974
1973
1972
1971
1970

10.

11.

($ MILLIONS)	1979	78	77	76	75	74	73	72	71	70
SALES	122.8	118.0	131.3	112.5	97.2	106.5	98.8	99.7	85.1	74.8
NET INCOME	2.8	6.6	9.6	8.6	3.8	4.6	6.3	5.7	4.6	3.0

CONSUMER PRODUCTS GROUP

The Consumer Products Group operates in the consumer electronic product industry. It had consisted primarily of three principal operations: Channel Master, B-I-C /Avnet and the music companies Guild and Meisel. In fiscal 1979 two custom manufacturing operations, Avnet International in Taiwan and Tenva in Mexico, overseas OEM offshoots of Channel Master and B-I-C/Avnet, started to become a factor in this Group.

Channel Master, the largest company in the Group, is the nation's leading manufacturer of TV antennas, which it sells through its national franchised distributor network, and TV replacement color tubes which it makes for most of the leading TV set manufacturers. B-I-C /Avnet sells hi-fidelity turntables, cassette decks, speaker systems, indoor FM antennas, and cored solder. Guild and Meisel supply guitars, stringed instruments and accessories. Avnet International manufactures receivers, cassette decks, 8-track and cassette mechanisms, in its Kaohsiung, Taiwan free-zone plant, and Tenva makes record changers in its Nogales, Mexico free-zone plant. Their primary customers are U.S., Japanese, and European based manufacturers and private label companies.

In 1979 Group sales were $122.8 million compared with $118 million in the prior year, with most of the sales increase coming from the two foreign operations and the newly introduced cassette decks. Earnings were down considerably at $2.8 million compared with $6.6 million last year due primarily to Far Eastern competition in the hi-fi business, startup and delivery problems in both its turntable businesses and to the sale by Avnet of Mountain Electronics, its former Southern-based radio parts distribution chain. Although sales are currently good at both OEM facilities they contributed little to profits last year.

Channel Master's outdoor TV and Master antenna business continued to be profitable. It increased its volume of Channel Master brand replacement tubes, picking up market share although its total tube business was off in a declining market. In 1979 it entered two exciting new fields for TV antennas, the supply of antennas and adaptor kits to the subscription TV industry, and the supply of sophisticated antennas and electronics for satellite-to-home TV reception.

For the new season B-I-C has restyled and simplified its automatic turntable line. Its 2-speed cassette tape deck line, which last year made a successful first entry into the U.S. and European markets, has been augmented by the addition of a low-end entry-level model, a high-end electronically operated metal-tape-capable model, and a high-end 2-speed car stereo tape player. It has retained its speaker line and has also introduced a unique new line of speakers called "Sound Span" which has 360° sound dispersion. This enables one to hear full stereo sound from any place in a room. The music companies, Guild, the leader in acoustic guitars, and Meisel, which distributes high quality stringed instruments and accessories, continued to improve their reputations, sales and earnings.

PROMOTION

ИСКУССТВО, ПОРАЖАЮЩЕЕ ГЛАЗ

Помещенные выше изображения глаз взяты из работ Ирвинга Блуменфелда, Уилльяма Голдона, Арта Кейна, Джея Майсела, Ирвинга Пенна, Карла Фишера, Фернанда Фонссагривса, Хиро и фирмы «Американ тайп фаундерс».

Искусство, поражающее глаз, искусство, ласкающее глаз! За последнее время в Соединенных Штатах прикладная графика достигла небывалого расцвета, и её произведения разнообразят и украшают повседневную жизнь. Всех — от типографа до упаковщика консервов — восхищают эти красочные произведения искусства. Передовая роль в развитии прикладной графики принадлежит Гербу Лубалину, известному мастеру художественного оформления. Его талант и новаторские идеи немало способствовали изменению внешнего вида американских журналов. На этих страницах Лубалин наглядно показывает нам, что происходит в области прикладной графики Соединенных Штатов.

2.

3.

4.

5.

6.

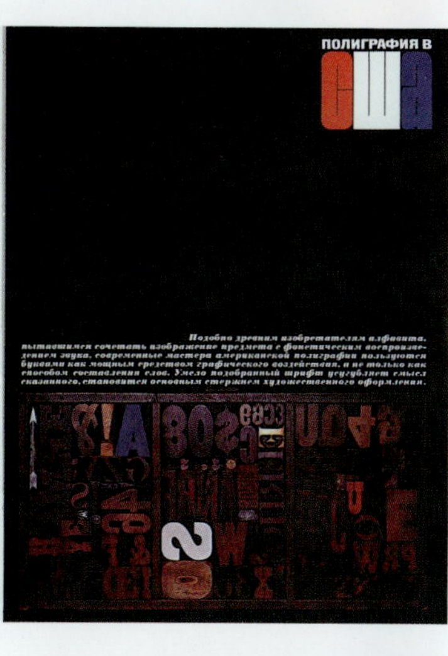

7.

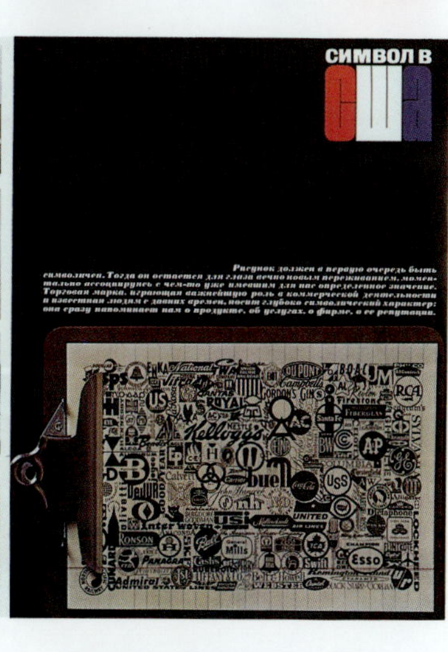

8.

9.

10.

1. Program for the film, "The Sound Of Music."

2.-10. Amerika was a United States propaganda magazine distributed in the USSR by the U.S. Information Agency. Lubalin designed an article on the graphic arts industry, showing work by the finest designers, illustrators and photographers.

11. This loose-leaf volume was designed for the Ministry of Tourism of the Island of Jamaica, and distributed to travel agents. Lubalin commissioned a photographer to take pictures of every hotel and guest cottage on the island.

12. Poster and advertisement for eight plays which were developed into films by The American Film Theatre. Lubalin designed a logo and poster for each play, and commissioned the art.

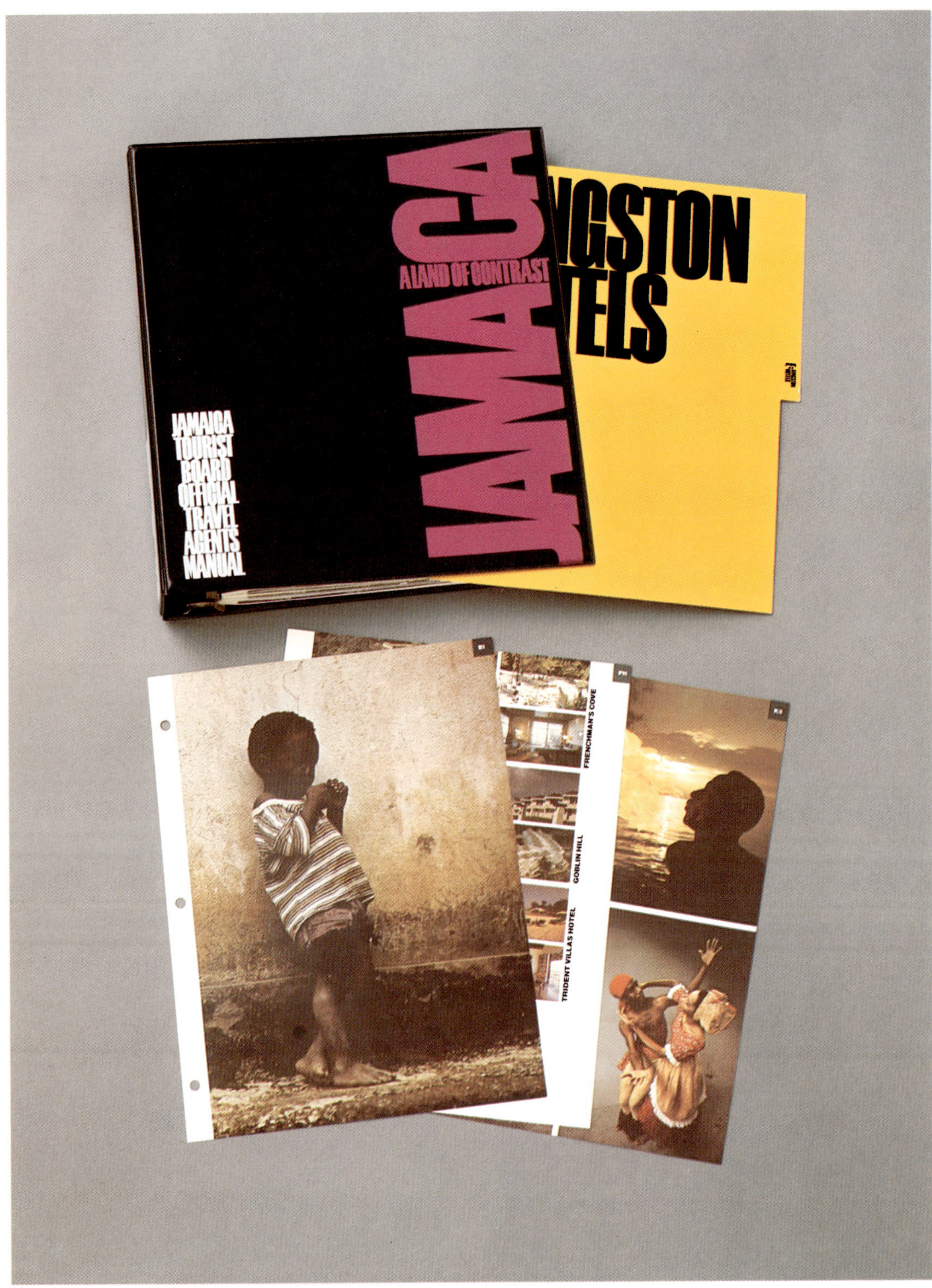

11.

AMERICAN EXPRESS FILMS, INC. AND THE ELY LANDAU ORGANIZATION, INC. PRESENT AFT THE AMERICAN FILM THEATRE

1

KATHARINE HEPBURN
PAUL SCOFIELD
LEE REMICK
KATE REID
JOSEPH COTTEN
BETSY BLAIR
IN
EDWARD ALBEE'S

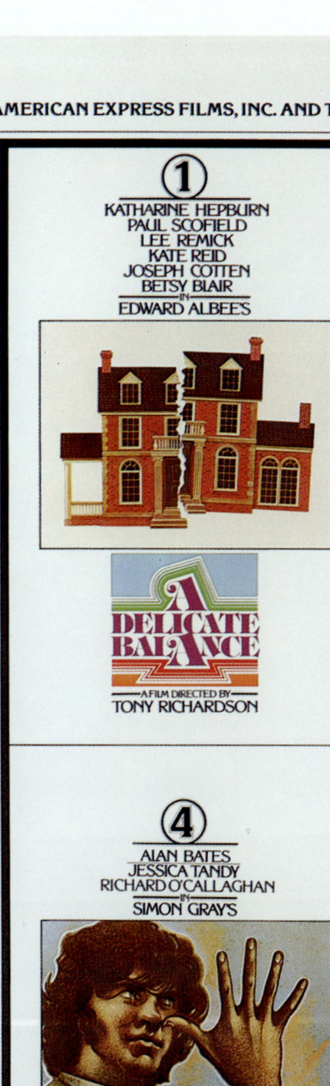

A FILM DIRECTED BY
TONY RICHARDSON

2

ZERO MOSTEL
GENE WILDER
AND KAREN BLACK
IN
EUGENE IONESCO'S

Rhinoceros

A FILM DIRECTED BY
TOM O'HORGAN
SCREENPLAY BY
JULIAN BARRY

3

CYRIL CUSACK
IAN HOLM
MICHAEL JAYSTON
VIVIEN MERCHANT
TERENCE RIGBY
PAUL ROGERS
IN
HAROLD PINTER'S

THE Homecoming

A FILM DIRECTED BY
PETER HALL

4

ALAN BATES
JESSICA TANDY
RICHARD O'CALLAGHAN
IN
SIMON GRAY'S

A FILM DIRECTED BY
HAROLD PINTER

This fall, in some 400 communities across our country, the houselights will dim and the curtain rise on a new era in motion pictures. World famous actors, playwrights and directors have joined in an uncommon enterprise: to bring the great plays of Broadway and London on film to men and women everywhere.

We invite you to take part in

EIGHT ENCHANTED EVENINGS

(OR EIGHT MARVELOUS MATINEES)

A SUBSCRIPTION SERIES OF EIGHT. TWO EVENING AND TWO MATINEE PERFORMANCES EVERY MONTH, OCTOBER THROUGH MAY.

5

STACY KEACH
ROBERT STEPHENS
HUGH GRIFFITH
IN
JOHN OSBORNE'S

A FILM DIRECTED BY
GUY GREEN
SCREENPLAY BY
EDWARD ANHALT

6

THE NATIONAL THEATRE
COMPANY OF ENGLAND
ALAN BATES
LAURENCE OLIVIER
JOAN PLOWRIGHT
IN
ANTON CHEKHOV'S

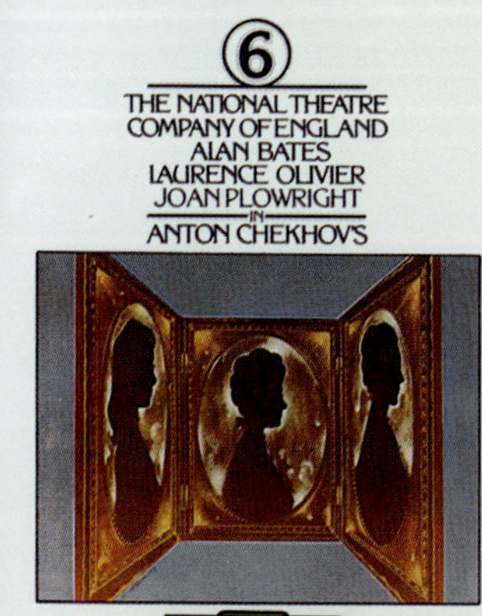

A FILM DIRECTED BY
LAURENCE OLIVIER

7

LEE MARVIN
FREDRIC MARCH
ROBERT RYAN
JEFF BRIDGES
BRADFORD DILLMAN
IN
EUGENE O'NEILL'S

A FILM DIRECTED BY
JOHN FRANKENHEIMER

8

BROCK PETERS
MELBA MOORE
RAYMOND ST. JACQUES
IN
KURT WEILL &
MAXWELL ANDERSON'S

A FILM DIRECTED BY
DANIEL MANN
SCREENPLAY BY
ALFRED HAYES

SUBSCRIPTION TICKET INFORMATION AT THE BOX OFFICE.

12.

VOTE
&
THE CHOICE IS YOURS
DON'T VOTE
& The Choice Is Theirs
Register
OR YOU
HAVE NO
CHOICE

13.

14.

13. Political poster used as a promotion by Drum Lithographers.

14.-16. Program for "The Country Wife" at the newly opened Repertory Theatre of Lincoln Center. A limited budget required it be printed in one color on brown craft paper.

15.

In 1640, the year of the Puritan Revolution, William Wycherley was born in Clive near Shrewsbury into a family of good estate. His first nine years witnessed the Great Civil War, the closing of the theaters and the beheading of Charles I. It was an England, split between Roundhead and Cavalier, in which tenant farmers followed their landlords into either camp. The strife was not due to "the collapse of an outworn society in a chaos of class hatred and greed but (to) a contest for political and religious ideals that divided every rank in a land socially and economically prosperous."*

Passionate piety did not blind Oliver Cromwell to rectitude. "I had rather," he asserted, "have a plain russet-coated captain that knows what he fights for and loves what he knows than what you call 'a gentleman' and is nothing else." However, not unlike other revolutions, once the Puritans were in power, they excluded dissidents from office and influence in the State, and "by making profession of religious zeal a shibboleth, they bred notorious hypocrites."*

The elder Wycherley, a Royalist, disliked the tone of English education and dispatched his son at the age of fifteen to be schooled in France. Young William spent five years in Paris, enjoying the plays of Molière and sampling the society of *Les Précieux* at the court of Louis XIV. With the coming of the Restoration in 1660, Wycherley converted to Catholicism and returned home in July to take up studies at Queen's College, Oxford. In November, he reembraced the Church of England and entered Inner Temple. Twenty-seven years later, he reconverted to Catholicism. "If he was not devout," said his friend, John Dennis, "at least he was not indifferent to religion."

King Charles and his court had returned in triumph to London. Sweeping the Puritans aside, the regime seemed to dedicate itself to youth, pleasure and the "new" philosophy, a skeptical materialism that held man's behavior to be governed not by a divine ideal but by his appetites, intellectual and sexual. Charles II spent his first evening in the City not at the royal palace but at the home of Sir Thomas Morland, a scientist and inventor. That night he slept with his favorite mistress, Barbara Palmer. This mixture of inquiring disbelief and sensuality lay at the base of Restoration comedy.

16.

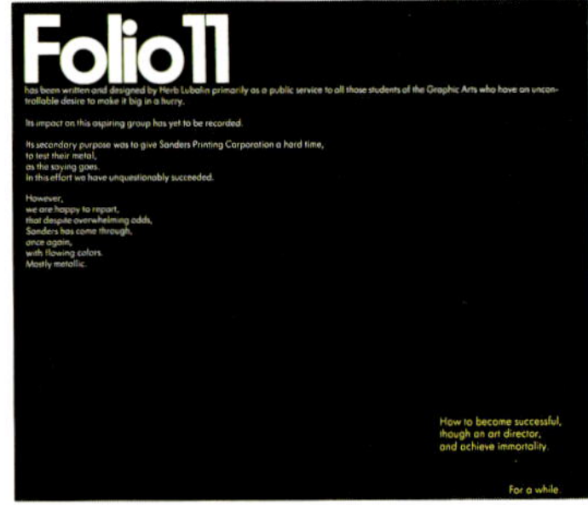

17.

17.-25. Sanders Printing Company promotion. The object of the design was to show the quality of their many printing processes. Lubalin wrote the copy as well.

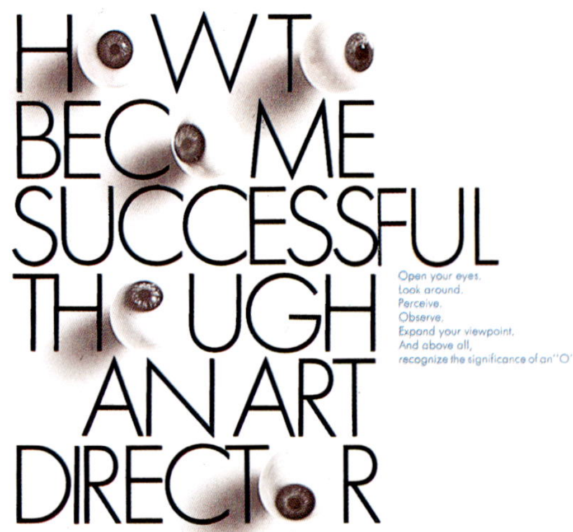

18.

HOW
TO
BECOME
SUCCESSFUL
THOUGH
AN ART DIRECTOR

Rearrange your life to accommodate an "O".
An "O" can be nothing . . . or something.
Or, it can be a bagel.
Or one sex symbol or another.

19.

HOW
TO
BECOME
SUCCESSFUL
THOUGH
AN ART DIRECTOR

An"O"can mean money.
Money talks.
A successful career is often built on a sound foundation of it.
Set your sights on this valuable commodity.

20.

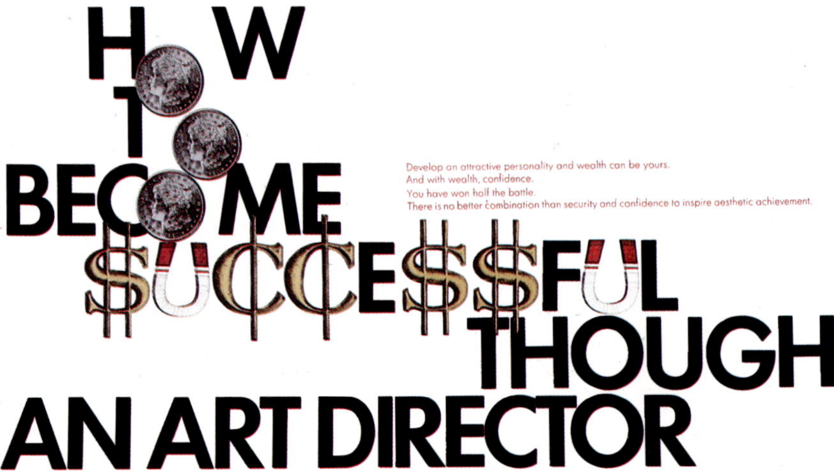

21.

22.

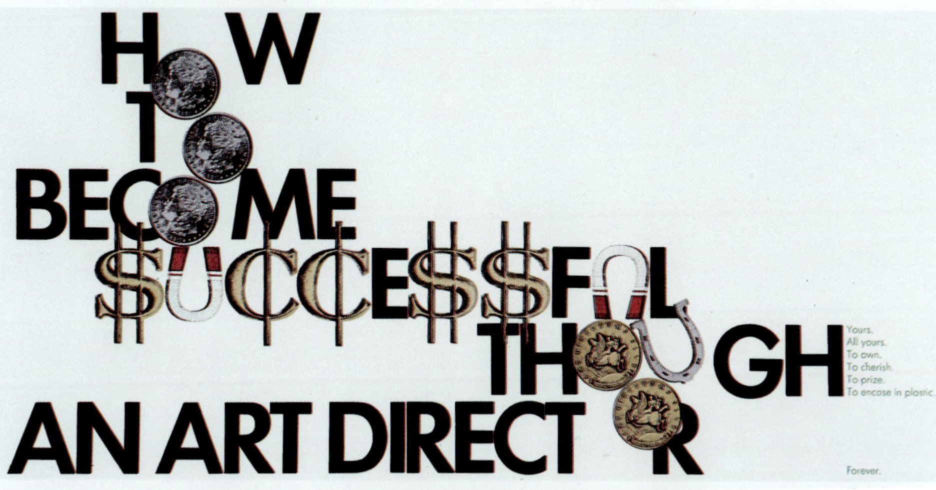

23.

OW TO BECOM
CESSFUL THOU
N ART DIRECTO

And with these kudos—fame.
Headlines,
travel,
speeches,
friends,
worshippers,
idolatry.
You are a hero.

24.

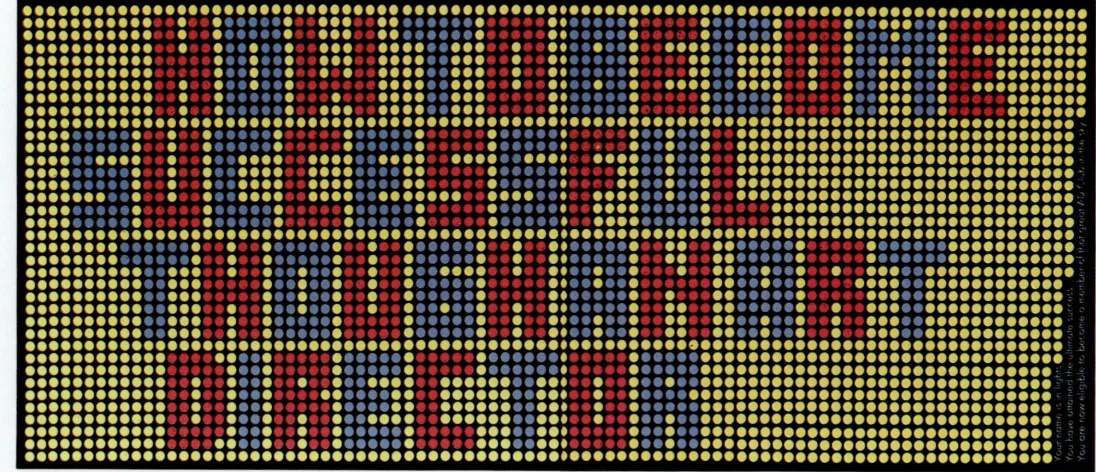

25.

Follow the leader: in reporting the news and in brin

The leadership of the Herald Tribune begins at the beginning — the reporting of the news. Fully. Intelligently. Accurately. But the Trib does more than that. It specializes in the kind of reporting that **makes** news. Creative journalism. Crusading journalism. Early in 1965, a team of Trib reporters and editors launched a series, **New York, City in Crisis,** a study in depth of urban sickness. John V. Lindsay, now Mayor of New York, said, "No one who really cares about the survival of New York can afford to miss reading it." And Franklin Delano Roosevelt Jr. said the series "...takes us to the very roots of the problems of urban government." In a few months, **New York, City in Crisis** won six major journalism awards, appeared in book form, and was a strong factor in the change of city administration.

The Trib leads in the ability to bring the news alive with breadth, scope and meaning. At the Herald Tribune, the meaning of the news is the province of perhaps the most gifted group of columnists ever assembled. The legendary **Walter Lippmann,** of wh U Thant has said, "He has set a standard of exceller in intellectual honesty which is recognized all over the world." **David Lawrence, Joseph Alsop, Roscoe Drummond.** And a pair of young Turks, **Rollie Evan** and **Bob Novak,** who are, as a news magazine recently put it, "the hottest political-reporting team since the Alsop brothers broke up." The local scene crackles with the Irish indignation and insight of **Jimmy Breslin. Red Smith** is that rarest of birds, a literate sports columnist. Anc **Art Buchwald.** As Newsweek said in its June cover story, Buchwald "has becon quite simply, the funniest U.S. newspap columnist published today and one of the nation's sharpest political satirists.'

26.

26. New York Herald Tribune promotion. The fourth figure from the right is Lubalin.

27. Cover design of a booklet for Mercedes-Benz, dealing with the history of the company.

28.-30. Cover and spreads for a Columbia University progress report.

27.

g it alive, on 7th, Park and B'way, Madison and Wall St.,

Eugenia Sheppard leads Seventh Avenue, and **Walter Kerr** leads Broadway. It's as simple as that. Eugenia, says Women's Wear Daily, is "Little Miss Fashion" and her pages in the Herald Tribune prove it. Her sense of style has made her unique in her ability to attract both readers and the trade. (A recent study* showed that 86% of Seventh Avenue top executives read Eugenia in the Trib.) Fashion leadership is a big reason why the Trib had the largest gain in retail advertising in 1965 of any New York newspaper. Leadership on Broadway belongs to the Trib's Walter Kerr. In December Variety wrote, "When it comes to readership and prestige, at least in theatrical circles, the Herald Trib is now generally regarded as the leading paper. That is largely because Walter Kerr, of the Herald Trib, has become the most-quoted, most-respected and most-influential critic."

Leadership in the business community runs from Madison Avenue to Wall Street. More than half of Madison Avenue executives, for example, read the Trib. And why not? No one reports on the world of advertising like **Joe Kaselow.** Time Magazine calls Kaselow "the dean of ad columnists." And it's the same story downtown. Among members of the New York Stock Exchange, a survey shows 63% read the Trib. Last year, Opinion Research did a study of the Trib's audience. It found 54% of the heads of Trib households employed in professional or managerial positions, a higher percentage than either the Wall Street Journal or Business Week. The same study showed that 72% of Trib reader-families have incomes in excess of $10,000. This is a higher percentage than Fortune or the New Yorker or Harper's.

*Market Dynamics, July-Aug. 1965

THE PROGRESS
AND PROMISE
OF COLUMBIA UNIVERSITY
IN THE CITY OF
NEW YORK

28.

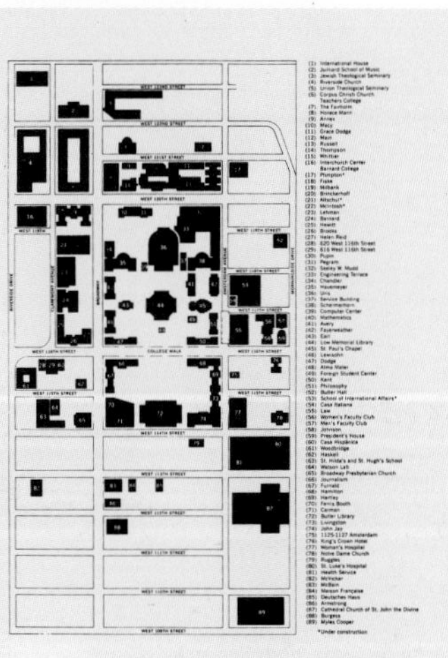

COLUMBIA—
THE GOING CONCERN

29.

Columbia University grew out of Columbia College, which in turn was originally named King's College, and was established during colonial times in a very modest way. As the first institution of its kind in New York, King's College was assigned by its charter "to promote a liberal education" in the British province which extended from the eastern tip of Long Island to the Iroquois hunting grounds in the north. It began to do so in 1754, with eight students and one professor, in a schoolhouse attached to Trinity Church. In 1760 the College acquired its first home, a three-story stone building with a small fenced-in park, near the shore of the Hudson River, at the foot of what became Park Place. There were twenty-four rooms where the president and his assistant tutor had their living quarters, and where the entire student body attended chapel and classes, made their home, and took their meals together. The gates to the grounds were locked soon after sundown. The following "Bill of Fare for Every Day in the Week" was approved and published by the Trustees—

"Sunday, Roast Beef and Pudding; Monday, Leg Mutton, and Roast Veal; Tuesday, Corn'd Beef and Mutton Chops; Wednesday, Pease Porridge and Beef Steaks; Thursday, Corn'd Beef and Mutton Pye; Friday, Leg Mutton and Soop [sic]; Saturday, Fish, fresh & salt, in their Season; Breakfast, Coffee & Tea, & Bread & Butter; Supper, Bread, Butter & Cheese, or Milk, or the Remainder of the Dinner."

King George the Second's ministers hoped the infant College would benefit not only the inhabitants of New York "but all our colonies and territories in America." They also had the public interest in mind, though not as we would define it today, for they expected that more and better education would "prevent the growth of republican principles which prevail already too much in the Colonies." In this King's College soon disappointed them. It produced a crop of American rebels and statesmen, loaned its telescope to General George Washington for use during the battle of Long Island and—as soon as independence was won—obtained from the Legislature of New York a new charter which contained this significant provision—"that the College within the City of New York heretofore called King's College shall be forever hereafter called and known by the name of Columbia College."

Thus the new American word "Columbia," recently coined by patriotic poets, was put to use for the first time in law and history.[7]

7. Brander Matthews et al, *A History of Columbia University 1754-1904* (Macmillan Company, 1904), p. 61.

30

The first home of Columbia, then King's College, was located on lower Broadway adjoining Trinity Church (top).
In 1760 it moved westward to Park Place at the Hudson River (bottom).

31

30.

31. Lubalin designed the cover, and acted as art director on this glossy covered, newsprint booklet project that he assigned to his Cooper Union class. The promotion piece dealt with the school's history as well as current architectural renovations. His class designed the inside pages.

31.

ADVERTISING

1.

get the lead out of your ads

2.

A prolific pencil is no substitute for a unique advertising idea.
Creativity is an art not a technique at SH&L. Call PLaza 1-1250.

In wooing a woman or a customer no single technique has yet been invented that, to our knowledge, is infallible. And yet the advertising business seems to develop periodic passions for a single font of wisdom. Unfortunately, when all products are dressed alike in a single advertising style and their messages addressed alike to all customers, their individual notes of me-me-me become indistinguishable in the chorus of me-toos. We don't believe in this kind of type-casting. To us, the heart of each ad is a simple, vital, selling idea. To convey it, our illustration can be art, photography or type: our sell can be soft or hard, our copy long or short. It takes all types. Call SH&L

3.

let's
talk
type

Some ads must whisper, some must shout. But whatever the tone of voice, creative typography speaks with a distinction that sets your advertising above the clamor of competing messages. If you share our interest in good typography, and the other creative tools that work with it, we would welcome the opportunity to show you how we at Sudler & Hennessey ● ● ●

let
type
talk

4.

5.

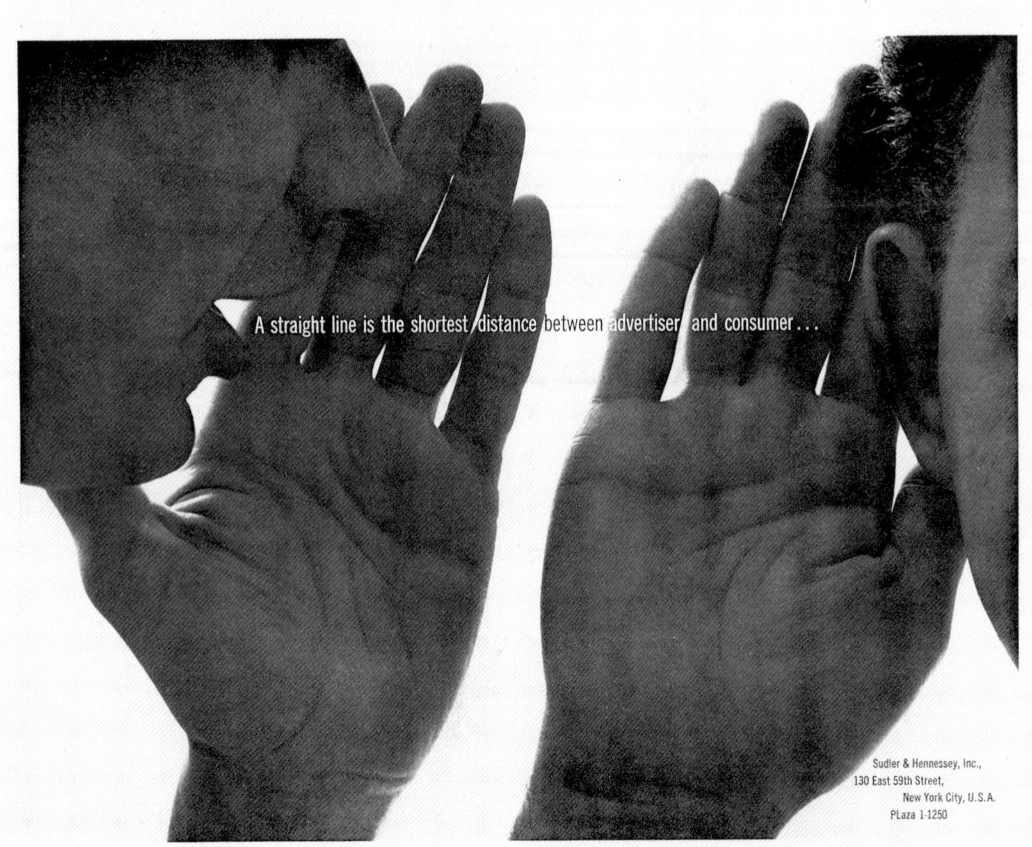

6.

1. An ad announcing the name change of the advertising agency Sudler & Hennessey to Sudler, Hennessey & Lubalin.

2. Trade ad for Sudler, Hennessey & Lubalin. This ad is as close as Herb came to stating his design philosophy: that technique or rendering were no substitute for good ideas.

3.-6. Trade ads for Sudler & Hennessey and Sudler, Hennessey & Lubalin.

7. Full page ad for Land Rover.

GOES ANYWHERE: the world's best 4-wheel drive takes the Land-Rover over any terrain, up and down incredible 45°-plus grades, through brush, swamp and desert. Yet on the highway, it cruises easily and comfortably at touring speeds. **DOES ANYTHING:** hauls, tows, operates portable and stationary machinery from three power take-off points. The Land-Rover has proved indispensable in agriculture, industry and private use around the world, in the armed services of over 23 countries and the police forces of 31. **LAND-ROVER** offers a wide range of body styles in two chassis lengths, plus a choice of gasoline or diesel engines. High and low gear ratios give a total of eight speeds forward and two reverse. Test-drive the Land-Rover to see for yourself why it is called "the world's most versatile vehicle."

7.

in senile agitation...

Her only comfort in life is her dog... Crowds distress her...She grows agitated when her pension check is late.

This anxious patient and others can feel more comfortable on Vistaril... because Vistaril calms smoothly, makes them feel better without the euphoria or psychic overgratification that fosters habituation.

What is Vistaril? Vistaril is hydroxyzine, a tranquilizer entity, totally different from the diazepines, meprobamates and the phenothiazines. While equal to the diazepines and meprobamates in effectiveness, Vistaril has been remarkably free of the unwanted psychic and somatic reactions associated with other tranquilizing agents because its primary effect is exerted at the seat of anxiety.

Vistaril tranquilizes with less complication than do the phenothiazines. Unwanted effects, such as hepatotoxicity, blood dyscrasias, skin pigmentation, and opacities of lens and cornea, are not characteristic of Vistaril activity.

Vistaril tranquilizes with less complication than do the minor tranquilizers. Withdrawal symptoms, possible psychotropic drug incompatibilities, blood dyscrasias and hepatotoxicity, seen with some minor tranquilizers, are not characteristic of Vistaril.

No other tranquilizer is as precise, as uncomplicated, as Vistaril®

(HYDROXYZINE)

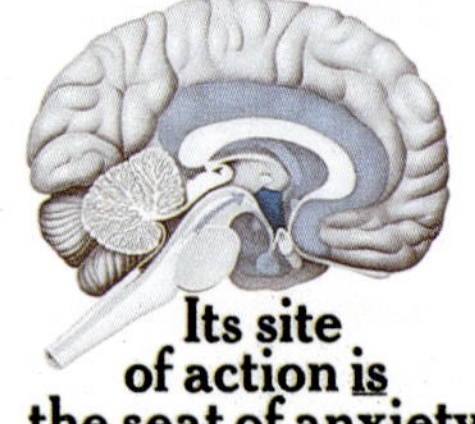

Its site of action is the seat of anxiety

Pfizer Since 1849
Science for the world's well-being®

Turn page for brief summary...

8.

IN PRE- AND POSTOPERATIVE INFECTIONS ...AND IN THE MORE SEVERE BACTERIAL INFECTIONS

Basic bactericidal, broad-spectrum therapy
Instead of tetracycline, chloramphenicol or penicillin/streptomycin, you can use the first parenteral broad-spectrum penicillin —Polycillin-N For Injection. It is indicated in many severe bacterial infections and before or after surgery.

Outstanding clinical record
In a series of 650 evaluated patients, Polycillin-N For Injection elicited cured or improved responses in 89.2%. This included 93.3% of 75 patients with bacterial meningitis and 95.3% of 170 patients with lower respiratory infections. Equally impressive results were achieved in bacteremia, in G.U. and soft-tissue infections.[1]

Action is rapid, thorough
Polycillin-N For Injection controls infection rapidly by producing highly bactericidal serum levels within 5 minutes after I.V. injection or ½–1 hour after I.M. injection, followed by extremely high and actively bactericidal urine levels.

This parenteral agent is thus a first choice in acute pyelonephritis,[2] if kidneys are damaged,[3] and when oral therapy is impractical after surgery.[3] In Gram-negative infections, Polycillin-N obviates resort to massive penicillin G doses.

A better tolerated antibiotic
I.M. or I.V.,[2] Polycillin-N For Injection is well tolerated and devoid of the toxic potential of tetracycline, chloramphenicol or streptomycin. As with any penicillin, the possibility of allergic response must be considered. Also note that Polycillin-N For Injection, like penicillin G, is not effective against resistant staph.

Available: Polycillin-N™ For Injection, vials of 250 and 500 mg.—for both I.M. and I.V. use.

Also: Polycillin® Capsules and Polycillin® for Oral Suspension (ampicillin trihydrate).

References: 1. Data on file, Medical Department, Bristol Laboratories. 2. Ruedy, J.: Canad. M.A.J. *92*:1029 (May 8) 1965. 3. Brumfitt, W.; Percival, A., and Williams, J.D.: Brit. J. Clin. Pract. *18*:503 (Sept.) 1964.

Bristol Therapeutic Summary:
For complete information consult Official Package Circular.

Effectiveness: Clinical experience has shown Polycillin-N For Injection to be effective in the treatment of infections due to susceptible strains of Gram-negative bacteria (including Shigella, *S. typhosa* and other Salmonellae, *E. coli*, *H. influenzae*, and *P. mirabilis*) as well as susceptible Gram-positive organisms such as streptococci, pneumococci, nonpenicillinase-producing staphylococci and most strains of enterococci. Polycillin-N For Injection is particularly indicated in urinary, respiratory and gastrointestinal tract infections.

Side Effects: Infrequently, skin rash, pruritus, urticaria and anaphylactic reactions. Mild SGOT elevations have occurred when I.M. injections have been larger and more frequent than usual and are attributed to a release of GOT at the site of injection. Increased amounts of this enzyme do not necessarily indicate liver involvement.

Precautions: Typical penicillin reactions may occur. Superinfections with mycotic organisms or other pathogens may also occur. Caution should be exercised in administering Polycillin-N For Injection to premature and newborn infants since experience with the drug in such patients is limited. Safety for use in pregnancy has not been established. It is advisable to reserve the parenteral form of this drug for moderately severe and severe infections and for patients who are unable to take the oral form.

Contraindications: A history of serious allergic reaction to penicillin contraindicates the use of this agent. It is also contraindicated in infections caused by penicillinase-producing staphylococci or other penicillinase-producing agents.

Usual Dose: Infections due to Gram-positive organisms and respiratory infections due to streptococci, pneumococci, nonpenicillinase-producing staphylococci and *H. influenzae*. Adults: 250-500 mg. q. 6 h. Infections of the genitourinary or gastrointestinal tract caused by sensitive Gram-positive or Gram-negative bacteria. Adults: 500 mg. q. 6 h.

BRISTOL
BRISTOL LABORATORIES
Division of Bristol-Myers Co.
Syracuse, New York

9.

8.-11. Sudler, Hennessey & Lubalin pharmaceutical ads.

10.

relax bronchioles, reduce histamine-induced congestion and irritation throughout the respiratory tract, liquefy thick, tenacious mucus.
PYRIBENZAMINE EXPECTORANT with Ephedrine
ALSO AVAILABLE: PYRIBENZAMINE EXPECTORANT WITH CODEINE AND EPHEDRINE (EXEMPT NARCOTICS). PYRIBENZAMINE CITRATE (TRIPELENNAMINE CITRATE CIBA)

11.

WHO'S

reaching the right ears in all network radio today? Listen: Cream of Wheat, Liggett & Myers, Mennen, Kitchens of Sara Lee, Chevrolet, William Underwood, Burlington Hosiery, Sylvania Electric, Abbott Laboratories, A. E. Staley, Midas Mufflers, Clairol, Best Foods, Tetley Tea, Kayser-Roth Hosiery, Hartz Mountain, Foster-Milburn, Nestle, Kitchen Art Foods, R.J. Reynolds, J. Nelson Prewitt, Oldsmobile, Pharmaco, General Foods, Eastern Products, Grove Laboratories, Kiwi Polish, Frank Tea & Spice, Gansco Products, Ex-Lax, Cat's Paw Rubber, Standard Brands, Mutual of Omaha, Mentholatum, du Pont, Warner-Lambert, Del Monte Foods, Rexall Drug, Corn Products, Bristol-Myers, Sperti Sun Lamps, Beltone & many others. That's

WHO!

Astute radio advertisers don't count noses. They count *ears:* people who really listen. On CBS Radio, you reach these tuned-in listeners, attracted by the exciting stars and programs, the superlative news. It's this, over and above the top-ranking *size* of audiences, that prompts so many different advertisers to make a larger investment here, minute for minute, than on any other radio network.

THE CBS RADIO NETWORK

9/24/'60/1:15/880/hike!

Tomorrow!..Hear the opening game of "Ivy League Football" brought to you every Saturday afternoon by TIME, The Weekly Newsmagazine. Tomorrow–Brown versus Columbia only on WCBS Radio 880, 1:15 P.M.

13.

12.-15. Series of ads for CBS Radio.

A Big Fish Story

This isn't a fable about a chicken. It's a true story about a fish. Its name is Breast-O'-Chicken tuna.

It all started last spring when sales of Breast-O'-Chicken (and other canned tunas) slumped badly. To turn the tide, the Westgate-California Corporation bought one 10-minute segment a week in "Arthur Godfrey Time." Just one a week...and it was the only national advertising for this product in 1963.

Arthur Godfrey started talking about Breast-O'-Chicken tuna on May 28th. Here's what happened—in the words of Milton F. Fillius, Jr., Executive Vice-President: "I am pleased to report that business is looking very good indeed...August and September showed an 80 to 100% improvement in share of market over the same period in 1962. We have concluded (and reports from the field bear it out) that your efforts on our behalf are responsible for a very substantial amount of our improvement."

And that's not the end of the story. Breast-O'-Chicken tuna and Godfrey will be together all of next year.

If you have a good product that's getting lost in a sea of good products, speak to Arthur Godfrey. Whatever you sell, you'll probably have a Big Fish Story to tell—one that really happened.

THE CBS RADIO NETWORK

14.

He Should Have Been A Mother

When Godfrey says eat, people eat.

"Only 20 weeks after Arthur Godfrey started advertising Morton House canned foods," says Mr. Lonnie V. Merrill, Vice President of Marketing, "our sales volume has increased 56.9%, and much of this increase we attribute to the splendid job that Godfrey is doing."

How does he do it? It's true, Godfrey has a way of describing food that makes your mouth water. But that's not all of it. The secret is that people trust Godfrey like a mother. When he says, "Try it. It's good," they do. And it is good. So sales go up.

If you have a good product, there's no one who can get people to eat it up like Arthur Godfrey. Try him. He's good.

The CBS Radio Network

15.

The American Way of Light. When the English, Dutch, French, Spanish first came to this country, they brought with them their own way of light. Now they're all at home in America. If you can afford an American antique—a Georgian chandelier, or Dutch lantern, or English oil lamp—by all

means buy it. If y
shown above are
cost much less. T

Lightolier dis

16.

16.-18. Lightolier, manufacturers of lighting fixtures.

you still don't have to do without. That's America. The Lightolier fixtures
ons of American antiques—in design, materials and craftsmanship. But they
erica, too. **LIGHTOLIER**® New York, Chicago, Dallas, Los Angeles.
ver America can show you these and other handsome Lightolier fixtures. The listing is on p. 00.

17.

18.

Some of our best friends are bigots.

For years the American bigot has loudly defended his Jim Crow-given right to persecute the Negro. For years the bigot has gotten away with murder. But thanks to a Supreme Court that believes in liberty and justice for all, the bigot is at the end of his rope. Every day he finds it tougher to practice what he preaches. Maybe that's why he's screaming louder than ever.

Or maybe it's because 20,000,000 Negroes earn $30 billion a year, and make up 28% of the central city aggregate population in 78 key cities, and represent huge percentages of the customers in downtown stores and retail outlets all over the country.

Whatever the reason, we consider it pretty white of the bigot to sound off. Because the more he rants, the more he calls attention to the growing affluence and size of the Negro market. And who are we to feel unkindly about a rave review? Ebony gets to the heart of the Negro market.

For example, every month Ebony reaches 43% of the Negro households in the country. 2,500,000 households. Of which 34.1% of the male heads earn more than $10,000 a year. An audience that includes a large percentage of professional people, managers, and business owners. People with a median income of $6,648 a year. Consumers who spend more of their income on food, home furnishings, and personal-care items than white people of comparable income do.

Ebony does more than reach the Negro. It gets to him in a way that no white-oriented mass media could: with reports on Negro Masons, Negro Elks, Negro weddings, with editorials on separate-but-unequal school systems, white-only jobs, and black-only ghettoes. In other words, Ebony gives the Negro what he hungers for: identification and recognition as a person.

That's why advertising in Ebony moves goods and services. Can any businessman be prejudiced against that?

Ebony.
The magazine that gets to the heart of the Negro market.

19.

You don't have to love us. Just give us your business.

Ebony.

20.

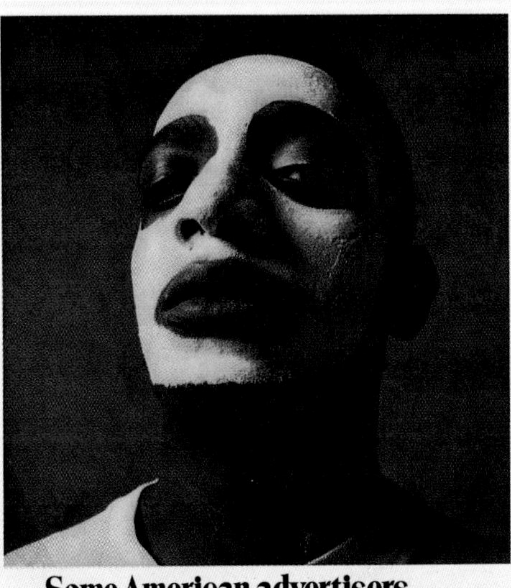

Some American advertisers are color-blind.

Some advertisers see the Negro as a black man in white-face. What a mistake! The Negro doesn't respond to lily-white advertising in mass media. How could he? The Negro thinks black, feels black, and lives black simply because Jim Crow is still the national custom.

If you want to reach the heart of a $30-billion-a-year market, you'll have to recognize that the Negro is nobody's fair-haired boy. You'll have to change the color of your advertising. And you'll have to advertise in a publication of the Negro, by the Negro, and for the Negro.

That's Ebony—a magazine as different from mass media as black is from white.

Ebony.
The magazine that gets to the heart of the Negro market.

21.

We're dreaming of a black Christmas.

Ebony.
The magazine that gets to the heart of the Negro market.

22.

19.-22. Lubalin was involved in writing and designing ads for Ebony magazine.

23.-24. Grumbacher, manufacturer of artists' paint brushes.

25. Bohn Duplicator Company, distributors of calculators. Lubalin placed this small ad where it would most likely be seen by the people who buy calculators—horizontally at the bottom of the New York World Telegram and Sun stock market report page.

WE GO TO GREATER LENGTHS TO MAKE GREATER BRUSHES.

How a hidden, extra quarter of an inch means better brush performance for you.

What makes a superior artist's brush is not always evident on the surface. Two brushes which appear to have the same length of hair on the outside may vary markedly on the inside.

The thousand dollar difference.

In our top-of-the line size ten red sable brushes, for example, we could easily use a 1¾ inch hair without changing outward appearance. But we choose to use 2-inch hair. At a difference in cost of over $1,000 a pound.

And we put this costly extra quarter of an inch inside the ferrule where you'll never see it.

Why? Because this places the widest part of each hair directly at the edge of the ferrule, enabling a brush of greater strength and resilience.

Hair from where?

But it isn't just length of hair that matters. It's also what kind of animal it came from and where the animal lived.

Red sable can mean different things depending upon who made the brush. Some brands use mink. Nice for a fur coat, but poor for an artist's brush. So poor that we won't use it.

Goodbye mink, hello kolinsky.

When you buy a Grumbacher red sable brush, its silky hair comes either from the northern marten or, in the case of our top-of-the-line brushes, from the North Asian Male Kolinsky.

Both these cold-weather animals produce an outstanding grade of hair. And the male kolinsky produces the finest sable in the world.

We're equally fussy about other types of brush hair. And we search the world for the best.

We use ox hair from oxen raised high in the Alps. We buy bristle that comes from Chinese wild boar. There are cheaper varieties, but they don't give the same properties in the brush.

Pride in every part.

Grumbacher brushes are handmade. We craft each part with the same care we give to hair.

Our ferrules are seamless to maintain a snug fit. We formulate special setting compounds to suit each type of hair. Our handles are shaped from birch for better balance, sealed and double-lacquered for longer life.

We even cement our handles inside the ferrule. And we're the only one who does.

Backing what we sell.

There are no time-and-motion studies. No automated assembly lines. The job is done with human hands and human eyes and 12 quality inspections. And when we're through, we're proud to stand by our product in writing.

Look for the Grumbacher warranty at your store. Choose the brush that gives you more.

Free booklet shows how brushes are made. A fascinating behind-the scene look at what goes into an artist's brush. Also tips on brush care.

Grumbacher Brush Booklet
460 W. 34th St.
New York, N.Y. 10001

Please send me your free booklet on brushes.

NAME

STREET

CITY STATE ZIP

Grumbacher *See what our art can do for yours.*

DESIGNED BY HERB LUBALIN
PHOTOGRAPHY BY PHIL MARCO

23.

In an era of faceless automation, every Grumbacher artist's brush is still made the way we did it in 1910—entirely by hand. Eleven pairs of hands, to be exact. That's how many craftsmen apply their talents to every brush. There are cheaper ways. There are easier ways. But there's no better way. At Grumbacher we never forget that the quality of our art is reflected in your art.

All artists' brushes are pretty much alike, aren't they? A brush is a brush, isn't it?

Believe that and you're headed for trouble.

There are many ways to skimp in the making of a brush. Ways that don't become evident until you're right in the middle of painting and a hair frays or falls out, or the brush fails to hold taper, or it grows "lazy" and loses resiliency.

That's why, at Grumbacher, we refuse to take shortcuts.

Every hair and every bristle of every Grumbacher brush is shampooed, vibrated, combed and shaped like the golden strands of a movie star.

The job is done with human hands and eyes and a damn-the-cost perfectionism that some believe died with Queen Victoria.

Ask Madame Labbe.

Master brushmaker Jeanette Labbe, for instance, has been inserting Grumbacher hairs into Grumbacher ferrules for 29 years.

Red sable is her speciality. Show Madame Labbe a tuft of red sable and she can tell you what kind of animal it came from, whether it was male or female, and from a frigid or moderate climate.

Why does it matter? Because there's a vast difference in how it will perform for you.

Mink, for example, makes a nice fur coat but a poor sable brush. Grumbacher won't use it.

On the other hand, the North Asian kolinsky, which roams the frigid steppes of Manchuria, produces the finest red sable in the world. And the very best kolinsky hair comes from the tail of a male.

This is the hair Madame Labbe uses exclusively in Grumbacher's top-of-the line red sable brushes.

Buried riches.

Madame Labbe knows we pay six times as much for a 2½ inch sable hair as for one that is half as long. Yet she buries over half of it inside the ferrule where no one will ever see it. Why?

This is the only way to make certain that the thickest, strongest part of the hair emerges precisely at the edge of the ferrule, so you get the maximum number of flexures a brush can give, the most snap, the best recovery.

Making quality stick.

At every stage we exert similar care. Cementing, for example, is crucial. We learned long ago that the major cause of hair loss is poor or improperly applied cement in the ferrule.

So we spent years developing setting compounds to suit the special characteristics of each type of hair. We use one formula for sable, another for bristle, another for ox hair and still another for camel hair. And we designed special equipment to apply and measure the compound so there's never too much or too little in the ferrule.

The seamless story.

Like stockings, the best ferrules are seamless. And for the same reason.

Seams tend to pull apart with use. Paint and thinner can work their way up inside the ferrule and play havoc. The handle may begin to wobble.

That's why Grumbacher artist's brushes have seamless ferrules. It costs us a few cents more. It costs you a few cents more. But if you've ever cursed out a wobbly brush, you know it's worth it.

Getting a better handle.

Even our handles are special. We shape them from selected New England birch to achieve the best balance in your hand. We seal the pores to prevent cracking and double-lacquer them for long life. And we're the only ones who also cement the handle in the ferrule so it won't loosen.

12 inspections.

As each Grumbacher brush travels from careful hand to careful hand, each craftsman makes his own inspection and may throw it out for the most trivial flaw. Then, after all eleven unofficial inspectors have inspected, our official inspector examines—aided by a ten-power magnifier.

These are just a few of the many reasons why a Grumbacher brush performs so well for you.

It all costs a little more. But it's what makes Grumbacher worth asking for.

Grumbacher *See what our art can do for yours.*

DESIGNED BY HERB LUBALIN
PHOTOGRAPHY BY PHIL MARCO

24.

American Stock Exchange

Latest Stock Prices

B—C

D to H

I to N

O to R

S to Z

Latest Bond Prices

FOREIGN

CITY OF NEW YORK

MISCELLANEOUS

B—C

D to O

P to Z

AMERICAN STOCK EXCHANGE BONDS

References.

Bond Table References

(u) Paid in 1960 plus stock. (v) Paid in 1960, no dividends in 1961 to date. (w) Paid in 1960, no dividend voted at last meeting. (x) Ex-dividend. (z) Paid in 1961, no dividend voted at last meeting. (†) Unit of trading less than 100 shares, sales reported in full. (†) Ex-rights. (spl) Special offering. (w-dist) With distribution. (ex-dist) Without distribution. (W.D.) When distributed. (w.i.) When issued. (N.D.) Next day delivery. (st) or (sta) Stamped. (rts) Rights. (war) Warrants. (‡) Voted for payment in 1961 in other than cash. (§) Ex-warrants. On stock dividends of 25 percent or less, high and low ranges for old stock are retained.

(w-c) With coupons. (ww) With Warrants. (x) Ex-interest. (x-c) Without coupons. (x-w) Without warrants.

'Big Board' Trend by Issues

	Total Traded.	Advances	Declines	Unchanged.	Shares Traded.
Mar. 13	1309	602	502	205	5,080,000
Mar. 10	1314	554	532	228	5,950,000
Mar. 9	1298	634	444	220	6,010,000
Mar. 8	1294	548	545	201	5,901,000
Mar. 7	1316	377	729	210	5,540,000
Mar. 6	1307	518	559	230	5,620,000
Mar. 3	1296	552	500	244	5,530,000
Mar. 2	1278	667	405	206	5,300,000
Mar. 1	1283	486	576	221	4,970,000
Feb. 28	1304	543	563	198	5,830,000
Feb. 27	1301	719	399	183	5,470,000
Feb. 24	1284	629	441	214	5,330,000
Feb. 23	1295	648	421	226	5,620,000
Feb. 21	1299	601	480	218	5,070,000
Feb. 20	1286	661	427	198	4,680,000
Feb. 17	1275	562	497	216	4,640,000
Feb. 16	1277	652	428	197	5,070,000
Feb. 15	1291	756	330	205	5,200,000
Feb. 14	1286	718	348	220	4,490,000
Feb. 13	1288	433	602	253	3,560,000
Feb. 10	1291	356	730	205	4,840,000
Feb. 9	1298	552	542	204	5,590,000
Feb. 8	1282	819	253	210	4,940,000
Feb. 7	1295	551	488	256	4,020,000
Feb. 6	1285	442	612	231	3,890,000
Feb. 3	1283	458	563	262	5,210,000
Feb. 2	1287	733	344	210	4,900,000
Feb. 1	1289	643	420	226	4,380,000
Jan. 31	1303	492	559	252	4,690,000
Jan. 30	1301	734	357	210	5,190,000
Jan. 27	1274	727	343	204	4,510,000
Jan. 26	1257	455	567	235	4,110,000
Jan. 25	1272	489	537	246	4,470,000
Jan. 24	1294	490	556	248	4,280,000
Jan. 23	1280	648	419	213	4,450,000
Jan. 20	1210	642	349	219	3,250,000
Jan. 19	1279	597	478	204	4,740,000
Jan. 18	1264	759	283	222	4,390,000

Stock Averages

	Dow, Jones 30 Ind.	Dow, Jones 20 R'ls.	Dow, Jones 15 Util.	Standard & Poor's 425 Ind.	Standard & Poor's 25 R'ls.	Standard & Poor's 50 Util.
Mar. 13	664.44	142.67	108.64	67.39	32.34	56.51
Mar. 10	663.56	143.00	108.38	67.17	32.47	56.45
Mar. 9	663.33	142.69	107.98	67.22	32.34	56.29
Mar. 8	666.15	142.24	108.26	67.21	32.05	56.02
Mar. 7	667.14	143.62	107.98	67.21	32.40	56.06
Mar. 6	674.46	144.77	108.70	67.87	32.67	56.39
Mar. 3	671.57	144.84	108.74	67.72	32.66	56.61
Mar. 2	669.39	145.65	108.42	67.58	32.77	56.60
Mar. 1	663.03	145.25	108.33	67.09	32.73	56.51
Feb. 28	662.08	146.01	108.49	67.08	32.96	56.61
Feb. 27	660.44	145.82	108.48	66.90	32.92	56.58
Feb. 24	655.60	145.49	107.89	66.38	32.82	56.37
Feb. 23	654.42	144.91	107.79	66.12	32.53	56.14
Feb. 21	652.40	143.86	107.53	65.90	32.47	55.85
Feb. 20	653.65	144.05	107.67	65.87	32.59	55.65
Feb. 17	651.67	144.32	107.56	65.63	32.56	55.49
Feb. 16	651.79	144.29	107.37	65.86	32.52	55.56
Feb. 15	648.89	143.31	107.44	65.45	32.26	55.30
Feb. 14	642.91	140.45	101.18	64.86	31.58	55.33
Feb. 13	637.04	139.68	107.29	65.54	31.41	55.30
Feb. 10	639.67	140.64	107.72	64.93	31.56	55.58
Feb. 9	645.12	141.76	107.94	65.54	31.80	55.66
Feb. 8	648.85	142.41	107.72	65.79	31.93	55.49
Feb. 7	643.94	141.66	107.56	65.19	31.58	55.14
Feb. 6	645.65	142.09	107.75	65.31	31.66	55.12
Feb. 3	652.97	143.10	107.79	65.81	32.02	55.46
Feb. 2	653.62	142.91	107.9-	65.89	32.07	55.49
Feb. 1	649.39	142.45	107.19	65.47	31.91	55.15
Jan. 31	648.20	141.71	106.50	65.38	31.77	54.81
Jan. 30	650.64	141.40	105.97	65.61	31.73	54.87
Jan. 27	643.59	140.54	105.14	64.86	31.58	53.97

25.

PACKAGING

1.

2.

Lubalin felt each package should look like an ad, and motivate the consumer to reach for it on the store shelf.

1. Cacharel of Paris. From a line of skin care products for men and women.

2. Mennen Company deodorant Vitamin E is the prime component.

3. Topps Chewing Gum. Lubalin tagged this new product, a softer, smoother bubble gum. The client liked the name Smooth and Juicy, but felt the design didn't strongly indicate the quality of smoothness.

4. The redesign of the package incorporated the O's to exaggerate the word "smooth."

SMOOTH
N'JUICY
BUBBLE
GUM BY
BAZOOKA
3.

Smoooth
N'Juicy
BUBBLE GUM
BY BAZOOKA
4.

5.

6.

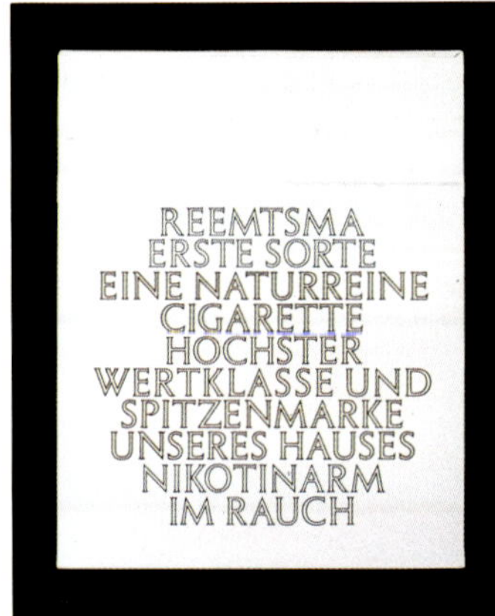

7.

8.

9.

5. Final design for a German cigarette package. Reemtsma Tobacco Company.

6.-9. Front and back of additional Reemtsma designs rejected by the client.

10.-11. Two early designs for the Eve cigarette package. The client loved the package, but the German division of the company astounded the designer when it insisted on a leafy cover-up for a naked Eve. Before distribution in Germany, a release had to be signed attesting that the model was over 25 years of age.

12. Liggett & Myers Incorporated. Final Eve package for a world-wide female cigarette market.

10.

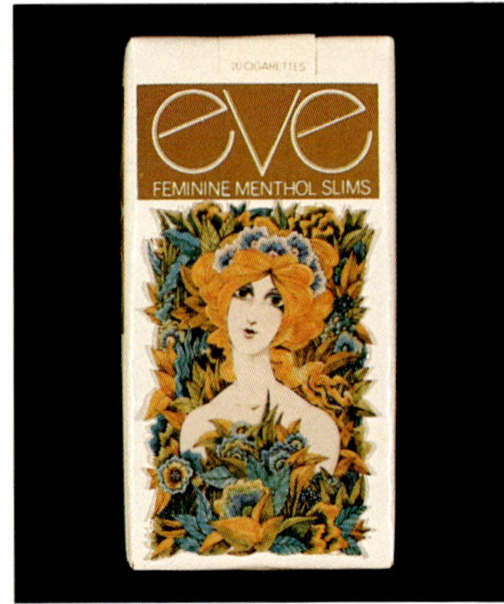

11.

12.

13. Rainier Brewing Company. Spur, a malt liquor.

14. The American Beverage Corporation wanted to keep the roots of its generically New York soft drink, and to redesign the line of 14 flavors for national sales in supermarkets. Lubalin worked on this while New York City was threatened with bankruptcy. So, he took the opportunity to plug the city he loved, and used old engravings of historical New York events.

13.

14.

DR. BROWN'S
NATURAL FLAVOR
CEL-RAY
THE ORIGINAL CELERY TONIC
DR. BROWN'S
NATURAL FLAVOR
BLACK CHERRY SODA
DR. BROWN'S
ORIGINAL
CREAM SODA
SINCE 1869
DR. BROWN'S
NATURAL FLAVOR
BLACK CHERRY
SODA WITH OTHER NATURAL
SINCE 1869
DR. BROWN'S
THE ORIGINAL
CREAM SODA
FLAVOR FAVORITE FOR GENERATIONS
28 FL. OZ.
(1 PT. 12 FL. OZ.)
827 ML.

15. Gaines Dog Food. Prototype for a new package for the oldest product of its kind produced in America. It was rejected by the client.

15.

BOOK JACKETS

1.

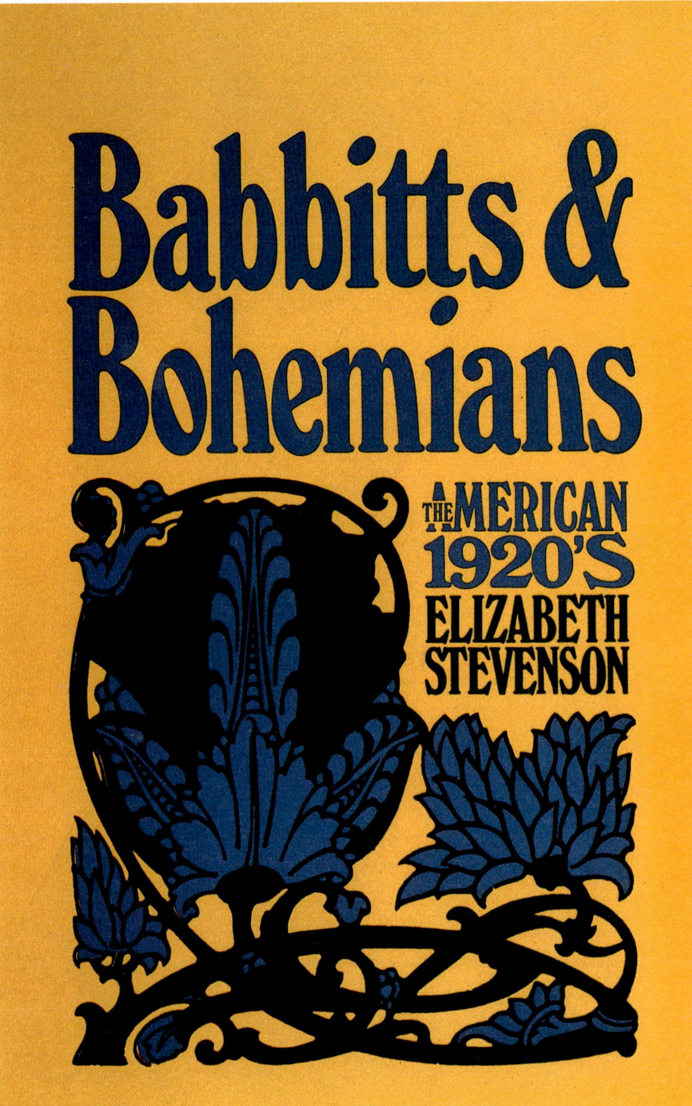

2.

1. Avon Books
2. MacMillan
3. Harcourt Brace Jovanovich
4. McGraw-Hill
5. Holt Rinehart Winston
6. Holt Rinehart Winston
7. E.P. Dutton
8. McGraw-Hill

3.

4.

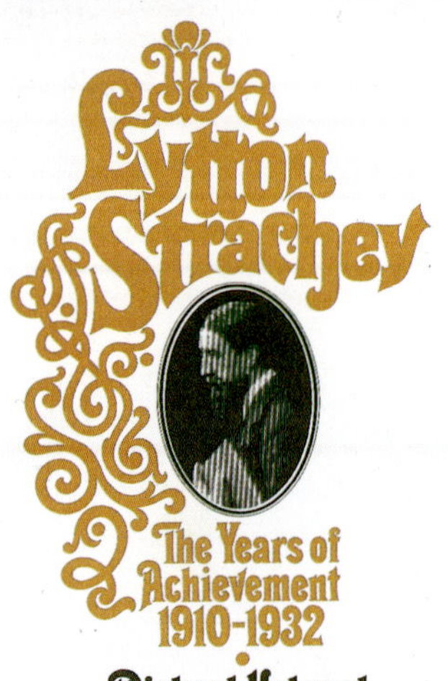

5.

6.

EDMUND
WHITE
STATES
OF
DESIRE
TRAVELS IN GAY AMERICA

7.

HAROLD
TAYLOR
STUDENTS
WITHOUT
TEACHERS
THE CRISIS
IN THE UNIVERSITY

8.

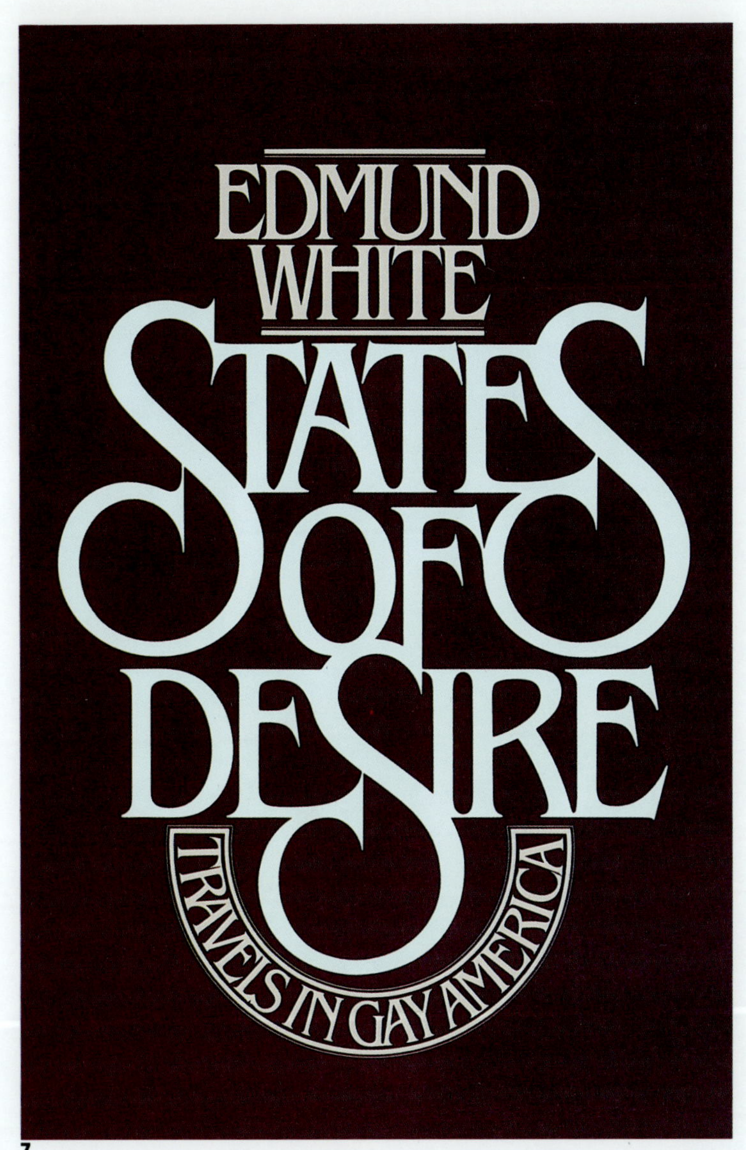

A Detective's Story. George Hatherill of Scotland Yard

DIEU ET MON DROIT

9.

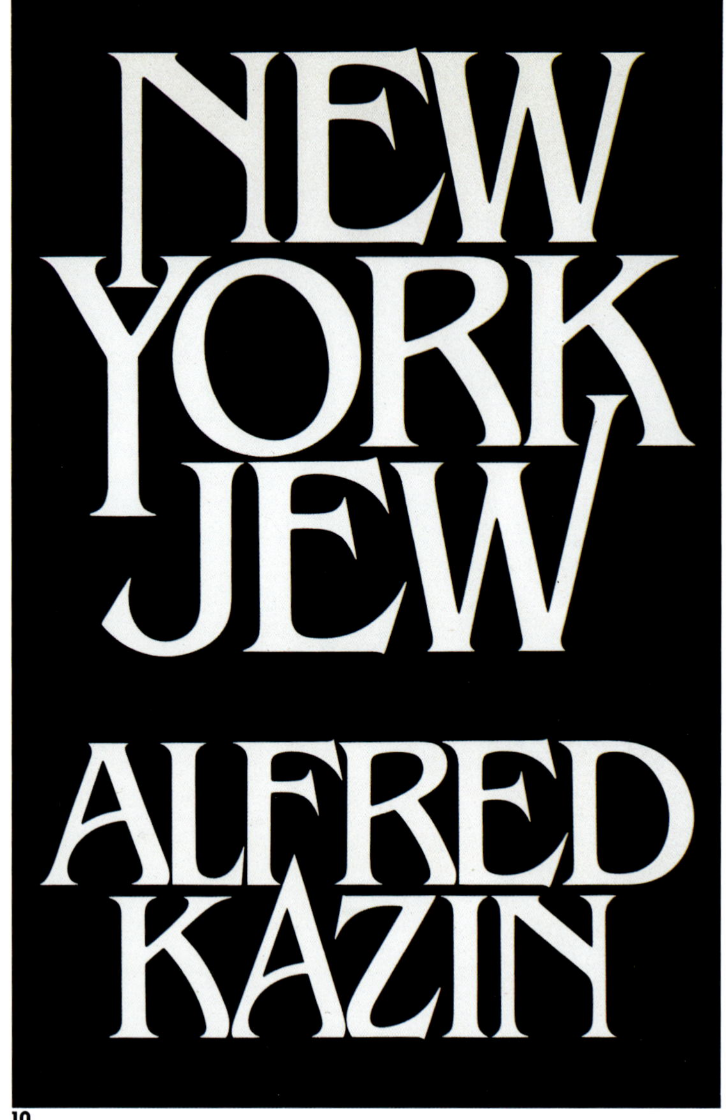

10.

9. McGraw-Hill

10. Alfred A. Knopf

11. Harbrace Paperbound Library

12. Harcourt Brace Jovanovich

13. McGraw-Hill

14. Saturday Press Review

15. Harcourt Brace Jovanovich

11.

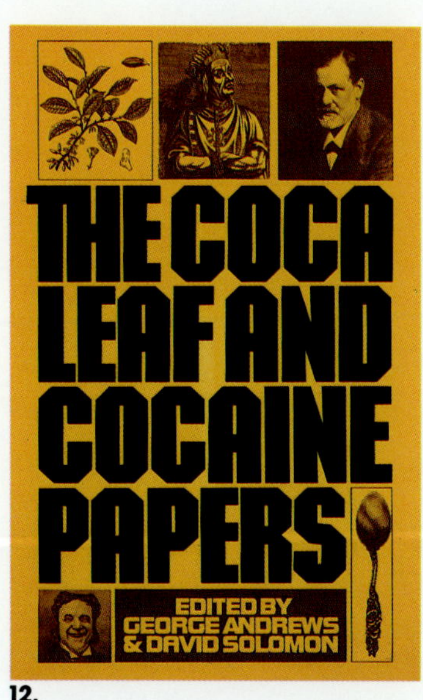

12.

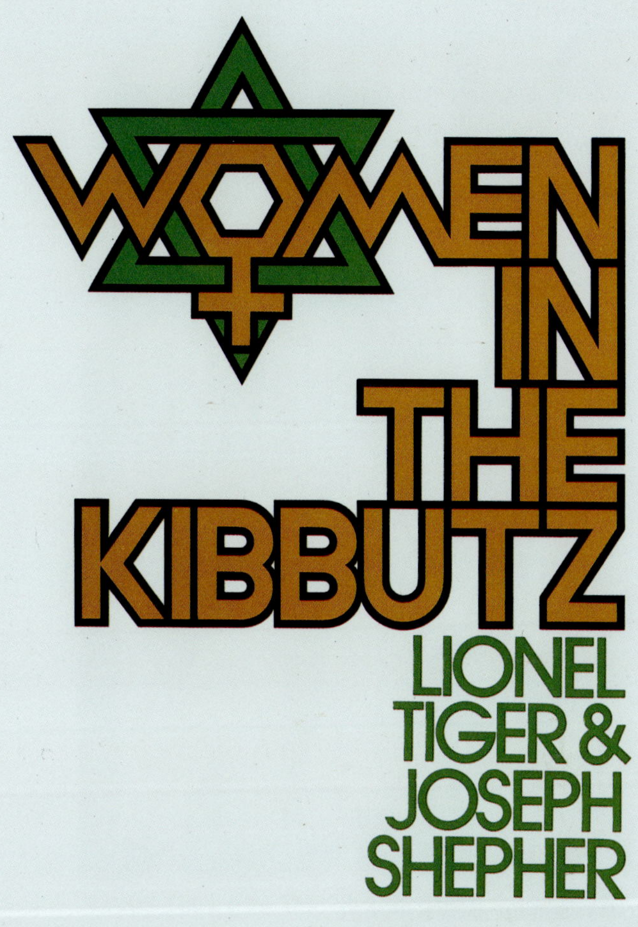

15.

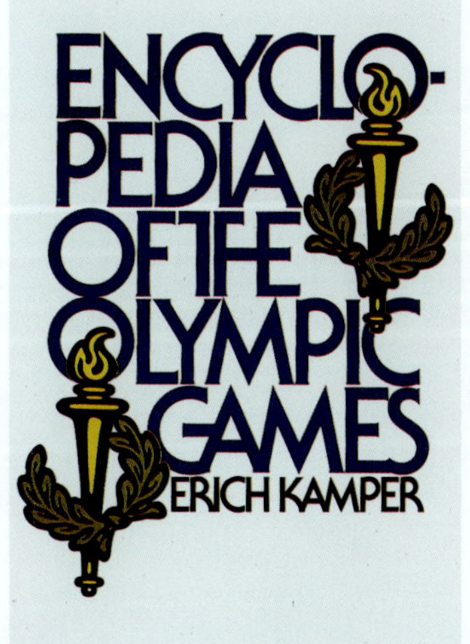

13.

YES,
MARRIED
A SAGA OF
LOVE AND
COMPLAINT
JUDITH
VIORST

14.

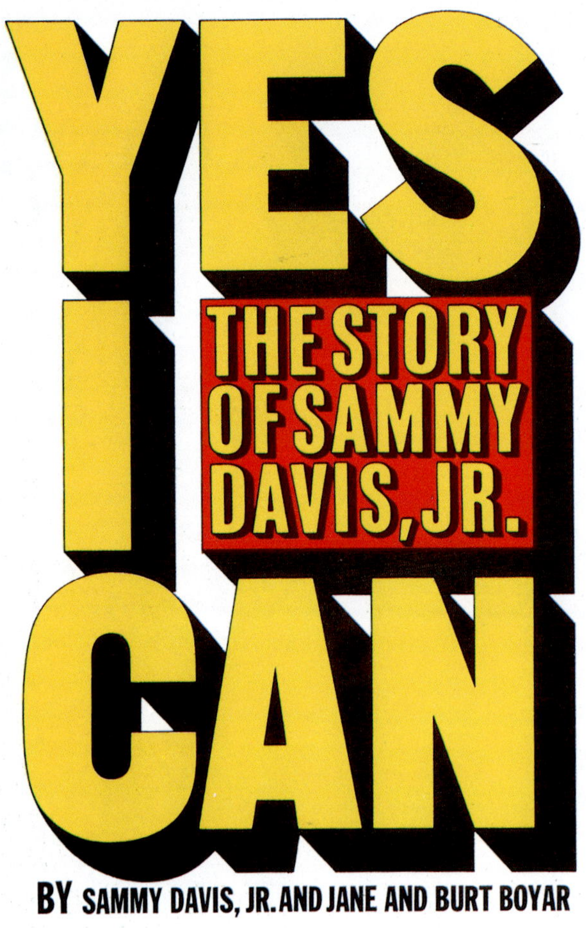

16.

16. Farrar, Straus & Giroux
17. World
18. World
19. Macmillan
20. Harcourt Brace Jovanovich

IT'S HARD TO BE HIP OVER THIRTY AND OTHER TRAGEDIES OF MARRIED LIFE

JUDITH VIORST

17.

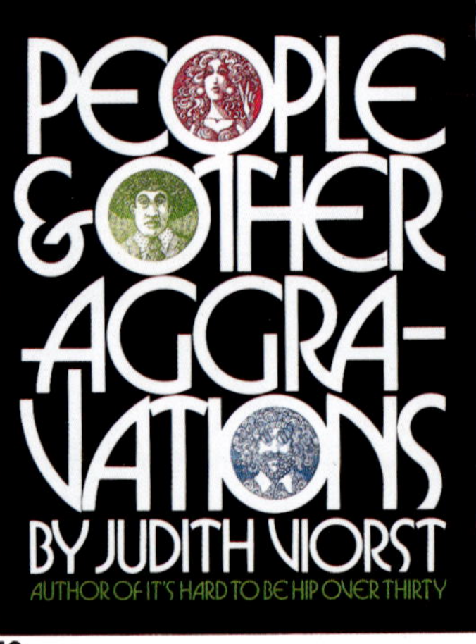

18.

The Silent Syndicate

by Hank Messick "puts the finger on" organized crime in America, especially the far-flung Cleveland Syndicate. Written with the aid of a $25,000 Ford Foundation grant, based on personal research that has been invaluable to law-enforcement agencies all over the country, this book names the names-from Las Vegas to "legit" takeovers in eastern real estate.

19.

GEORGES SIMENON
LETTER TO MY MOTHER

Dear Mama,
It has been close to three and a half years since you died, at the age of ninety-one, and perhaps it's only now that I'm beginning to understand you. Throughout my childhood and adolescence I lived under one roof with you, I lived with you, but when I left for Paris at the age of about nineteen, you were still a stranger to me.

20.

FANNY HILL

BOOK DESIGN

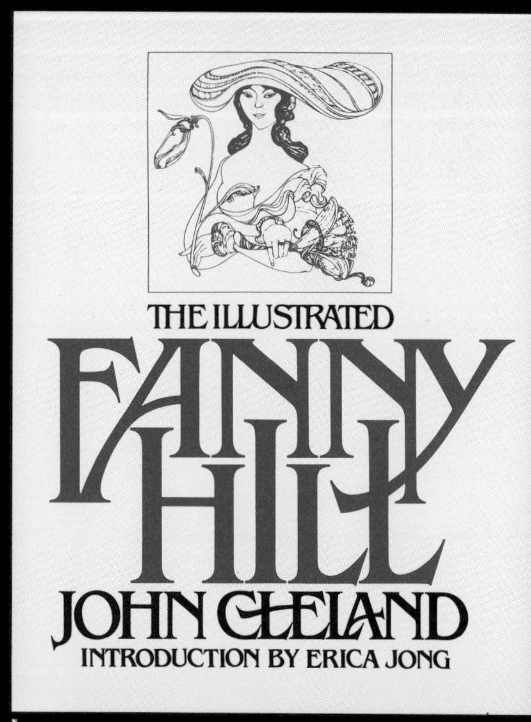

1.

Lubalin felt that book design should suggest the subject matter, even subtly, through the choice of type, page layout and illustration.

1.-4. Lubalin updated this mid-18th-century book with contemporary typography and illustration. The Erotic Book Society.

2.

I concluded that I had fallen into the hands of the kindest mistress in the world

Letter the First

MADAM: I sit down to give you an undeniable proof of my considering your desires as indispensable orders. Ungracious then as the task may be, I shall recall to view those scandalous stages of my life, out of which I emerg'd, at length, to the enjoyment of every blessing in the power of love, health, and fortune to bestow; whilst yet in the flower of youth, and not too late to employ the leisure afforded me by great ease and affluence, to cultivate an understanding, naturally not a despicable one, and which had, even amidst the whirl of loose pleasures I had been tost in, exerted more observation on the characters and manners of the world than what is common to those of my unhappy profession, who looking on all thought or reflection as their capital enemy, keep it at as great a distance as they can, or destroy it without mercy.

Hating, as I mortally do, all long unnecessary preface, I shall give you good quarter in this, and use no farther apology, than to prepare you for seeing the loose part of my life, wrote with the same liberty that I led it.

Truth! stark, naked truth, is the word; and I will not so much as take the pains to bestow the strip of a gauze wrapper on it, but paint situations such as they actually rose to me in nature, careless of violating those laws of decency that were never made for such unreserved intimacies as ours; and you have too much sense, too much knowledge of the *originals* themselves, to sniff prudishly and out of character at the *pictures* of them. The greatest men, those of the first and most leading taste, will not scruple adorning their private closets with nudities, though, in compliance with vulgar prejudices, they may not think them decent decorations of the staircase, or salon.

This, and enough, premised, I go souse into my personal history. My maiden name was *Frances Hill*. I was born at a small village near *Liverpool*, in *Lancashire*, of parents extremely poor, and, I piously believe, extremely honest.

My father, who had received a maim on his limbs that disabled him from following the more laborious branches of country-drudgery, got, by making of nets, a scanty subsistence, which was not much enlarg'd by my mother's keeping a little day-school for the girls in her neighbourhood. They had had several children; but none lived to any age except myself, who had received from nature a constitution perfectly healthy.

My education, till past fourteen, was no better than very vulgar; reading, or rather spelling, an illegible scrawl, and a little ordinary plain work composed the whole system of it; and

The Illustrated Fanny Hill — *Page 9*

3.

there was a great deal of youth and freshness in it.

"The frolic and various play of all his polish'd limbs, as they appeared above the surface, in the course of his swimming or wantoning with the water, amus'd and insensibly delighted me: sometimes he lay motionless, on his back, waterborne, and dragging after him a fine head of hair, that, floating, swept the stream in a bush of black curls. Then the over-flowing water would make a separation between his breast and glossy white belly; at the bottom of which I could not escape observing so remarkable a distinction as a black mossy tuft, out of which appeared to emerge a round, softish, limber, white something, that played every way, with ever the least motion or whirling eddy. I cannot say but that part chiefly, by a kind of natural instinct, attracted, detain'd, captivated my attention: it was out of the power of all my modesty to command my eye away from it; and seeing nothing so very dreadful in its appearance, I insensibly lock'd away all my fears: but as fast as they gave way, new desires and strange wishes took place, and I melted as I gazed. The fire of nature, that had so long lain dormant or conceal'd, began to break out, and made me feel my sex the first time.

Fearing him drown'd, she fainted dead away, whereupon he ravished her. So penitent was he afterwards that she forgave, nay loved him for it. Soon they were entwined again.

"He had now changed his posture, and swam prone on his belly, striking out with his legs and arms, finer modell'd than which could not have been cast, whilst his floating locks played over a neck and shoulders whose whiteness they delightfully set off.

"Then the luxuriant swell of flesh that rose from the small of his back, and terminated its double cope at where the thighs are sent off, perfectly dazzled one with its watery glistening gloss.

"By this time I was so affected by this inward involution of sentiments, so soften'd by this sight, that now, betrayed into a sudden transition from extreme fears to extreme desires, I found these last so strong upon me, the heat of the weather too perhaps conspiring to exalt their rage, that nature almost fainted under them.

"Not that I so much as knew precisely what was wanting to me: my only thought was that so sweet a creature as this youth seemed to me could only make me happy; but then, the little likelihood there was of compassing an acquaintance with him, or perhaps of ever seeing him again, dash'd my desires, and turn'd them into torments. I was still gazing, with all the powers of my sight, on this bewitching object, when, in an instant, down he went.

"I had heard of such things as a cramp seizing on even the best swimmers, and occasioning their being drowned; and imagining this so sudden eclipse to be owing to it, the inconceivable fondness this unknown lad had given birth to distracted me with the most killing terrors; insomuch, that my concern giving the wings, I flew to the door, open'd it, ran down to the canal, guided thither by the madness of my fears for him, and the intense desire of being an instrument to save him, though I was ignorant how, or by what means to effect it: but was it for fears, and a passion so sudden as mine, to reason?

"All this took up scarce the space of a few moments. I had then just life enough to reach the green borders of the waterpiece, where wildly looking round for the young man, and missing him still, my fright and concern sunk me down in a deep swoon, which must have lasted me some time; for I did not come to myself till I was rous'd out of it by a sense of pain that pierced me to the vitals, and awaked me to the most surprising circumstance of finding myself not only in the arms of this very same young gentleman I had been so solicitous to save, but taken at such an advantage in my unresisting condition that he had actually completed his entrance into me so far, that weakened as I was by all the preceding conflicts of mind I had suffer'd, and struck dumb by the violence of my surprise, I had neither the power to cry out, nor the strength to disengage myself from his strenuous embraces, before, urging his point, he had forced his way and completely triumphed over my virginity, as he might now as well see by the streams of blood that follow'd his drawing out, as he had felt by the difficulties he had met with consummating his penetration.

"But the sight of the blood, and the sense of my condition, had (as he told me afterwards), since the ungovernable rage of his passion was somewhat appeas'd, now wrought so far on him that at all risks, even of the worst consequences, he could not find in his heart to leave me, and make off, which he might easily have done.

"I still lay all discompos'd in bleeding ruin, palpitating, speechless, unable to get off, and frightened, and fluttering like a poor wounded partridge, and ready to faint away at the sense of what had befallen me. The young gentleman was by me, kneeling, kissing my hand, and with tears in his eyes beseeching me to forgive him, and offering all the reparation in his power. It is certain that could I, at the instant of regaining my senses, have called out, or taken the bloodiest revenge, I would not have stuck at it: the violation was attended too with such aggravating circumstances, though he was ignorant of them, since it was to my concern for the preservation of his life that I owed my ruin.

"But how quick is the shift of passions from one extreme to another! and how little are they acquainted with the human heart who dispute it! I could not see this amiable criminal, so suddenly the first object of my love, and as suddenly of my just hate, on his knees, bedewing my hand with his tears, without relenting.

"He was still stark-naked, but my modesty had been already too much wounded, in essentials, to be so much shocked as I should have otherwise been with appearances only; in short, my anger ebbed so fast, and the tide of love return'd so strong upon me, that I felt it a point of my own happiness to forgive him.

"The reproaches I made him were murmur'd in so soft a tone, my eyes met his with such glances, expressing more languor than resentment, that he could not but presume his forgiveness was at no desperate distance; but still he would not quit his posture of submission, till I had pronounced his pardon in form; which after the most fervent entreaties, protestations, and promises, I had not the power to withhold. On which, with the utmost marks of a fear of again offending, he ventured to kiss my lips, which I neither declined nor resented: but on my mild expostulations with him upon the barbarity of his treatment, he explain'd the mystery of my ruin, if not entirely to the clearance, at least much to the alleviation of his guilt, in the eyes of a judge so partial in his favour as I was grown.

"It seems that the circumstance of his going down, or sinking, which in my extreme ignorance I had mistaken for something very fatal, was no other than a trick of diving which I had not ever heard, or at least attended to, the mention of: and he was so long-breath'd at it, that in the few moments in which I ran out to save him, he had not yet emerged, before I fell into the swoon, in which, as he rose, seeing me extended on the bank, his first idea was that some young woman was upon some design of frolic or diversion with him, for he knew I could not have fallen a-sleep there without his having seen me before: agreeably to which notion he had ventured to approach, and finding me without sign of life, and still perplex'd as he was what to think of the adventure, he took me in his arms at all hazards, and carried me into the summer-house, of which he observed the door open: there he laid me down on the couch, and tried, as he protested in good faith, by several means to bring me to myself again, till fired, as he said, beyond all bearing by the sight and touch of several parts of me which were unguardedly exposed to him, he could no longer govern his passion; and the less, as he was not quite sure that his first idea of this swoon being a feint was not the very truth of the case: seduced then by this flattering notion, and overcome by the present, as he styled them, superhuman temptations, combined with the solitude and seeming security of the attempt, he was not enough his own master not to make it.

"Leaving me then just only whilst he fastened the door, he returned with redoubled eagerness to his prey: when, finding me still entranced, he ventured to place me as he pleased, whilst I felt, no more than the dead, what he was about, till the pain he put me to roused me just in time enough to be witness of a triumph I was not able to defeat, and now scarce regretted: for as he talked, the tone of his voice sounded, methought, so sweetly in my ears, the sensible nearness of so new and interesting an object to me wrought so powerfully upon me, that, in the rising perception of things in a new and pleasing light, I lost all sense of the past injury.

"The young gentleman soon discern'd the symptoms of a reconciliation in my softened looks, and hastening to receive the seal of it from my lips, press'd them tenderly to pass his pardon in the return of a kiss so fiery, that the impression of it being carried to my heart, and thence to my sphere of Venus, I was melted into a softness that could refuse him nothing.

The young gentleman press'd fiery kisses on the now undone Harriet and secured her willing complicity in a fresh and passionate interchange. Injury was forgot and extatic pleasure took its place.

"When now he managed his caresses and endearments so artfully as to insinuate the most soothing consolations for the past pain and the most pleasing expectations of future pleasure, but whilst mere modesty kept my eyes from seeing his and rather declined them, I had a glimpse of that instrument of the mischief which was now, obviously even to me, who had scarce had snatches of a comparative observation of it, resuming its capacity to renew it, and grew greatly alarming with its increase

The Illustrated Fanny Hill — *Page 74*

The Illustrated Fanny Hill — *Page 75*

4.

5.-9. For this book about late 19th-century immigrants, Lubalin used brown wrapping paper for the jacket and endpapers. He felt this suggested the inverted paper bags that the immigrants used as signs for their pushcarts, a symbol of life on Manhattan's lower East Side.

5.

7.

6.

8.

I Discover America

9.

10.-13. Cover, endpaper, and spreads from book of whimsical poetry. Simon and Schuster.

10.

11.

12.

Self-Improvement Program

I've finished six pillows in Needlepoint,
And I'm reading Jane Austen and Kant,
And I'm up to the pork with black beans in Advanced Chinese Cooking.
I don't have to struggle to find myself
For I already know what I want.
I want to be healthy and wise and extremely good-looking.

I'm learning new glazes in Pottery Class,
And I'm playing new chords in Guitar,
And in Yoga I'm starting to master the lotus position.
I don't have to ponder priorities
For I already know what they are:
To be good-looking, healthy, and wise.
And adored in addition.

I'm improving my serve with a tennis pro,
And I'm practicing verb forms in Greek,
And in Primal Scream Therapy all my frustrations are vented.
I don't have to ask what I'm searching for
Since I already know that I seek
To be good-looking, healthy, and wise.
And adored.
And contented.

I've bloomed in Organic Gardening,
And in Dance I have tightened my thighs,
And in Consciousness Raising there's no one around who can top me.
And I'm working all day and I'm working all night
To be good-looking, healthy, and wise.
And adored.
And contented.
And brave.
And well-read.
And a marvelous hostess,
Fantastic in bed,
And bilingual,
Athletic,
Artistic ...
Won't someone please stop me?

44 45

13.

ETIENNE DELESSERT FOREWORD BY JEAN PIAGET
HOW
THE MOUSE
WAS HIT ON
THE HEAD BY A
STONE AND SO
DISCOVERED
THE WORLD

14.

14.-18. Good Book was a publishing venture Lubalin formed with Etienne Delessert to create children's books. Front cover, title page and spreads from one of the few children's books Lubalin designed.

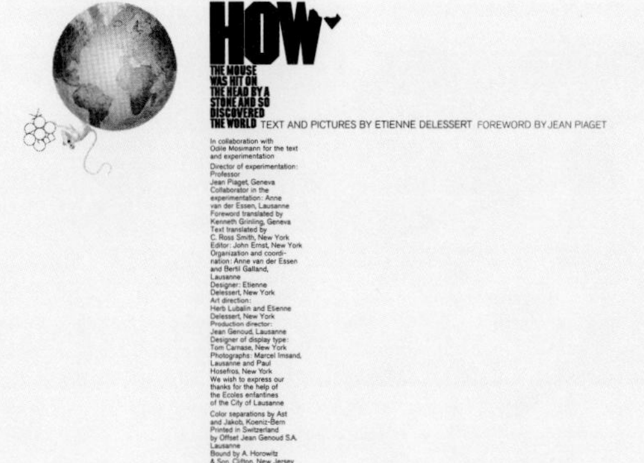

HOW THE MOUSE WAS HIT ON THE HEAD BY A STONE AND SO DISCOVERED THE WORLD TEXT AND PICTURES BY ETIENNE DELESSERT FOREWORD BY JEAN PIAGET

In collaboration with Odile Mosimann for the text and experimentation

Director of experimentation: Professor Jean Piaget, Geneva
Collaborator in the experimentation: Anne van der Essen, Lausanne
Foreword translated by Kenneth Grinling, Geneva
Text translated by C. Ross Smith, New York
Editor: John Ernst, New York
Organization and coordination: Anne van der Essen and Bertil Galland, Lausanne
Designer: Etienne Delessert, New York
Art direction: Herb Lubalin and Etienne Delessert, New York
Production director: Jean Genoud, Lausanne
Designer of display type: Tom Carnase, New York
Photographs: Marcel Imsand, Lausanne and Paul Hosefros, New York
We wish to express our thanks for the help of the Ecoles enfantines of the City of Lausanne

Color separations by Ast and Jakob, Koeniz-Bern
Printed in Switzerland by Offset Jean Genoud S.A. Lausanne
Bound by A. Horowitz & Son, Clifton, New Jersey

Produced by Good Book, Inc., New York
Doubleday & Company, Inc., Garden City, New York

Copyright © 1971 by Etienne Delessert
All rights reserved
Library of Congress Catalog Card Number 79-158138
Printed in Switzerland

15.

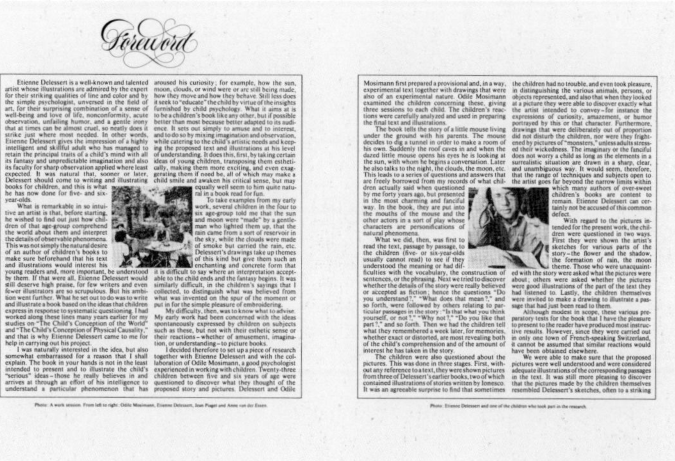

Foreword

Etienne Delessert is a well-known and talented artist whose illustrations are admired by the expert for their striking qualities of line and color and by the simple psychologist, unversed in the field of art, for their surprising combination of a sense of well-being and love of life, nonconformity, acute observation, unfailing humor, and a gentle irony that at times can be almost cruel, so neatly does it strike just where most needed. In other words, Etienne Delessert gives the impression of a highly intelligent and skillful adult who has managed to retain the principal traits of a child's mind with all its fantasy and unpredictable imagination and also its faculty for sharp observation applied where least expected. It was natural that, sooner or later, Delessert should come to writing and illustrating books for children, and this is what he has now done for five- and six-year-olds.

What is remarkable in so intuitive an artist is that, before starting, he wished to find out just how children of that age-group comprehend the world about them and interpret the details of observable phenomena. This was not simply the natural desire of an author of children's books to make sure beforehand that his text and illustrations would interest his young readers and, more important, be understood by them. If that were all, Etienne Delessert would still deserve high praise, for few writers and even fewer illustrators are so scrupulous. But his ambition went further. What he set out to do was to write and illustrate a book based on the ideas that children express in response to systematic questioning. I had worked along these lines many years earlier for my studies on "The Child's Conception of the World" and "The Child's Conception of Physical Causality," and that is why Etienne Delessert came to me for help in carrying out his project.

I was naturally interested in the idea, but also somewhat embarrassed for a reason that I shall explain. The book in your hands is not in the least intended to present and to illustrate the child's "serious" ideas – those he really believes in and arrives at through an effort of his intelligence to understand a particular phenomenon that has aroused his curiosity; for example, how the sun, moon, clouds, or wind were or are still being made, how they move and how they behave. Still less does it seek to "educate" the child by virtue of the insights furnished by child psychology. What it aims at is to be a children's book like any other, but if possible better than most because better adapted to its audience. It sets out simply to amuse and to interest, and to do so by mixing imagination and observation, while catering to the child's artistic needs and keeping the proposed text and illustrations at his level of understanding. It does this, first, by taking certain ideas of young children, transposing them esthetically, making them more exciting, and even exaggerating them if need be, all of which may make a child smile and awaken his critical sense, but may equally well seem to him quite natural in a book read for fun.

To take examples from my early work, several children in the four to six age-group told me that the sun and moon were "made" by a gentleman who lighted them up, that the rain came from a sort of reservoir in the sky, while the clouds were made of smoke but carried the rain, etc. Delessert's drawings take up themes of this kind but give them such an enchanting and concrete form that it is difficult to say where an interpretation acceptable to the child ends and the fantasy begins. It was similarly difficult, in the children's sayings that I collected, to distinguish what was believed from what was invented on the spur of the moment or put in for the simple pleasure of embroidering.

My difficulty, then, was to know what to advise. My early work had been concerned with the ideas spontaneously expressed by children on subjects such as these, but not with their esthetic sense or their reactions – whether of amusement, imagination, or understanding – to picture books.

I decided therefore to set up a piece of research together with Etienne Delessert and with the collaboration of Odile Mosimann, a good psychologist experienced in working with children. Twenty-three children between five and six years of age were questioned to discover what they thought of the proposed story and pictures. Delessert and Odile Mosimann first prepared a provisional and, in a way, experimental text together with drawings that were also of an experimental nature. Odile Mosimann examined the children concerning these, giving three sessions to each child. The children's reactions were carefully analyzed and used in preparing the final text and illustrations.

The book tells the story of a little mouse living under the ground with his parents. The mouse decides to dig a tunnel in order to make a room of his own. Suddenly the roof caves in and when the dazed little mouse opens his eyes he is looking at the sun, with whom he begins a conversation. Later he also talks to the night, the clouds, the moon, etc. This leads to a series of questions and answers that are freely borrowed from my records of what children actually said when questioned by me forty years ago, but presented in the most charming and fanciful way. In the book, they are put into the mouths of the mouse and the other actors in a sort of play whose characters are personifications of natural phenomena.

What we did, then, was first to read the text, passage by passage, to the children (five- or six-year-olds usually cannot read) to see if they understood the meaning or had difficulties with the vocabulary, the construction of sentences, or the phrasing. Next we tried to discover whether the details of the story were really believed or accepted as fiction; hence the questions "Do you understand?," "What does that mean?," and so forth, were followed by others relating to particular passages in the story: "Is that what you think yourself, or not?," "Why not?," "Do you like that part?," and so forth. Then we had the children tell what they remembered a week later, for memories, whether exact or distorted, are most revealing both of the child's comprehension and of the amount of interest he has taken in the story.

The children were also questioned about the pictures. This was done in three stages. First, without any reference to a text, they were shown pictures from three of Delessert's earlier books, two of which contained illustrations of stories written by Ionesco. It was an agreeable surprise to find that sometimes the children had no trouble, and even took pleasure, in distinguishing the various animals, persons, or objects represented, and also that when they looked at a picture they were able to discover exactly what the artist intended to convey – for instance the expressions of curiosity, amazement, or humor portrayed by this or that character. Furthermore, drawings that were deliberately out of proportion did not disturb the children, nor were they frightened by pictures of "monsters," unless adults stressed their wickedness. The imaginary or the fanciful does not worry a child as long as the elements in a surrealistic situation are drawn in a sharp, clear, and unambiguous way. It would seem, therefore, that the range of techniques and subjects open to the artist goes far beyond the narrow limits within which many authors of over-sweet children's books are content to remain. Etienne Delessert can certainly not be accused of this common defect.

With regard to the pictures intended for the present work, the children were questioned in two ways. First they were shown the artist's sketches for various parts of the story – the flower and the shadow, the formation of rain, the moon theme. Those who were unacquainted with the story were asked what the pictures were about; others were asked whether the pictures were good illustrations of the part of the text they had listened to. Lastly, the children themselves were invited to make a drawing to illustrate a passage that had just been read to them.

Although modest in scope, these various preparatory tests for the book that I have the pleasure to present to the reader have produced most instructive results. However, since they were carried out in only one town of French-speaking Switzerland, it cannot be assumed that similar reactions would have been obtained elsewhere.

We were able to make sure that the proposed pictures were well understood and were considered adequate illustrations of the corresponding passages in the text. It was still more pleasing to discover that the pictures made by the children themselves resembled Delessert's sketches, often to a striking

Photo: A work session. From left to right: Odile Mosimann, Etienne Delessert, Jean Piaget and Anne van der Essen

Photo: Etienne Delessert and one of the children who took part in the research.

16.

17.

18.

19.-23. Harlem on My Mind was produced in conjunction with an exhibit at the Metropolitan Museum of Art, New York, documenting the struggle to establish an urban black culture in the midst of a 20th-century industrialized society. Random House.

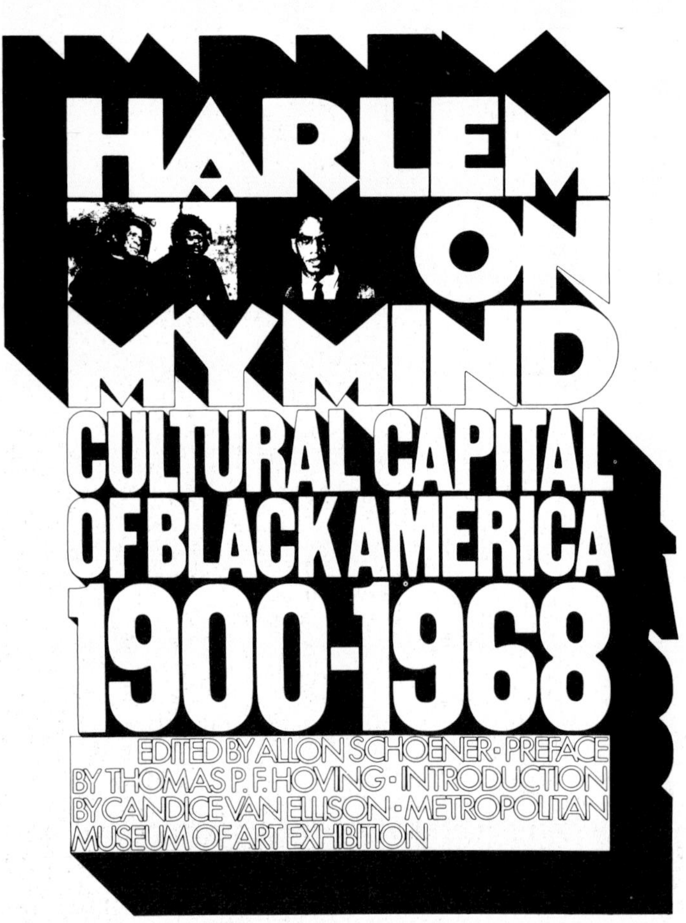

19.

20.

what he doesn't care about. Instead of being a passive recipient who digests what is directed to him, the individual becomes an active participant by making his own choices. As a result of his unique reactions, the individual who responds to an experience becomes as important in the communication process as the one who organizes it. In other words, the audience itself becomes a creative force. Participation implies more effective communication.

This suggests a new aesthetic hierarchy. It is time to think about such things. Electronic mass communication media transmit information effectively on all levels to people with a variety of backgrounds. This exhibition and book have been guided by a new aesthetic—that it is possible to communicate to individuals as unique and differentiated factors within a mass audience. Communication pattern (more information than can be received by an individual within the fixed time available) has replaced communication message (a clear, precise set of facts stated in a logical order).

This book is an extension of the exhibition. It is not necessary to see the exhibition to appreciate the book, but if one has, the structure and technique of the book are recognizably parallel. In both there is a selective barrage of information. In the exhibition, it is images and sounds; in the book, it is text and pictures. No attempt has been made to describe the sixty-eight-year history of Harlem as a continuing sequence of events. It is presented through a cluster of documentary newspaper stories and photographs assembled as units interpreting the character of each decade. Thus, without being rewritten, the history of Harlem does fall into a pattern of distinct sections.

The visitor to the exhibition can move through it as quickly or as slowly as he chooses. The reader of this book can use it as he chooses. He can skim through it and get the essential outlines of Harlem's history, or he can read slowly and extract details. As the editor, I hope that everyone uses this book differently. I hope that each person injects some of his own personality and style into the way that he reads it. The book accommodates itself to people; it does not dictate to them. It functions as an element in today's communications experiences, and it should serve as an invitation to probe further into this subject.

The objective of this exhibition and book is to prove that the black community in Harlem is a major cultural environment with enormous strength and potential, that there is a continuing leadership tradition, that there is a stable social community which supports civic and social institutions, that this community has made major contributions to the mainstream of American culture in music, theater and literature, and that there is an enormous reservoir of untapped talent. If the white community can stop expiating its guilt by rebuilding Harlem to mirror a white middle-class image, both black and white America will be happier.

Human attitudes are not inflexible. They can be influenced by a variety of circumstances and conditions. The attitudes governing social behavior in America can be questioned because the problems which confront us today are not being resolved. We are in the midst of a period of fundamental change. Where do we go from here? If we—both black and white—can accept the reality of Harlem as an important fact in our lives, we will have accomplished something.

ALLON SCHOENER

FROM WHITE TO BLACK HARLEM 1900-1919

21.

THE NEW YORK TIMES, APRIL 8, 1968

HARLEM YOUTHS EXHIBIT LOOT, TAKEN "TO GET BACK AT WHITEY"

While a memorial march honoring the Rev. Dr. Martin Luther King Jr. moved yesterday along Seventh Avenue in Harlem, an 18-year-old Negro youth at the corner of 122nd Street showed off a navy-blue double-breasted cashmere blazer to several admirers. "That's a beautiful blazer, a boss piece of stitching," one admirer said. "I've been making payments on one like that for weeks." The youth with the jacket smiled broadly. "I picked this one up for little or nothing," he said. The group laughed, understanding that the garment had been snatched from a clothing store during the looting that followed the slaying of Dr. King on Thursday.

Desire, need and an eagerness to "get back at whitey" were the primary reasons expressed by those who acknowledged they had looted clothing, food, liquor and appliance stores here. One young anti-poverty worker who was pummeled by other youths when he tried to convince them they should not risk death "for a damn cheap suit in a credit house along 125th Street" said later: "What whitey don't understand is that America is a damn rich country and she flashes this richness in the brother's face and tells him, 'It ain't for you.' The brother gets out and grabs a bit of it now and then—I wish he'd learn to grab himself a lot instead of a little.'"

✣ ✣ ✣

AMSTERDAM NEWS, MAY 4, 1968

HARLEM BACKED COLUMBIA STUDENTS

The Harlem community rallied to the aid and defense of the Black Columbia University students who took over Hamilton Hall in unprecedented numbers. Harlem mothers made sure students ate well. Daily, since the more than 150 Black student protestors laid siege, Harlemites visited with them behind their barricaded doors, advised them, gave them moral support, food and money to buy food. Speaking for many others, one Harlem mother said while standing in the rain during a Black student rally in front of Hamilton Hall the second night students occupied the building: "Rain or no rain, I don't care. We must support these young people. They went out on the limb for us. That's part of the reason they're here now. I for one am coming back and bringing them hot, nourishing food."

✣ ✣ ✣

AMSTERDAM NEWS, JUNE 15, 1968

COMMUNITY REACTS TO ANOTHER KILLING

The assassination of Senator Robert F. Kennedy drew more response from the black community than that of any other prominent white American since the tragic death of the senator's brother, the late President Kennedy. Afro-Americans of all walks of life were shocked, dismayed, angered, anguished and troubled over the latest shooting, and one so close to the death of the late Dr. Martin Luther King. The views of the average man in the street were varied—as expected—but they all expressed a common denominator of worry and fear about the times that now surround us.

✣ ✣ ✣

22.

23.

LETTERHEADS

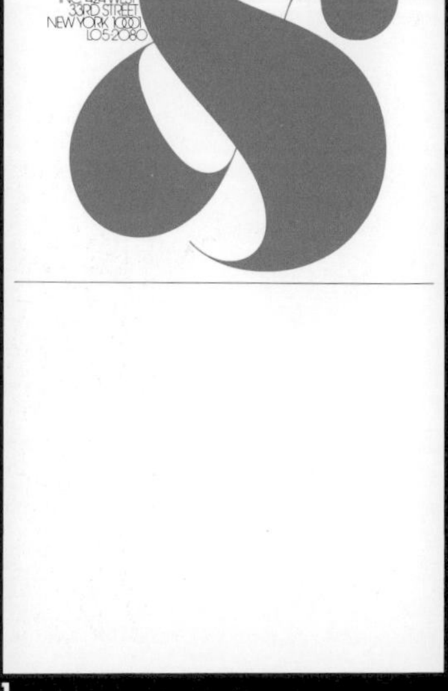

1.

2.

3.

4.

5.

1. Ampersand Productions Inc., film producers.

2. Meier Bernstein, book dealer.

3. America Unlimited, non-profit research and public education organization.

4. Rhoda Sparber.

5. Gerry Gersten, illustrator. Lubalin asked Gersten to draw 12 symbols, which were printed on adhesive-backed paper. Each month, Gersten placed a new symbol in the box beneath his name.

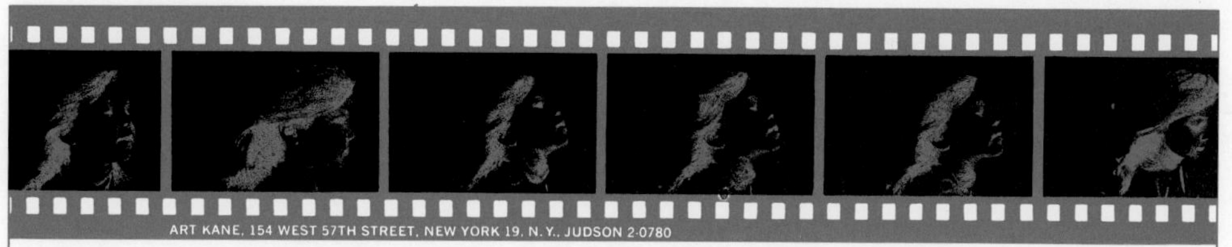

6.

6. Art Kane, photographer. The sprockets were die-cut in the strip of negative film on the letterhead, and on the envelope. Before postage, it cost Kane $1.25 for each letter.

7. Man, international newspaper.

8. Typographic Innovations, Inc., typesetter.

9. Ronchetti & Day, advertising agency.

10. Volk Corporation, stock art publishers.

7.

8.

9.

10.

11. Anthony Hyde, Jr., photographer. The use of initials indicates a favorable response to the artist's photos.

12. Li-Lian Oh, representative for Mr. Hyde.

12.

anthony hyde, jr., photography!
223 east 31st street, new york 10016,
murray hill 6-0431-2

11.

TYP

TYPEFACE DESIGN

HERB LUBALIN & TONY DI SPIGNA HAVE DESIGNED A NEW TYPEFACE THAT COMBINES GOTHIC SIMPLICITY WITH ROMAN ELEGANCE: SERIF GOTHIC & BOLD

1.

A
BCD
ETC.

2.

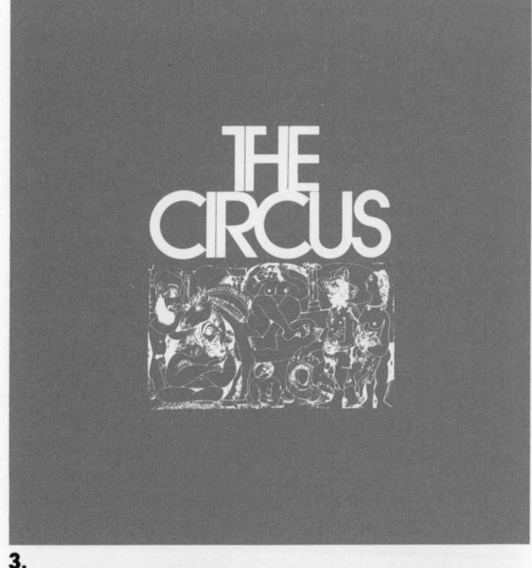

3.

THE
MUSES

4.

5.

6.

The typeface Avant Garde was an outgrowth of the masthead logo for Avant Garde magazine. More and more, Lubalin found that, in designing the interior pages, he used characters based on the logo. The number of letters grew significantly, and were developed into a complete alphabet and innovative ligatures by Tom Carnase. Avant Garde was intended for use only in the magazine, and only in upper case. Lower case characters had to be developed before the typeface was available for commercial distribution after 1970.

1. Cover of a brochure announcing the new Serif Gothic typeface.

2.-6. Interior pages for Avant Garde magazine showing the typeface in its first use.

CA EA FA FR
GA HT KA LA
NT PR RA SS
ST TH UT W

LUBALIN GRAPH

A
BCD
ETC.

Lubalin Graph is a serif version of Avant Garde. It was developed by Tony Di Spigna.

7.

7. An illustration from a page of an ITC type promotion showing Lubalin's use of Lubalin Graph.

ÆC

CA EA FA GA

HT KA LA NT

RA SS TH UT

SERIF GOTHIC

A BCD ETC.

I WISH THE BALD EAGLE HAD NOT BEEN CHOSEN AS THE REPRESENTATIVE OF OUR COUNTRY; HE IS A BIRD OF BAD MORAL CHARACTER; LIKE THOSE AMONG MEN WHO LIVE BY SHARPING & ROBBING, HE IS GENERALLY POOR AND OFTEN VERY LOUSY. THE TURKEY IS A MUCH MORE RESPECTABLE BIRD, & WITHAL A TRUE ORIGI-NAL NATIVE OF AMERICA.

8.

Lubalin felt that the industry needed a typeface to fill the gap between Gothic and Roman. So, he and Tony Di Spigna developed Serif Gothic.

8. Lubalin used Serif Gothic to re-design a 1966 poster for a page in U&lc. See page 38, #18.

aaee
ffkkrr
sstzz

CHRONOLOGY OF HERB LUBALIN 1918-1981

1918: Born in New York City.

1939: Graduated The Cooper Union.

1939: Designer, Display Guild.

1941: Art Director, Deutsch & Shea Advertising.

1942: Art Director, Fairchild Publications.

1943: Art Director, Reiss Advertising.

1945: Vice President, Art Director and Creative Director of Sudler & Hennessey, Inc.

1952-80: Nine Gold Medals and Eight Silver Medals, Art Directors Club of New York.

Over 500 Awards for Professional Excellence from the Art Directors Club, Type Directors Club, AIGA, Society of Publication Designers, Society of Illustrators and CA Annual Exhibition.

1952-81: Annual Group Shows, American Institute of Graphic Arts, New York Art Directors Club, Type Directors Club.

1958-81: Annual Group Shows, C.A., Communication Arts Magazine.

1962: Art Director of the Year, NSAD, National Society of Art Directors.

1962-81: Annual Group Shows, Society of Publication Designers.

1963: Cleo Award, Best TV Commercial at American Television Festival.

Three medals, Advertising Club of New York.

U.S. Government Citation for Design of Airmail Stamps.

The Lotus Club Award.

1964: One Man Exhibition, Overseas Press Club.

1964-67: President, Herb Lubalin, Inc.

1964-70: Executive Vice President, Lubalin, Burns & Co., Inc. Advisory Board, Hampshire College, Massachusetts.

1967-75: President, Lubalin, Smith, Carnase, Inc.

1968: One Man Exhibition, Gallery 303.

1971: Executive Vice President, International Typeface Corporation.

Vice President, Lubalin, Delpire et Cie, Paris.

Vice President, Lubalin, Maxwell, Ltd., London.

Vice President, Good Book, Inc., Publishing.

1972: Cooper Union Professional Achievement Citation.

Graphics Teacher, Cornell University.

1973: Augustus St. Gaudens Medal for Professional Achievement, Cooper Union Alumni Association.

1974: Vice President, Aki, Lubalin, Hawaii.

1975: One Man Exhibition, TGI Gallery, New York; Ryder Gallery, Chicago; Advisory Board, Kean College, New Jersey; Visiting Graphic Arts Instructor, Syracuse University.

1975-78: President, LSC&P Design Group, Inc.

1976: One Man Exhibition, Hampshire College, Massachusetts.

1976-81: Professor of Design, The Cooper Union.

1977: Chairman, Design Processing International, Inc., Art Directors Club Hall of Fame.

1978: One Man Exhibition, Galerie Robert Clarence, Paris.

1978-80: President, Herb Lubalin Associates, Inc.

1979: One Man Exhibition, Pompidou Center for the Arts, Paris.

1980: The Cooper Union Alumnus of the Year Award.

One Man Exhibition, ITC Center, New York.

1980-81: Chairman of the Board, Lubalin, Peckolick, Associates, Inc.

1981: The American Institute of Graphic Arts (AIGA) Medal.

PERMANENT COLLECTIONS: Whitney Museum of American Art, Library of Congress, Museum of Modern Art, New York; Smithsonian Institution, National Gallery, Washington, D.C.

PROFESSIONAL ORGANIZATIONS: American Institute of Graphic Arts, Member of the Board.

New York Art Directors Club, President, Vice President and Board Member.

AGI (Alliance Graphique Internationale), International Vice President.

SAFFT, Scandinavian Society of Designers, Honorary Member.

Society of Typographic Artists, Chicago, Honorary Member.

Society of Publication Designers.

Society of Illustrators.

National Society of Art Directors.

New York Type Directors Club.

AIA, American Institute of Architects.

LECTURES: Toronto School of Art, Canada; Alberta School of Art, Canada; Sheridan College of Art, Canada; Pratt Institute, New York; Parsons, New York; School of Visual Arts, New York; City College of New York, New York; New York University, New York; Harlem Preparatory, New York; State University of New York, Albany; State University of New York, Stonybrook, L.I.; Drake University, Iowa; University of Miami, Florida; Kansas City School of Art, Missouri; Art Center, Los Angeles; Rhode Island School of Design, Switzerland; Barcelona College of Architecture; Spain, Oregon State University.

CONFERENCES: A.TY.P. 1 Conference, Barcelona and Sao Paulo; World Advertising Conference, Sweden; Ad Age Conference, Chicago; Aspen Conference, Colorado; Typomundus Conference, Stuttgart; American Society of Magazine Photographers Conference, Miami; Art Directors Communication Conference, New York.

BIBLIOGRAPHY

1961: Gebrauchsgraphik Magazine, January.

1969: C.A. Magazine, Vol 11 #4.

Idea Magazine.

Print Magazine, January-February.

1970: Gebrauchsgraphik Magazine, January.

1971: Cree, September-October.

1974: Idea Magazine, Issue #127.

1974-81: U&lc—Upper and lower case, The International Journal of Typographics.

1976: Graphics Today, July-August.

1977: Vision Magazine, October.

1978: American Artist Magazine, December.

1979: Graphic Art News, Vol #11, November; Graphics, New York, July-August; Print Magazine, May-June; Projekt, Issue #129, February.

1979-80: Graphis Magazine, Issue #204.

1981: Idea Magazine, Issue #164, January.

Additional articles sans publishing dates: Advertising Age Magazine, Advertising Requirements Magazine, Advertising Week Magazine, Art Direction Magazine, Lightworks Magazine, The New York Times, Printers Ink.

ESTABLISHED IN 1984 IT WILL BE THE WORLD'S FIRST STUDY CENTER FOR THE GRAPHIC ARTS. IT WILL BE AN INTERNATIONAL EDUCATIONAL RESOURCE, UNPRECEDENTED IN IT'S MAGNITUDE. INITIALLY, THE LUBALIN CENTER WILL HOUSE HERB'S VAST ARCHIVE OF WORK. WORKS OF THE MOST PROMINENT NAMES IN OUR INDUSTRY WILL BE ADDED TO FORM A PERMANENT COLLECTION. THE LUBALIN STUDY CENTER WILL PROVIDE THE MEANS WHEREBY THE ENTIRE DESIGN COMMUNITY CAN STUDY INNOVATIVE WORK & IDEAS PRODUCED BY LEADING COMMUNICATORS. IT IS A MONUMENTAL WAY **TO HONOR HERB LUBALIN**

ACKNOWLEDGEMENTS

FOR SHOWING THE WILLINGNESS TO SEARCH MEMORIES WITH PATIENCE AND GOOD HUMOR, WE THANK THOSE WHO WERE INTERVIEWED:

Michael Aron
John Alcorn
Matthew Baumwell
Ed Benquiat
Aaron Burns
Fay Barrows
Seymour Chwast
Tony Di Spigna
Lou Dorfsman
Roger Ferriter
Louise Fili
Carl Fischer
Julius Galian
Gerry Gersten
Ralph Ginzburg
Irwin Glusker
George Lois
Irwin Lubalin
Peter Lubalin
Rhoda Lubalin
Larry Muller
Marian Muller
Seth McCormick
Russ Pinieri
John Pistilli
George Sadek
Art Schlosser
Ellen Shapiro
Ira Shapiro
Arthur Singer
Ernie Smith
Lois Wyse
Karen Zaimen

A.P./G.G.S.

THANKS ARE DUE THE FOLLOWING WHO HELPED

Eugenie Anderson
Herbert Bayer
Tony Di Spigna
Keith Gemerek
Gerry Gersten
Ralph Ginzburg
Marilyn Hoffner
International Typeface Corporation
Art Kane
Kirsch Beverages Inc.
Rhoda Lubalin
PAS Graphics, Inc.
Pushpin Lubalin Peckolick, Inc.
Michael Aron
Cleveland Dobson
Kevin Gatta
Ronald Smith James
Hugh Montgomery
Mary Louise Muehlhausen
Judy Paloferro
Russ Pinieri
Debbie Schuler
Gail Stampar
Juan Tenorio
Robin Nedboy
Paul Rand
The Estate of Norman Rockwell
The Saturday Evening Post
Schaedler/Pinwheel
Steelograph Company
Bert Stern
Sudler & Hennessey, Inc.
TypoGraphic Innovations, Inc.
U.S. Information Service
Diana Raquel Vasquez
Jessica Weber

An especially warm thanks to my assistant Doris Neulinger for her talent, sensitivity and capacity to transform my rough scribbles into something I know Herb would have been proud of.

A.P.

INDEX

CLIENTS

ILLUSTRATORS

LETTERERS

PHOTOGRAPHERS

Gertrude Goodrich Snyder, a close friend of the late Herbert Lubalin, has had rich and varied experiences in the field of the graphic arts.

She has been an exhibiting painter and muralist, a magazine art director, President of her own design promotion corporation, and author of the feature, "Pro.Files," in U&lc. She is currently a featured writer in the Swiss publication, Graphis.

Ms. Snyder is married to William Weinberger, Creative Director of a fragrance company. They live in the outreach of New Jersey, on the New York-Pennsylvania border, "knee-deep in books, birds, bees and beavers."

Alan Peckolick is a graphic designer working with international clients in areas from print and film to environmental design. He has received numerous design awards and has been exhibited around the world.

In 1972, he became a partner of Herb Lubalin. Currently, he is president of his own design firm, Peckolick + Partners.

Mr. Peckolick is a member of the New York Art Directors' Club, New York Type Directors' Club, The American Institute of Graphic Arts, Alliance Graphique Internationale, and an honorary member of the Art Directors' Club of Bergen, Norway. He is also on the Advisory Boards of Design World magazine in Australia and The Herb Lubalin Study Center of Design and Typography at Cooper Union. In addition, he lectures to art students and professional organizations.

Mr. Peckolick is married to Jessica Weber, who also has her own firm, Jessica Weber Design. They reside in New York City.

PRODUCTION

Major Color Photography:
Robin Nedboy, Inc.

Black & White Graphic Arts Photography:
Schaedler/Pinwheel

Typesetting:
TypoGraphic Innovations, Inc.
Rules:
Cardinal Type Service, Inc.

Color Prints:
Mann & Greene Color Inc.

Retouching:
Kerry Meyer

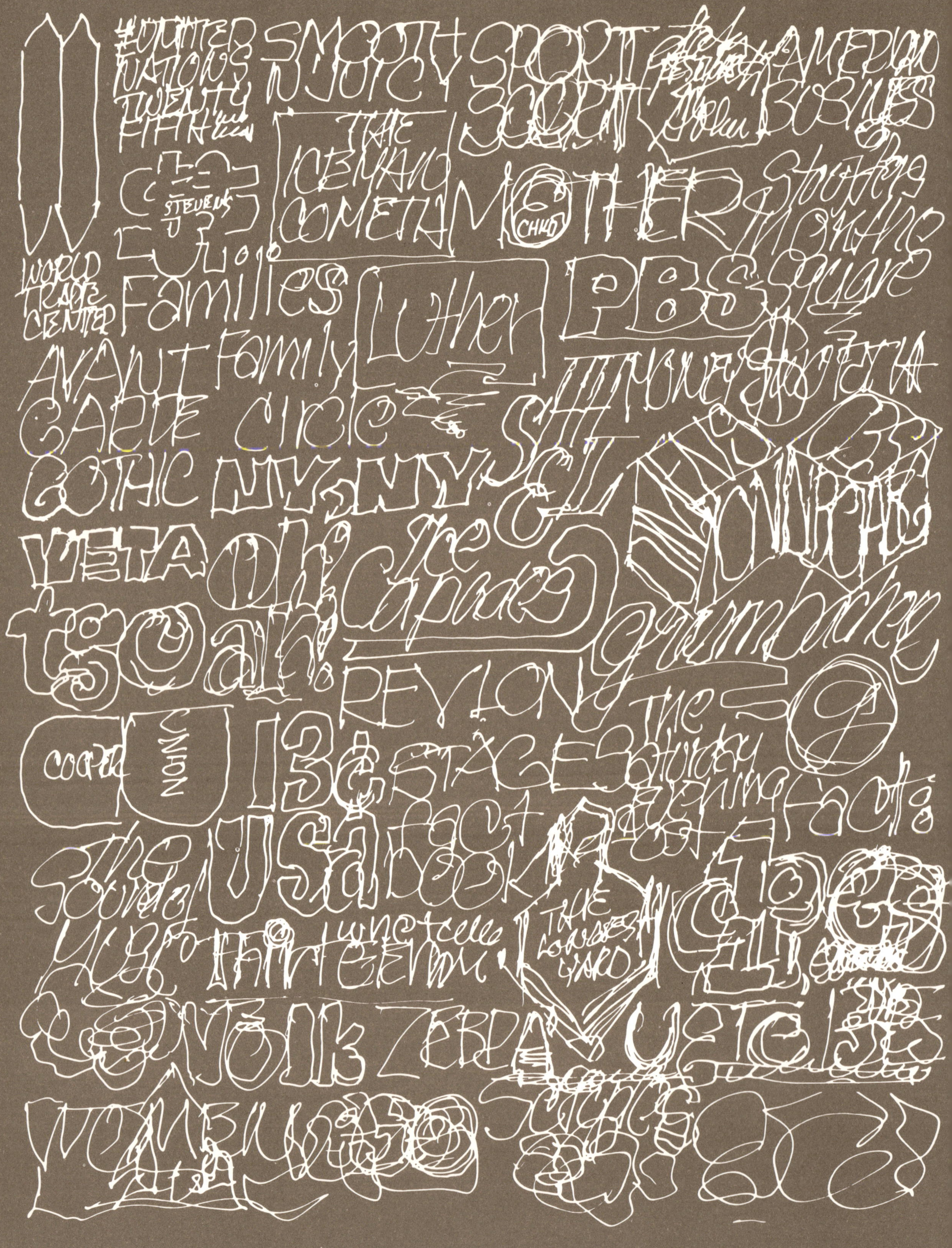

UNITED NATIONS TWENTY FIFTH
SMOOTH N JUICY
THE ICEMAN COMETH
STEVENS
MOTHER
CHILD
WORLD TRADE CENTER
Families
Luther
PBS
AVANT GARDE GOTHIC
Family Circle
NY NY
REVLON
UNION
USA
thirteen
ZEBRA